W9-BPP-024

_____ Antifoundationalism Old and New

Antifoundationalism
Old and New

Edited by

Tom Rockmore
and Beth J. Singer

Temple University Press
Philadelphia

Temple University Press, Philadelphia 19122
Copyright © 1992 by Temple University. All rights reserved
Published 1992
Printed in the United States of America

The paper used in this publication meets the minimum requirements of
American National Standard for Information Sciences—Permanence of
Paper for Printed Library Materials, ANSI Z39.48-1984

Library of Congress Cataloging-in-Publication Data
Antifoundationalism old and new / edited by Tom Rockmore and Beth J.
Singer.
       p.   cm.
  Includes bibliographical references and index.
  ISBN 0-87722-881-7 (alk. paper)
    1. Knowledge, Theory of.   I. Rockmore, Tom, 1942–   .
II. Singer, Beth J., 1927–   .
BD181.A57   1992
121—dc20   91-3117
                                           CIP

Contents

Acknowledgments

None of the papers in this volume has previously appeared in print and most were written expressly for this collection. Editing such a book can be an arduous task, but we were fortunate enough to be working with an enthusiastic and able group of scholars who met deadlines efficiently and uncomplainingly and did more than their part to forward our collective enterprise. All of us owe a debt to our editor, Jane Cullen, whose support and good judgment contributed immeasurably.

—————————————— *Antifoundationalism Old and New*

Introduction

TOM ROCKMORE

My task here is to introduce a collection of original essays, arranged in historical order, concerning various issues of foundationalism and antifoundationalism throughout the philosophical tradition. An introduction should seek to present the book to follow, to lead into it, to induce the reader to follow along in the book; it should not seek to take the place of the book, by anticipating the arguments to follow. For that reason, rather than providing another essay on foundationalism and antifoundationalism, I limit myself here to preliminary remarks intended to characterize these alternatives, to show why they are problematic, and to justify the historical approach taken in the essays.

It will be useful to comment on four points: First, we must indicate why, at this late date, one should continue to think about antifoundationalism; why the issues surrounding this concept require still further attention; in a word, why this is not a case of driving still another nail into the foundationalist coffin. If everyone, or nearly everyone, has switched to antifoundationalism, if most of the recalcitrants have now been converted to this new religion, is there still something that needs to be said? Second, it needs to be shown why this volume takes a resolutely historical perspective; why it does not simply restrict itself, as is so often the case in modern philosophy, to a discussion of the latest views, on the assumption that it is finally only in recent thought, in the latest views to emerge, that philosophy has achieved a sound footing. To put this point in even sharper form: If foundationalism is a view that some writers have defended because they were uncritical, now that we are critical, now that we have reached the present stage, is there any need to examine earlier mistakes? Why cannot we just

1

start over again in blissful ignorance of the history of philosophy, content in our conviction that philosophy in any significant sense is independent of its history? Third, we must ask whether all the critiques of foundationalism address the same issue or complex of issues. As becomes apparent from the various essays, behind the width of views concerning antifoundationalism there lurks an even wider understanding of the nature of the genus, a remarkable disparity of the sense and reference of the basic terms, in short, the familiar diversity of opinion that has been characteristic of philosophy throughout its long tradition. Accordingly, we can at best provide only a general indication of how these terms are to be understood, as each contributor redefines them in the course of his or her contribution to the volume.

I

Among the many reasons that could be cited in support of this anthology on antifoundationalism, two are particularly important. On the one hand, this term is in the air, it is part of the current philosophical discussion; but it is unclear what it means and there is a danger that the inquiry is moving faster than the comprehension of the topic. The chaotic state of the discussion is indicated by the burgeoning literature about it, which seems to be developing exceedingly rapidly in comparison with the philosophical tradition, where discussions often continue for centuries. In just the recent literature antifoundationalism at one time or another has been associated with an almost bewildering assortment of current trends, including, in no particular order, incommensurability, hermeneutics, objectivism, relativism, postmodernism, forms of literary theory, deconstruction, and so on, and with writers such as G. W. F. Hegel, Friedrich Nietzsche, Karl Marx, Martin Heidegger, Hans-Georg Gadamer, Jacques Derrida, and Michel Foucault, W. V. O. Quine, Richard Rorty, and Jean-François Lyotard.

The wide, but not always careful, reference to antifoundationalism suggests that possible confusions lurk behind facile allusions. A single example will suffice for present purposes. In a recent volume on the relation of antifoundationalism and practical reasoning from the perspectives of hermeneutics and analysis, antifoundationalism is described as a "slogan" popularized by Rorty "for a complex of ideas previously lacking resonant expression."[1] Although this description reflects the current state of the rapidly moving debate on antifoundationalism, on reflection it seems highly questionable on at least four grounds.

First, it is not the case that Rorty initially coined the term "antifoundationalism," as might be inferred. In fact, even his use of the term is uncharacteristic, as he is concerned almost exclusively in his work with the supposed failure of the analytic approach to epistemology, which he mistakenly equates with theory of knowledge in general.[2] For Rorty, then, antifoundationalism is not a viable philosophical option but, rather, the consequence of the failure of the only correct philosophical approach.

Second, and even more important, it is vital to stress that the cluster of issues captured by this term was not somehow brought into being by its coinage or sudden surge in popularity. Discussion of the foundations of knowledge, including the antifoundationalist option, as the present volume shows, goes back in the tradition to early Greek thought. Plato's theory of ideas and Aristotle's doctrine of *ousía* are concerned with versions of this problem, in reaction to still earlier views proposed by Heraclitus, Anaximander, and Parmenides. In different forms and in other terminology the debate between the proponents of foundationalism and antifoundationalism is a main current of the entire philosophical tradition.

Third, the suggestion that the debate in question runs throughout the history of philosophy should suggest the value of rereading it in whole or part from this angle of vision. But if anything, Rorty's work has decreased attention to such problems since he thinks that philosophy, at least in the traditional sense, is no longer a live option. He has, hence, served as a lightning rod for philosophers skeptical about philosophical prospects, those uninterested in further pursuit of the discipline, in a word, for disgruntled practitioners of the art, not as a stimulus to further reflection about the foundations of knowledge. If Rorty is right, there is simply nothing interesting to say about the foundations of knowledge, about the conflict between foundationalism and antifoundationalism, because the entire theme is a sort of nonissue, the kind of topic invented for edifying discussion by philosophers who have nothing better to do.

Fourth, it is emphatically not the case that the debate between foundationalism and antifoundationalism is over, that there is simply nothing further interesting to say, that proponents of the latter view have definitively vanquished their opponents. The history of philosophy is replete with overly rapid declarations of victory, statements that an argument, tendency, even a major current of the tradition is moribund, most recently evident in Jürgen Habermas's claim that German idealism (*Bewusstseinsphilosophie*) is over.[3] But the future evolution of the tradition on occasion corrects such pronouncements by revealing them to be premature. It is, hence, by no means certain that antifoundationalism is the only way to go or that the nature and limits of this perspective can be adequately studied within the confines of these two strands of contemporary philosophy. Indeed, even at this late date there are still important proponents of certain types of foundationalism, including Karl-Otto Apel, Habermas, and, most prominently, Roderick M. Chisholm.[4]

On the other hand, there is a concealed danger in proceeding to the specialized discussion of variant types of antifoundationalism before adequate clarification of the raison d'être of this epistemological option. It is a mistake to treat the rejection of other approaches to knowledge in favor of this perspective as something over and done with. Not only is this discussion not finally decided in favor of antifoundationalism, since there are still important writers who reject this idea in some or all of its forms; there is further a considerable difference of opinion as to what this term means, and how to draw the limits. It is, then, premature, to table on the specialized exploration of this terra nuova, to attempt to map this terra incognita merely from the viewpoints of hermeneutics or analysis, since it is still an open question as to whether what some see as a new continent is terra firma or simply a mirage.

II

One of the results of the discussion to follow is to indicate the genuine variety of approaches to antifoundationalism in the philosophical literature. Since the terms "antifoundationalism" and "foundationalism" are not natural, but normative, there is no one way to draw the distinction between them. Antifoundationalism and foundationalism are correlative concepts. Just as there are types of foundationalism, say, epistemological and metaphysical, so there are epistemological and metaphysical forms of antifoundationalism. Metaphysical antifoundationalism, for instance, in opposition to metaphysical foundationalism, denies any ultimate reality or fundamental kind of being, although the denial is not necessarily couched in epistemological terms. With some notable exceptions, in recent times philosophy has turned increasingly against the idea of an ultimate reality. Forms of metaphysical antifoundationalism are especially well developed in modern times in the views of the pragmatists and their conceptual bedfellows. But pragmatic forms of antifoundationalism are not to be classed as epistemological, at least not without a struggle, since numerous pragmatists, such as John Dewey and George Herbert Mead, take an avowedly anti-epistemological stance.

It is perhaps more common to understand foundationalism and antifoundationalism from an epistemological angle of vision. Roughly speaking, we can understand foundationalism as the epistemological doctrine that there are or can be secure foundations for knowledge. This doctrine functions widely within philosophy. It is often singled out as the basis for epistemology, for system in those views that hold that philosophy must assume form as a system and system requires an epistemological ground, and for still others as the condition of the possibility of philosophy itself. Conversely, antifoundationalism is, roughly speaking, the view that there are and can be no secure foundations for knowledge, which in turn implies the denial that a grounded system is possible as well as the denial of the possibility of philosophy if philosophy in general is held to depend on an epistemological ground.

Foundationalism and a fortiori antifoundationalism are not meaningful in themselves; they are meaningful only as methodological strategies for knowledge, whose purpose is to secure validity for philosophic discourse and to justify its claims to truth. Viewing philosophy as the study, along with logic, of the underlying presuppositions of all other disciplines, foundationalists typically contend that all knowledge claims, including those of philosophy itself, must rest on and be justified by an epistemology that guarantees certainty. But epistemology has taken both foundationalist and antifoundationalist forms.

Now, there are about as many views of epistemology in the history of philosophy as there are thinkers interested in this theme. But from another perspective, the various theories of knowledge are variations on a very small number of basic themes. Historically speaking, if we exclude skepticism, or the denial of knowledge— more precisely, the minimal claim to know that we can know only that we cannot know, which is rarely disclaimed—we can discern three main approaches to knowledge in the philosophical tradition: intuitionism, foundationalism, and antifoundationalism. Intuition- ism is the view that knowledge can be grasped directly, in an act of direct "mental seizure" of the object, what the Greeks called the Forms or reality. This strategy, which depends for its claims to truth on the subjacent ontological level, is found widely in modern thought, in our time most prominently in the phenomenological theories of Edmund Husserl and Heidegger.

Historically, foundationalism and antifoundationalism arose to take the place of intuitionism, with which in some of its forms it, however, retains a distinct link. With respect to the intuition- ist approach to knowledge, foundationalism is an epistemological theory intended to be independent of ontological claims, a theory in which reason is meant to justify its own claim to know. "Foun- dationalism" can be understood in different ways. Here we will understand "foundationalism" to mean the assumption that "there are secure foundations, that is a firm, unshakable basis, on which to erect any edifice of knowledge." Knowledge, from this angle of vision, is understood as like a building or structure that reposes directly on a conceptual underpinning. For both a building and the theory of knowledge, if the underpinnings of the edifice can be made secure, then nothing can shake the higher stories.

If foundationalism is understood in this manner, we can distin- guish three ideal-typical forms of foundationalism. These sweep- ing descriptions are intended more as a way of collecting often rather different types of epistemological strategy than as a definite description of a particular position. Ontological foundationalism typically appeals to a direct, intuitive grasp of an underlying sphere of reality, as in the Platonic theory of ideas in which thought pene- trates from appearance to essence. Phenomenology in this century, in the work of Husserl and Heidegger, is an effort to restate a simi- lar claim to direct grasp of essences in the absence of an underlying ontological framework in the Greek sense.

A second form of foundationalism requires the appeal to indefeasible perceptual statements, which are, hence, necessarily true. The perceptual form of foundationalism is exemplified in the Cartesian view by René Descartes's emphasis on clear and distinct perceptions, as well as by the ongoing concern in classical and more recent British empiricism with perceptions resistant to problems of illusion and delusion. Descartes's discussion of unerring perception, and later discussions by John Locke, George Berkeley, and David Hume, and more recently by John Austin and a host of writers, including Ludwig Wittgenstein, all represent efforts to plumb the depths of claims to knowledge from immediate experience.

A third type of foundationalism is based on principles of some kind, for instance, the idea of a principle that is necessary or necessarily true. Examples include the Aristotelian idea that as a condition of rational discourse the law of excluded middle is a necessary basis of all discussion,[5] or the Cartesian view of the *cogito* as indeniable, or even the Hegelian idea of Being. A later form of this approach is a categorial framework as providing the form of all knowledge, for instance, in the Kantian, Fichtean, and Hegelian positions. The post-Kantian quarrel about the proper form of systematic philosophy and the deduction of the categories was concerned with a form of foundationalism based on a necessary principle or set of principles supposed to ground all claims to know.

These remarks concerning a systematic approach to the idea of foundationalism can be supplemented by some equally general historical remarks. Foundationalism, which reaches back into the early Greek tradition, is often seen as emerging with modern philosophy, above all in Descartes's writings. It would be more accurate to say that foundationalism is popularized, but not invented, by Descartes. In the Cartesian position we find the terms "fundamentum" and "fondement" as well as "fundamentum inconcussum," "Archimedean point," and the like. Although the term "foundationalism" does not occur, Descartes's view is widely regarded as the paradigm of foundationalism, which, in his thought, takes the form of the rigorous deduction of an entire theory from an initial principle known to be true, more precisely in his position from the *cogito* that cannot be doubted. Descartes's theory exemplifies the foundationalist approach to knowledge as requiring an unshakable foundation as the necessary condition of claims to know in the full, or traditional sense, in Cartesian language of apodictic knowledge. Later forms of foundationalism can be regarded as efforts to make good on his approach to knowledge in the full, or traditional, sense while responding to criticisms raised against his position.

The Cartesian approach has historically been widely influential in later thought. Descartes's influence reaches into both the English and the continental tradition. For the former, we need go no further than the obviously Cartesian form of Thomas Hobbes's view of certainty as based on the certainty of the prior stages in the reasoning[6] and in his description of "sense and memory" as "absolute knowledge" of "fact."[7] Other theories retain the Cartesian commitment to knowledge in the full sense, or apodicticity, but abandon his reliance on an a priori principle known to be true. Examples in the German tradition that invoke this variety of the Cartesian approach include Karl Leonhard Reinhold's appeal to an a posteriori principle of presentation (*Vorstellungsvermögen*) and, as we have noted, the repeated efforts by Immanuel Kant, Johann Gottlieb Fichte, and Hegel to deduce a categorial set adequate for the interpretation of any and all experience.

Antifoundationalism can be understood as the negation of one of the various forms of foundationalism. Antifoundationalism is plausible as an effort to justify claims to know, but now in a new, often weaker than traditional sense, if there can be no final unshakable ground for knowledge. We can characterize it in general as any effort to validate knowledge claims without appealing to an absolute or ultimate basis known with certainty, whether the latter is held to be unattainable or the model of knowledge as a unified structure resting on a foundation of certainty is rejected in principle. One of the themes of this book is that antifoundationalism is not new, that it has been around for a long time, about as long as foundationalism, which, like its denial, did not suddenly appear and was not in fact constituted by the adoption of the canonical term. If, to simplify things, we understand antifoundationalism as the contrary to the Cartesian approach to knowledge, we can describe it simply as any effort to attain knowledge in the absence of secure foundations.

Although it is relatively easy to grasp antifoundationalism as the rejection of Cartesian foundationalism, this description rests on an evident simplification. Not all forms of foundationalism can be assimilated to forms of Cartesianism, so antifoundationalism in general cannot adequately be defined as anti-Cartesianism. Although Giovanni Battista Vico was one of the first and most prominent anti-Cartesians, it is difficult to classify his view as antifoundationalist. In fact, although most antifoundationalists weaken traditional claims for knowledge, some attempt to maintain such claims while rejecting either the intuitionist or foundationalist epistemological strategies. This is certainly the base for positivism in general, which typically bases its claims to know on the claimed validity of modern science.

Like foundationalism, antifoundationalism comes in more than one size or variety. Forms of antifoundationalism, although not necessarily under that name, are widespread in philosophy, particularly modern philosophy. An example is the recent concern with postmodernism, which Lyotard understands as the denial of the so-called "méta-récit" or overriding myth, a form of antifoundationalism that in this case is a transparently anti-Cartesian position. Other forms of antifoundationalism include Aristotle's practical theory, classical American pragmatism, such forms of post-Husserlian phenomenology as Heidegger's fundamental ontology or Gadamer's hermeneutics, as well as the neo-American pragmatism of Rorty, Quine, Joseph Margolis, and others.

III

In this introduction and in the essays below, there is discussion of the foundations of knowledge not only from a systematic but also from a historical or historical and systematic angle of vision. Now, even the limited appeal to a historical perspective requires comment for two reasons. First, it has often been thought, especially in the modern philosophical tradition, that the foundations of knowledge are susceptible to a purely systematic treatment. A historical approach conflicts with the profoundly antihistorical *Zeitgeist* of the present moment, which is largely unaware of its past. As concerns philosophy, the antihistorical tendency now prevalent is the result of a conscious belief concerning the nature of acceptable theory.

This belief is predicated on the dual conviction that we must choose between systematic and historical approaches to philosophy that are incompatible and hence cannot fairly be combined. The assumption that philosophy needs to select a systematic, nonhistorical form of theory, clearly represented in such central modern writers as Descartes and Kant, is widely current in recent thought. In the critical philosophy it is present in the stated preference for a priori as opposed to a posteriori knowledge, in Kant's insistence on *cognitio ex principiis* as distinguished from *cognitio ex datis*, in the Cartesian position in the description of history as a *fabula mundi*. It is exemplified elsewhere in recent thought, in Marxism by the qualification of what Marxists call bourgeois thought as irrational, in Husserl's relative lack of interest in the prior history of philosophy, and with rare exceptions in the analytic approach to philosophy in general. So in a recent work John R. Searle straightforwardly indicates that he has seen fit to examine the conception of intentionality without reference to the extensive discussion already available.[8]

With respect to the issues canvassed in this book, the widespread preference of analytic thinkers for a mainly or even wholly systematic form of inquiry is significant as so much of the recent debate about the foundations of knowledge has been analytic. Even if at present there are signs of change, analytic thought has obviously long been hostile to the prior history of philosophy. It is no secret that the founders of analytic philosophy, including Bertrand Russell, George Edward Moore, and Wittgenstein, wanted to start over: the first by abandoning his earlier adherence to British Hegelianism, Moore through the discernment of a basic error (the reputed naturalistic fallacy, said to infect earlier ethical theory),[9] and the last in the effort to diagnose the supposed error intrinsic not only to ethics but to philosophy itself, in order, in his own arresting words, to let the fly out of the fly bottle.

This same disinclination to give serious attention to nonanalytic efforts is present in the unfortunate tendency to write as if no one other than analytic thinkers had ever attempted to scrutinize the issues concerning the foundations of knowledge. It is a startling fact that, with the exception of such writers as Chisholm, standard analytic works concerning this topic by such authors as Alfred Jules Ayer, Rorty, or Quine confine the discussion mainly or wholly to other theories in the analytic tradition.[10]

In respect to the historical approach in evidence here, two points need to be made. First, it is simply the case that no account of the problem of knowledge can be even reasonably complete that fails to address relevant aspects of the long discussion of the foundations of knowledge interspersed in many of the main texts throughout the philosophical tradition. As the studies below remind us, a central theme in the discussion of knowledge over some twenty-five centuries has been the continuing struggle between proponents of foundationalism and antifoundationalism. Second, it would be an error to infer that chronologically earlier discussion is somehow conceptually prior, that is, less rigorous or no longer worthy of consideration.

I believe that we tend to overstate the claims for contemporary thought at the expense of its predecessors. But this insensitivity to prior views is dangerous for several reasons. On the one hand, a lack of awareness of what has gone before can lead to the necessity of repeating what has already been accomplished, as Gottfried Wilhelm Leibniz is said to have rewritten earlier papers in his corpus that he later forgot. On the other hand, as the discussion to follow shows in detail, the history of philosophy is replete with insights and arguments that need to be kept in mind if we are to profit from what has already been done. It is with this idea in mind that we invite you to consider the following essays on aspects of antifoundationalism in the history of philosophy.

Notes

1. Evan Hunter, ed., *Anti-Foundationalism and Practical Reasoning: Conversations between Hermeneutics and Analysis* (Edmonton, Alberta: Academic Publishing and Printing, 1987), p. 2.

2. See Richard Rorty, *Philosophy and the Mirror of Nature* (Princeton: Princeton University Press, 1979).

3. See Jürgen Habermas, *Nachmetaphysisches Denken: Philosophische Aufsätze* (Frankfort a. M.: Suhrkamp, 1988).

4. See Roderick M. Chisholm, *The Foundations of Knowing* (Minneapolis: University of Minnesota Press, 1982).

5. See Aristotle, *Metaphysics*, Gamma iv.

6. See Hobbes, *Leviathan*, chap. 5.

7. See ibid., chap. 9.

8. See John R. Searle, *Intentionality: An Essay in the Philosophy of Mind* (Cambridge: Cambridge University Press, 1983), pp. ix–x.

9. For Searle's influential later rejection of the fallacy of the naturalistic fallacy from a stance well within analytic thought, see his *Speech Acts* (Cambridge: Cambridge University Press, 1968), pp. 132–36.

10. To the extent that Rorty and Quine regard themselves as pragmatists, they break with an earlier generation of American pragmatists better informed about the history of philosophy, including William James, to a greater extent Charles Sanders Peirce, and above all Dewey. The antifoundationalism that runs throughout Dewey's corpus is particularly apparent in two books, *The Quest for Certainty* and *Reconstruction in Philosophy*.

One

The Limits of Metaphysics and the Limits of Certainty

JOSEPH MARGOLIS

I

Possibly the most mysterious and provocative remark in the whole of pre-Socratic philosophy is the famous fragment from Anaximander: "Out of those things whence is the generation of existing things, into them also does their destruction take place, as is right and due; for they make retribution and pay the penalty to one another for their offense [or 'injustice,' *adikía*], according to the ordering of time."[1] Martin Heidegger, following Friedrich Nietzsche, struggles manfully with the task of finding an ancient anticipation of his own insistence on the puzzle of the separation of plural things from the formless source of all being.[2] It is, in fact, Anaximander's *Apeiron* itself (the Boundless, the Unlimited, the immense, the "untraversible"[3]) that ineluctably provides the source of this conceptual intrigue. Even the mischief of Heidegger's presumption, therefore, is worth an inning.

The reason Anaximander's remark is so important is that, of the entire pre-Socratic corpus, it is the only one, faltering though it may be, that challenges (or may be made to challenge) the canon of Greek philosophy "from the outside." The canon, the *archic* canon as it may be named, threads its inexorable way from Parmenides through Plato and Aristotle down to our own day. It maintains that whatever is real is unchanging and is intelligible in virtue of and to the extent only of possessing invariant structures. The canon was reflectively challenged "from the inside," in ancient times, by

13

Protagoras.[4] But that challenge was also nearly suppressed or discounted by ridicule. Anaximander challenges the canon (or may be interpreted to challenge it) "from the outside," so to say—in the sense that what he says goes beyond the admitted resources of enunciative discourse. There is, however, every reason to believe Anaximander was not entirely clear about the radical import of what he affirms. For he supposes the very *invariances* of what was to become the canon *could* be secured by his own "external" program. But that is either impossible or arbitrary. Protagoras was much clearer about the significances of his own attack on the Parmenidean canon, proposing that "man is the measure" and that coherent discourse could be made to support the denial of an invariant reality and the affirmation of relativism. Still, Anaximander and Protagoras together set the stage for every challenge that the later history of philosophy was to collect against the presumptions of the *fixed ontic and epistemic foundations* of philosophy and science. And that is no small achievement.

There seems to be no hope of recovering precisely what Anaximander meant by his new term; what we can make of it, given the ancient commentaries, baffles every easy reading. For example, Anaximander may (as the pupil and successor of Thales) have meant the *Apeiron* to be "material" in some sense: Aristotle clearly takes it that the Milesians were committed to such a source.[5]

Anaximander straddles two sorts of conceptual innovation: one, that of the *cosmologist,* proposing an "external" source for whatever is determinate in accord with the *archai* "internal" to or regulative of the familiar observable world *and* for those *archai* themselves— a source (the *Apeiron*) possessing its own (unknown) *archai* utterly different from what governs what has been "separated" from it; and the other, that of a distinct, still uncatalogued sort of *philosopher* who realized that any *Apeiron* thus characterized invites an infinite regress of similar speculations confined only by our ignorance of what lies beyond the *archai* of the (or any such) "separated" world.[6] The first is now thought to be clearly what Anaximander confined himself to.[7] And indeed, on the textual evidence we now have, it is a conclusion difficult to avoid. Nevertheless, it is also difficult to believe that a mind apt enough to grasp the "philosopher's" theme implicated in the "cosmologist's" would not have been tempted at all to construe the *Apeiron* (once formulated in the first sense) also as an inarticulable source, a surd, that could not be captured by any *archai* at all. This *is*, of course, related to the point of the natural (somewhat Orphic) speculation of Nietzsche and Heidegger (and of others);[8] and it is clearly opposed to the archic limitation of Plato's and Aristotle's thought. Whatever the textual errors of the theorists who favor the "philosopher" over the "cosmologist," the irresistibility of the conceptual linkage just noted seems entirely compelling. *If so*, then Anaximander *is* indeed the originator, however incipient and faltering, of a distinct line of thought challenging in advance—from an intractably "external" vantage—what was to become the full archic canon of Greek philosophy, a canon to which, as a cosmologist and otherwise conventional philosopher, Anaximander himself obviously also subscribed (as by his use of the notion of *adikía* or transgression).[9]

This reading may make initially plausible the idea that the manifold of discrete things—forming the intelligible order of the world by way of the *archai* of the "opposites"—was, in some sense, "separated from" or "torn away" from the "infinite" source, *to which* it (and they) must return (by way of some sort of "justice" rendered to one another within that order). But if so, it fails to provide an *arche* for that very process, and it fails to explain what its conceptual gain is over the alternative Milesian options. Also, if we succumb to Nietzsche's and Heidegger's (imperfect) intuition that the *Apeiron* must be utterly unlike anything to which intelligible principles ranging over plural, structured things obtain—which is certainly attractive—then we need to understand the sense in which the *Apeiron* thus construed is discursible (subject to enunciative discourse) at all; why the Greeks, particularly Aristotle, did not pursue the matter; how such a reading bears on the fact that Anaximander makes the "penalty" refer to the plurality of things affected rather than to the Boundless itself; and what the function of such a speculation might be.

Now, having entered the proper caveats about how to read Anaximander, we may permit ourselves a speculation that no longer pretends to be bound by the actual fragmentary text or the usual interpretation but attempts instead, adventurously, to preserve the point of what we have tried to salvage as the query that "must" have driven Anaximander's more restricted cosmology. The reason for doing so is simply that *that* line of speculation is valid on its own, unavoidable, plausibly linked to Anaximander's own thought, spontaneously so construed by modern readers, and distinctly telling when applied to all forms of the archic canon. So let us take the extra step and treat all reference to Anaximander and the *Apeiron* under the color of the novel "philosophy" we hinted at.

II

Anaximander appears to regard the *Apeiron* as "the original material of existing things," "everlasting and ageless," "immortal and indestructible."[10] Aristotle considers and confirms the notion that "there is no body which is *actually* infinite."[11] He is particularly careful, however, to retain a use for the concept of the infinite after rejecting the notion of sensible or material objects of infinite magnitude: "the infinite cannot be an actual thing and a substance and principle."[12] But he does pause long enough to worry the idea that "belief in the existence of the infinite" rests in part on the thought that "what is outside [the universe or this universe] is infinite";[13] that may be as close as Aristotle comes to the line of speculation that Nietzsche and Heidegger take up and that Anaximander rather weakly hints at.

It certainly seems reasonable to suppose that Nietzsche and Heidegger were attracted to Asian, possibly Buddhist, notions of the Void—the doctrine of śunyātā ("emptiness") for instance—in reading Anaximander; it is certainly just that doctrine that specifically recommends Nietzsche and Heidegger to the philosophers of the Kyoto School.[14] But observations of these sorts are merely forms of learned ignorance, avoiding straightforward accounts of what the *Apeiron could or must mean* if adjusted well enough to escape the obvious paradoxes that commentators like Aristotle find so easy to collect, and that commentators like Nietzsche and Heidegger find so easy to press into transparently self-serving roles.

What can be said in favor of recovering a role for *something* like Anaximander's notion once and for all freed from the obviously offending paradoxes? The beginning surely lies here:

(i) The *Apeiron* cannot be a particular principle (or *arche*) coherently fitted to other similarly (limited) principles for descrip-

tion or explanation, for it cannot apply directly to distributed things of any kind whose intelligible structures change
or persist in formulably limited ways;

(ii) the *Apeiron* cannot possess number, cannot be a particular
thing or substance (*ousía*) subject to description or explanation as are particular things, for it would then be subject to
the same principles as would other things and would then
similarly raise the question of its own comparable sources;

(iii) the *Apeiron* cannot be conceived discursively since it cannot
be a numerically identifiable referent—or, since it cannot
be aggregatively or holistically defined with respect to any
such referents—and nothing may be predicated of it qua
referent.

Aristotle dismisses all would-be thought or talk that is not in
clear accord with such (enunciative) constraints; he is thoroughly
convinced that what is real is archically accessible. That is what
Anaximander threatens. But Heidegger, of course, does try to salvage some distinct sort of intelligibility for what *he* took the *Apeiron*
to be: "what if that which is early [Anaximander] outdistanced
everything late," he asks in his most cryptic way; "if the very earli-
est surpassed the very latest [the metaphysics of our own day]?"
Heidegger does a little conceptual jig thereupon, about how to recover the meaning of history without reverting to historiography
(that is, archized history); and he arrives at the following pronouncement—a preamble to his own favored view, of course: "The
Being of beings is gathered [*legesthai, logos*] in the ultimacy of its
destiny." [15]

Our concern, here, is hardly to follow Heidegger. But if we
honor the point of his speculation while setting aside the particular message he himself would have us take away, and if we bring
that speculation to bear on a possible improvement of Anaximander's own problematic remark, then we may add a little more to
our initial tally of constraints:

(iv) As the source of what is, or of what is real, the *Apeiron* itself *is*, or *is real*, but (if that is granted) then it is
not real in the same sense in which whatever "originates"

from or "returns" to it *is* or is real—namely, the sense in which the manifold of things is subject to the referential and predicative functions of enunciative discourse; hence, even the expressions "originating" and "returning" are *not* used predicatively *of* the *Apeiron* in Anaximander's utterance, and (the verb) "is" is sui generis there and never enters into enunciative discourse;

(v) the *Apeiron* is intelligible (to the extent that it *is* intelligible) only by virtue of a conceptual *via negativa* that affirms the inapplicability of the functions of enunciative discourse to "itself" *and* by way of a dialectical demonstration of the inherent incompleteness (without "it") of every effort to collect the *archai* of all possible descriptions and explanations ranging over all discursible things; so a totalized system of *archai* ranging over everything is conceptually impossible in science and philosophy;

(vi) the *Apeiron*, then, provides a sense of conceptual closure ranging over all that is real, over all that is thought to be real, over all (however unfathomed) that is possible to be real and possible to be thought to be real—but only in a way that cannot be formalized, cannot be treated discursively, cannot be taken as an entailment or transcendental condition or revealed source or the like of the other;

(vii) the *Apeiron* cannot be bound by necessity, either in "itself" or in "relation" to the discursibly many things that originate from it and return to it, for it would then have to be said to possess determinate structures of its own in virtue of which such necessity could be discursibly affirmed of it;

(viii) all thought or talk about the *Apeiron* must be conceptually parasitic, must masquerade as, or figuratively adopt the alien form of, enunciative discourse, because no linguistic resource can function independently of the referential and predicative resources of natural language.

Conditions (i)–(viii) represent the leanest, most coherent reading of Anaximander's dictum that is possible. It repudiates the discursive conjunction of the merely material and the infinite that is not subject at all to discursive predication; it denies all distributed attributions to, and relations regarding, the *Apeiron* and the many things of the world; and it reserves an as yet unspecified function for a certain use of language that seems to be, but is not, a form of enunciative discourse itself. In some sense, Nietzsche and Heidegger do *identify* the Void that is the *Apeiron* (thus construed), for they characteristically privilege the need on *our* part to respect the Void (or *Sein*) over *any* articulated order of plural beings.[16]

Jacques Derrida, by contrast, comes closer to our reading, in developing his surd *"différance,"* by providing a nondiscursive intimation of an analogue of the denial of the completeness of *any* and *every* possible conceptual scheme—dialectically, by way of discursively supplementing every would-be such scheme. His intervention, then, functions distributively; but he wishes to avoid all appearance of making any affirmative claim about the ultimate "source" of all such operative schemata (against Heidegger himself), and therefore he avoids any positive doctrine of the Void or *Apeiron*.[17] Nevertheless, Derrida actually analyzes Heidegger's "Anaximander Fragment"; and, in that context, he says, first, seemingly against the ontology of *Being and Time*, that *"différance* is neither a word nor a concept," and, second, reaffirming Heidegger's later analysis, he says that the ultimate question, the question of Being (*Seinsfrage*), concerns "the alliance of speech and Being in the unique word, in the finally proper name." That question he finds "inscribed in the simulated affirmation of *différance*[, which] bears [on] each member of this sentence: 'Being speaks / always and everywhere / throughout / language'."[18] The formulation, "inscribed in the simulated affirmation," is a distinctly felicitous anticipation of the *philosophical* theme we are trying to rescue here.

III

There is only one linguistically possible strategy by which to satisfy the constraints of (i)–(viii), to avoid the paradoxes and seeming mistakes of Anaximander's account, to go beyond Aristotle's model of the archic limit of philosophy, to reject outright the excessive optimism of Heidegger's *Being and Time* while acknowledging the correction (in this regard only) of his later adjustment, and to go beyond Derrida's refusal to address explicitly the positive linkage between metaphysics and the implication of its deconstruction.

That is to recognize straight out that the *Apeiron* (and all of its surrogates: Being or *Sein* itself) *is a mythic posit, not the referent of a discursive assertion.*

Mention of "mythic posits" offers a strenuous but a most promising clue. Think only of the essential difference, ubiquitous in enunciative discourse, between sentences and the use of sentences, between mere strings of words composing well-formed or meaningful propositions and the actual utterance of such strings in this or that context of use in order to make a particular assertion capable of acquiring truth-values as a result—the distinction, in fact, that P. F. Strawson introduced with such remarkable effect in exposing the inherent limitations of Bertrand Russell's classic account of denotation (which, of course, Russell confused or conflated with reference).[19] Enunciative discourse, the sine qua non of every linguistic site that can be assigned cognitive import, functions as such only in an implied context of use that is not, and cannot be, exhaustively specified in any particular further such utterance. In that sense, there is an anticipation of the ultimate *Apeiron* in every contexted utterance—which is perhaps just what Derrida insinuates in his pronouncement regarding *différance*. Whether *every* such context of use can, in principle, be so recovered by way of a linkage to a cognitively privileged set of claims that can assure us that context need never disturb (may even vouchsafe) the ampliative truth of all pertinent claims identifies the fundamental conceptual problem of what is known as *foundationalism*.[20]

For our present purpose, we are *not* directly interested in challenges to foundationalism generated from "within" the range or context of all distributed truth-claims. There can be no doubt that the history of recent philosophy has overwhelmingly recommended the repudiation of every form of foundationalism and cognitive privilege on "internal" or "internalist" grounds.[21] But in introducing the conceptual puzzle of the *Apeiron*, we specifically hinted at the sense in which we might recover what should have been Anaximander's "external" attack on the reliability of the archic canon—Protagoras having been in a way the effective progenitor of the critique of that same canon on "internal" grounds. That is, what Protagoras managed to do was to demonstrate (we may at least conjecture) the coherence of treating the entire distribution of particular truth-claims as *not* requiring the cognitive privilege built into the presumption of the classical (the Parmenidean) canon: the canon that holds that reality possesses invariant structures and that human science is capable of—indeed, is formed specifically for—discerning just those structures. What we mean to consider instead is the bearing of our own version of the *Apeiron* on the question of context, now viewed "externally."

We said that the *Apeiron* was a *mythic* posit, not the referent of a discursive claim. By "mythic," we intend a distinction of art fixing a certain use of language, a use that can never be separated from the enunciative use but that is entirely different from it. It is an obvious use of language, but one neglected in most analyses of the functions of discourse. We may even guess at the reason. If we understand the archic canon to be committed to "transparency," committed to some foundationalist or cognitively privileged presumption, then, indeed, in accepting the canon, the *Apeiron*—which would, of course, threaten transparency—must be effectively replaced by a congenial myth that accords with transparency. In the West the most famous version of such a myth is the doctrine of correspondence.[22] It or its analogues (Aristotle's for instance[23]) is the archic myth that the *Apeiron* upsets. Once distributed truth-claims are admitted to be privileged or foundational *on "internal" grounds*, there is no further need to make the "external" myth it implicates explicit—*but it is there nevertheless*. The doctrine of the *Apeiron*—at least as recovered in accord with our constraints (i)–(viii)—is the first great "external" mythic posit by which all versions of transparency are placed in jeopardy. But the *arguments* against transparency are not directly drawn *from* the myth but only, dialectically, from more local contexts of utterance in which archic discourse may be distributively challenged. The baffling thing about Anaximander is simply that, having introduced the notion, he himself then goes on to favor the main lines of the archic canon. Hence, unaccountably, he speaks of some necessary, invariant order of justice that connects the origination of a world rendered intelligible by the *archai* of the opposites and *their* ultimate source, which source must be "an-archic"—hence, challenges *ab initio* all archic necessity.

IV

Seen thus, a *myth* may be said to exhibit the following features:

(a) It posits but does not (cannot) affirm a context of all contexts for enunciative discourse;

(b) it posits such a context holistically, that is, in a way that no distributed truth-claims can be said to be derived from, to be directly confirmed by reference to, or to be ensured, authorized, or strengthened by cognitively locating their own enunciative contexts within, the context of all contexts;

(c) the context of all contexts that it posits provides a totalized vision rather than an all-inclusive system holding between cognized world and cognizing subject and the supposed source of the entire order of that symbiotized pair apt for all enunciative discourse.[24]

Two illustrations, one drawn from René Descartes, the other from Heidegger, may serve to fix the function of mythic posits.

The famous quarrel about the analysis of the supposed circularity of Descartes's appeal to the *cogito* and to God's benevolence usually resists conceding that the first is meant to be a distributed truth-claim of a foundational sort, where the second signifies only the mythic source of the independent self-evidence of the first. On the reading just suggested, Descartes's argument would be plainly illicit: his reading of God's creation would instantly violate (b) of the tally given above. For he would provide a mythic vision of the context of all contexts (God's providential order) and then proceed to affirm, distributively, a direct assurance of the *cogito* itself (against all possible efforts of the Evil Demon) *from* the vantage of holistic myth. That *would be* foundationalism from an "external" source—that an adjusted doctrine of the *Apeiron* would effortlessly expose.

Consider, for example, the following remark of Descartes's, which shows that Descartes was at least sometimes worried about the truth and indubitability of what appeared most certain to him:

> whether I am awake or asleep, two and three together always form five, and the square can never have more than four sides, and it does

not seem possible that truths so clear and apparent can be suspected of any falsity or uncertainty.

Nevertheless I have long had fixed in my mind the belief that an all-powerful God existed by whom I have been created such as I am. But how do I know that He has not brought it to pass that there is no earth, no heaven, no extended body, no magnitude, no place, and that nevertheless I possess the perceptions of all these things and that they seem to me to exist just exactly as I now see them. And, besides, as I sometimes imagine that others deceive themselves in the things which they think they know best, how do I know that I am not deceived every time that I add two and three, or count the sides of a square, or judge of things yet simpler, if anything simpler can be imagined? But possibly God has not desired that I should be thus deceived, for He is said to be supremely good.[25]

If there are, distributively, indubitably true propositions—for instance, that a square has four sides, that God exists, or the notorious "I think, hence I am, or I exist" (construed as uttered by someone)—then such propositions do not require the logically prior services of a benevolent God in order to disallow the possible deception (*even apart from doubt*) of an Evil Demon. But *if even the* "simplest" (read. least dubitable) things may *somehow* be subject to deception (though *we* cannot fathom how, and though we may not even be able to doubt that they are so), then the relevant propositions *are* indubitable *only on the sufferance of a benevolent God.* This could conceivably be made to extend *to the cogito* itself. Descartes's discussion is not always or altogether felicitous.

For example, in his "Reply to the Second Set of Objections" to the *Meditations* (collected by Marin Mersenne), Descartes says:

when I said that *we could know nothing with certainty unless we were first aware that God existed,* I announced in express terms that I referred only to the science apprehending such conclusions *as can recur in memory without attending further to the proofs which led me to make them.* Further, knowledge of first principles is not usually called science by dialecticians. But when we become aware that we are thinking beings, this is a primitive act of knowledge derived from no syllogistic reasoning. He who says, '*I think, hence I am, or exist,*' does not deduce existence from thought by a syllogism, but, by a simple act of mental vision, recognizes it as if it were a thing that is known *per se.* This is evident from the fact that if it were syllogistically deduced, the major premise, *that everything that thinks is, or exists,* would have to be known previously; but yet that has rather been learned from the experience of the individual—that unless he exists he cannot think. For our mind is so constituted by nature that general propositions are formed out of the knowledge of particulars.[26]

Here, we must pose a pertinent dilemma. Either the *cogito* falls directly under the authorizing priority of God's benevolence or its certainty is unique and independent of all such assurance. If the first strategy is favored, then Descartes violates condition (b) on mythic posits; if the certainty of the *cogito* (somehow) depends on the prior certainty of God's existence (that is, that His existence is entailed by His essence, given that we *can* think of God, however "inadequately" to His perfection[27]), then the would-be certainty of the first remains hostage to all the known difficulties that dog the latter (which, at the very least, would generate reasonable doubt about God's existence and about the adequacy of our grounds for believing that He exists). If, on the other hand, the *cogito* is sui generis and does not *presuppose* God's benevolence as the necessary or adequate cognitive ground for its own certainty, then that I exist (*my existence*) must be directly, incorrigibly "intuited" as true in the very event of (my) *thinking*. But Descartes says very plainly that *existence* is never directly observed by us; in fact, the mode of existence of *all* existing things ("substances") *is inferred* from whatever we are aware of. In that case, the validity of the *cogito* depends on an inference and must, for that reason, be subject to ordinary doubt and must depend on the privileging benevolence of God—violating (b) once again.

Consider what Descartes says in *Principles of Philosophy*:

Created substances, . . . whether corporeal or thinking, may be conceived under this common concept [substance]; for they are things which need only the concurrence of God in order to exist. But yet substance cannot be first discovered merely from the fact that it is a thing that exists, for that fact alone is not observed by us. We may, however, easily discover it by means of any one of its attributes, because it is a common notion that nothing is possessed of no attributes, properties, or qualities. For this reason, when we perceive any attribute, we therefore conclude that some existing thing or substance to which it may be attributed, is necessarily present.[28]

In his replies to the objections to the *Meditations* Descartes affirms: "neither do we have any other idea of substance itself, precisely taken, than that it is a thing in which this something that we perceive or which is present objectively in some of our ideas, exists formally or eminently. For by means of our natural light we know that a real attribute cannot be an attribute of nothing."[29] Here, Descartes clearly adheres to the archic canon of Aristotle's *Metaphysics*. More than that, he renders the *cogito* hostage to inferences regarding existence and existing substances. There are other pertinent subtleties concerning the identity and permanence of the *ego* that Descartes does not satisfactorily resolve,[30] but to discuss them would lead us too far afield. It suffices to say that neither strategy offered can save Descartes from violating condition (b).

V

It is not merely that Descartes's argument is defective. It is the principal exemplar of all foundational and transparentist arguments, and is defective as such. For one thing, in accord with the characteristic orientation of all philosophy since the Renaissance, Descartes does not countenance disjoining (in the manner of Parmenides, Plato, and Aristotle) ontological and epistemological questions. And for another, he effectively divides all questions of indubitable truth into the exhaustive alternatives of those (like the number of sides of a square) that depend on God's benevolence and those (like the *cogito*) that (on the strongest argument) do not. Our counterargument, therefore, shows the sense in which either strategy is bound to fail, violating condition (b) of our tally on mythic posits. For the *cogito* is surely the leanest possible candidate for indubitable self-evidence: yet it cannot ensure the existence and persistence of any determinate "substance"; and any enhancement of its content along those lines renders it at once subject to the dubiety of all conjectures regarding existence and substance.

All other transparentist arguments are bound to enlarge the dependence of particular claims on God's benevolence or on some alternative myth (even if unnamed). For instance, Saint Thomas Aquinas's claim about the full compatibility of assent to truths disjunctively grounded in faith and reason, where both are competent sources for the same truths, cannot possibly fail to rest on God's benevolence; hence, it cannot possibly fail to violate condition (b).[31]

More interestingly, in Roderick Chisholm's extended defense of foundationalism—without a doubt the last original sustained version of foundationalism in Western philosophy, the Cartesian difficulties mentioned are not overcome. For Chisholm opposes his foundationalism to phenomenalism, that is, to the thesis that what is evident to us in terms of "self-awareness" ("more particularly, . . . [in terms of] the ways in which one is appeared to") provides for the paraphrastic reduction—to the content of such awareness—of what may be said about ordinary macroscopic things ("material objects");[32] also, Chisholm does not advance any particular or unique proposition in Descartes's manner but provides instead general criteria for various forms of foundationalist and nonfoundationalist beliefs.[33] He does indeed consider the concept and existence of the intuiting self: here, he follows both Descartes and Franz Brentano. But to cite what he says is to see at once that his arguments are not stronger than Descartes's, and that, as a consequence, he is bound to rely on some mythically supplied source of certainty (not necessarily the God of Saint Thomas or of Descartes): [34]

> The person's self-presenting properties, then, are such that he can be absolutely certain that they are all had by one and the same thing— namely, himself. And this is the closest he comes—and can come—to apprehending himself directly. But this awareness that there is something having the properties in question is what constitutes our basis, at any time, for all the other things that we may be said to know at that time.[35]

In effect, Chisholm reverses the direction of Descartes's argument and makes the certainty of *what* is "presented" in awareness depend on its being "considered" *by* the persistent real self to which it is presented. But this brings into play all the full (Cartesian) doubts about the analysis of what the nature of that self is and about what the evidence is that such a self reliably persists as self-identical through time.

There seem to be no other distinctive lines of argument of these sorts to consider.

VI

The issue Heidegger's argument raises is of another sort, because it never descends explicitly to Cartesian-like dicta; and yet, of course, particularly in *Being and Time*, it does posit certain "ontic" truths about *Dasein* that, in effect, recover the archic canon in an attenuated way—against Heidegger's own project of subverting the pretensions of canonical metaphysics and epistemology. For Heidegger's concern, at least against Descartes and Kant, is to explain the sense in which the standard bifurcation of cognizing subject and cognized world falsifies our understanding of *Dasein*—a fortiori, our understanding of ourselves and our mode of inquiry—even though the categories of our cognitive grasp of the world are deployed as they are as a result of *Dasein*'s career:

> Ontically, of course, Dasein is not only close to us—even that which is closest: we *are* it, each of us, we ourselves. In spite of this, or rather for just this reason, it is ontologically that which is farthest. . . . The kind of Being which belongs to Dasein is rather such that, in understanding its own Being, it has a tendency to do so in terms of that entity towards which it comports itself proximally and in a way which is essentially constant—in terms of the 'world'. In Dasein itself, and therefore in its own understanding of Being, the way the world is understood is . . . reflected back ontologically again upon the way in which Dasein itself gets interpreted.
>
> Thus because Dasein is ontico-ontologically prior, its own specific state of Being (if we understand this in the sense of Dasein's 'categorial structure') remains concealed from it. Dasein is ontically 'closest' to itself and ontologically farthest: but pre-ontologically it is surely not a stranger.[36]

Heidegger's point is that the formative conditions of *Dasein*'s being (its "ontological" structure) are obscured by prioritizing or fixing as essential and unchanging the canonical subject-object oppositions of standard metaphysics and epistemology (its "ontic" structure), which it does indeed spawn:

> For what is more obvious than that a 'subject' is related to an 'Object' and *vice versa*? This 'subject-Object-relationship' must be presupposed. But while this presupposition is unimpeachable in its facticity, this

makes it indeed a baleful one, if its ontological necessity and especially its ontological meaning are to be left in the dark.

Thus the phenomenon of Being-in [Being-in-the-world] has for the most part been represented exclusively by a single exemplar—knowing the world.[37]

In a word, "the question of the kind of Being which belongs to this knowing subject is left entirely unasked, though whenever its knowing gets handled, its way of Being is already included tacitly in one's theme."[38]

All forms of certitude, invariant structure, the totalized closure and fixity of concepts are put entirely at risk by Heidegger's account. The Cartesian venture, all foundationalism, all transparency, is outflanked. Furthermore, once we follow Heidegger himself in construing "the task of Interpreting Being as such" as "working out the [radical] *Temporality of Being*," we grasp the sense in which totalized closure is impossible, in which "*the central problematic of all ontology*" leads us to consider that inquiry itself (and whatever it discloses) *is* "an ontical possibility of Dasein."[39]

All this may be put more compendiously. Heidegger holds that the seeming fixity of the subject-object relationship basic to canonical metaphysics and epistemology is itself an artifactual posit drawn from the contingent preformational conditions forming *Dasein* as it is in-the-world (*in-der-Welt-sein*). The independent *relationship* of subject to object (epistemologically) is *not* (existentially) the same as, or congruent with, the internal *interrelatedness* of *Dasein* and "world" within the whole of Being (*Sein*):

The 'problem of Reality' in the sense of the question whether an external world is present-at-hand and whether such a world can be proved, turns out to be an impossible one, not because its consequences lead to inextricable impasses, but because the very entity which serves as its theme [*Dasein as Being-in-the-world*], is one which, as it were, repudiates any such formulation of the question. . . . After the primordial phenomenon of Being-in-the-world has been shattered, the isolated subject is all that remains, and this becomes the basis on which it gets joined together with a 'world'.[40]

In this sense, Heidegger completely subverts the archic projects of Descartes, Kant, and Edmund Husserl without subverting the possibility of metaphysics and epistemology.[41]

The "world" is not merely *present* (in some timeless, invariant, detached, external, complete, and independent way) *to* plural active and cognizing agents. It is present-to-*Dasein*, but only in that "primordial" sense in which "*Dasein*'s Being" is itself the "*Temporality of Being.*"[42] Effectively, this means that the internal relatedness of *Dasein* to *Sein* is posited "mythically" by Heidegger in terms of some precognitive, premetaphysical condition of time, *such that* every determinate structure of world and cognition enunciated archically (presuming the bifurcation of subject and object) is tacitly, even blindly, and in a radically contingent way preformed by the way in which *Dasein*'s Being is itself preformed by its own temporal career in-the-world. That is what Heidegger means by "historicality" (*Geschichtlichkeit*): "historiology—or more precisely historicity [*Historizität*]—is possible as a kind of Being which the inquiring Dasein may possess, only because historicity is a determining characteristic for Dasein in the very basis of its Being."[43]

At this point a curious but ineluctable puzzle arises. We have just construed Heidegger's vision of the "relationship" of *Dasein* to *Sein*, affecting all enunciative discourse, all truth-claims, as a *mythic* posit. It could not be otherwise for Heidegger himself, since the purpose of his intervention is to subvert the presumption of all archic discourse and to restore ontology to a much more modest function *within* "historicality." But *if* that is granted, then there is no way of privileging Heidegger's own *analysis* of the distortions of the archic tradition: *it* must be similarly subject to the "historizing" influences that his own myth so effectively collects. Nevertheless, that, for one thing, is hardly the impression *Being and Time* affords; for another, Heidegger is obviously worried about the import of just this reflexive challenge; and for a third, there is no longer any way in which to privilege *any* "existential-hermeneutic" account of historical *Dasein* over the "objectivist" claims of canonical metaphysics and epistemology: at any point in time they must have the same limited standing. That means that, in a very real sense, Heidegger's own analysis is itself inescapably infected by the "subject-object relationship" he means to expose; also, that there is no way of escaping it altogether.

This is the implicitly circular threat of Heidegger's own patient explanation of the relationship that holds between "objective" and "existential" analysis:

whenever an ontology takes for its theme entities whose character of Being is other than that of Dasein, it has its own foundation and motivation in Dasein's own ontical structure, in which a pre-ontological understanding of Being is comprised as a definite characteristic.

Therefore, *fundamental ontology*, from which alone all other ontologies can take their rise, must be sought in the *existential analytic of Dasein*.

Dasein accordingly takes priority over all other entities in several ways. . . . But the roots of the existential analytic, on its part, are ultimately *existentiell*, that is, *ontical*.[44]

The upshot is that the symbiosis of enunciative and mythic language is ineliminable: the enunciative functions within the mythic; and the mythic is posited from the ever-changing vantage of particular enunciative claims. There is no escape from this circle (except at the price of some transparentist presumption).

Nevertheless, Heidegger intends his doctrine to obviate all forms of historicism, relativism, incommensurabilism; or, better, he intends all enunciated forms of historicism and the like to be constrained by the *invariantly unified historicality* of *Dasein*.[45] The necessity of that constitutive unity is nowhere explained. It is in fact particularly problematic, since, as Heidegger remarks, "subject and object do not coincide with Dasein and the world."[46] The thesis is also, as it happens (through the meaning of history), curiously suggestive of Donald Davidson's altogether different undefended rejection of incommensurabilism.[47] For, if moderate conceptual divergences yielding incommensurabilism can arise without risking intelligibility, then the counterinsistence of different thinkers like Heidegger and Davidson and others becomes entirely arbitrary.[48] The charge holds for every insistence on the all-encompassing *unity* (or closed system) of *Dasein* (Heidegger), understanding (Immanuel Kant), conceivability (Husserl), interpretation (Hans-Georg Gadamer), communication (Jürgen Habermas), meaningfulness (Davidson). In any case, the insistence is the last-ditch claim of a foundationalism for which there can no longer be the slightest defense.[49] Its defeat prepares the ground for the various sorts of relativisms that Heidegger certainly meant to oppose—but could not, without betraying a commitment to the very "ontic" fixities he wished to "destroy." For, the necessary unity of the "knowing subject" is made (by Heidegger) to depend on the necessary unity of *Dasein* (which, of course, is simply constructed in the other's image).[50] In Donald Davidson's case, a metaphysically and epistemologically relaxed pragmatism is somehow made to preclude, even against W. V. Quine's concessions, any drift in the direction of plural conceptual schemes that cannot, demonstrably, satisfy the impossible test of "translat*ability*."

VII

In a fair sense, the drama of the Cartesian and Heideggerean strategies confirms the need to interpret Anaximander's *Apeiron* along the lines we have. In fact, in the "Letter on Humanism," which provides one of the most sustained commitments to the theme of the *Kehre*, Heidegger explicitly says: "if man is to find his way once again into the nearness of Being he must first learn to exist in the nameless. In the same way he must recognize the seductions of the public realm [*die Öffenlichkeit*, with which *Dasein* is occupied in *Being and Time*] as well as the impotence of the private. Before he speaks man must first let himself be claimed again by Being, taking the risk that under this claim he will seldom have much to say. Only thus will the preciousness of its essence be once more bestowed upon the word, and upon man a home for dwelling in the truth of Being."[51] Decoded, Heidegger's somewhat florid pronouncement signifies the turn from *Entschlossenheit* (the "resoluteness" of *Dasein* in the face of what is revealed only *to* and *through Dasein*'s essential mode of existential "care" for Being)[52] to *Gelassenheit* ("release" or freedom, that is, escape from every "technical" or "representational" scheme of categories governing enunciative discourse about, and the manipulation of, reality; or, again, receptiveness to an encounter with Being no longer encumbered by a metaphysics of any kind).[53]

Heidegger abandons, here, the mediating Kantian-like function *Dasein* plays (and must play) in *Being and Time*.[54] Either, therefore, he intends *Gelassenheit* in a fully mythic (hence, *not* enunciative) way that may still yield a suitable "ethic" or natural "piety" for man;[55] or else, by privileging the "revelations" of Being (*alētheia*), *sans Dasein*, he risks violating the inherent (Kantian-like) constraints on enunciative discourse itself.

That is, after the *Kehre*, Heidegger is obliged to treat the "dis-

closedness" of any structured world of things as, somehow, *not*
inherently conditioned or constrained by the symbiotized involve-
ment of human understanding, but as (rather) an originary revela-
tion that *human* "thinking" must (then) address in addressing the
greater mystery of its being disclosed at all:

> But does not *Being and Time* say on p. 212 [in the German pagination],
> where the "there is / it gives" comes to language, "Only so long as
> Dasein is, is there [*gibt es*] Being"? To be sure. It means that only so
> long as the lighting of Being comes to pass does Being convey itself to
> man. But the fact that the *Da*, the lighting as the truth of Being itself,
> comes to pass is the dispensation of Being itself. This is the destiny of
> the lighting. But the sentence does not mean that the Dasein of man in
> the traditional sense of *existentia*, and thought in modern philosophy
> as the actuality of the *ego cogito*, is that being through which Being is
> first fashioned. The sentence does not say that Being is the product of
> man. . . . For all that, Being is thought on the basis of beings, a conse-
> quence of the approach—at first unavoidable—within a metaphysics
> that is still dominant. Only from such a perspective does Being show
> itself in and as a transcending.[56]

The issue is a vexed one and has such an improbable air about
it that it is hard to take it seriously. But stay a moment longer
with it. In *Being and Time*, Heidegger says very plainly: "Being (not
entities) is something which 'there is' only insofar as truth is. And
truth *is* only insofar as and as long as Dasein is. Being and truth
'are' equiprimordially. What does it signify that Being 'is', where
Being is to be distinguished from every entity? One can ask this
concretely only if the meaning of Being and the full scope of the
understanding of Being have in general been clarified. . . . By
laying bare the phenomenon of care, we have clarified the state
of Being of that entity to whose Being [*Dasein*] something like an
understanding of Being belongs. At the same time the Being of Dasein has thus been distinguished from modes of Being (readiness-
to-hand, presence-at-hand, Reality) which characterized entities
with a character other than that of Dasein."[57] Heidegger mentions
this passage in the "Letter on Humanism." But, there, he makes
"the truth of Being" *effect*—draw into effectiveness—man's function *as Dasein* at the same time it effects *Dasein*'s (passive) reception
of whatever Being discloses in ways suitable for language:

Being is illuminated for man in the ecstatic projection [*Entwurf*]. But this projection does not create Being. Moreover, the projection is essentially a thrown projection. What throws in projection is not man but Being itself, which sends man into the ek-sistence of Dasein that is his essence. This destiny comes to pass as the lighting of Being, as which it is. The lighting grants nearness [but only nearness] to Being.[58]

In this peculiarly convoluted way, Heidegger manages to construe the destiny of the West ("man's approaching destiny") as, somehow, man's discovery (*qua Dasein*) of "the history of Being"— disclosed to him but not constructed by him: "As the destiny that sends truth, ... In the face of the essential homelessness of man [that is, his oblivion of the truth of Being], man's approaching destiny reveals itself to thought on the history of Being in this, that man find his way into the truth of Being and set out on this find. . . . Man is not the lord of Beings. Man is the shepherd of Being."[59]

Two remarks serve to bring this account to a proper close. The first is an aside, namely, that we cannot fail to see in the "Letter" Heidegger's metaphysical contortions in the service of his own brand of National Socialism. The second is simply that we cannot fail to see that Heidegger's later thought ruinously confuses and conflates enunciative and mythic talk. For, in some very strange way, although "Language is the house of Being. In its home man dwells,"[60] it is not of *human* language that Heidegger first speaks, but of a "language" (the language of the "truth" of Being) that man can (somehow) bring *his* own language to grasp. Hence, the mythic source, Being, somehow "sends" discernible messages to man (his historical "destiny," for instance) in a way that can be enunciatively proclaimed. But that is utterly preposterous and brings us back again to Anaximander.

VIII

The critical insight of Anaximander's groping improvement on the Milesian cosmology rests with his recognition of the dialectical significance of the Opposites or paired concepts by which any perceivable order of things is rendered intelligible. The insight is this:

    (i) that all concepts are privative;

and

    (ii) that to specify what of reality is not captured by particular sets of concepts is to employ other concepts that are equally privative.

The *Apeiron* is intended, cosmologically, to do justice to (ii) beyond the palpable incompleteness of Thales's cosmology confined to (i); naively, it leaves all concepts within the scope of (ii) unspecified. In a deeper philosophical sense, the *Apeiron* signifies that the application of concepts is necessarily contextual and, therefore, incapable of achieving any systematic comprehensiveness, any totalized closure regarding what is or *is* real. That, very plausibly, is part of the sense in which particular things "make retribution and pay the penalty to one another for their offense, according to the ordering of time." For, every order is privative of other possible orderings that may be drawn from the *Apeiron*.

    Now, the archic presumption maintains that, although this is indeed true, the contingent, *apparent* ordering of the processes of change—say, according to some provisional version of (i)—obscures the deeper truth that there is an as yet unknown but fixed and necessary order of change in accord with the *archai* of the ultimate *Apeiron*—say, according to some totalized version of (ii)—that renders the whole of reality an intelligible invariant plenum or closed system. Anaximander *is* a party to this vision since he is committed to *adikía*. But if so, then he *cannot* consistently suppose that the categories of (ii) are logically different in any pertinent sense from those of (i): only our ignorance makes for the difference between the Bounded and the Boundless. And that is hardly enough: it means that, ultimately, Anaximander has *not* gone very far beyond Thales. Ultimately, perhaps surprisingly, the Milesian vision is the same as that of the modern unity of science program, that is, that knowledge takes, in principle, a thoroughly *homonomic* form: the vocabulary of description is the vocabulary of explanation under changeless and exceptionless laws.[61] From this point of view, it is true enough that particular concepts are, if taken distributively, privative—they give no assurance that other *possible* parsings of reality (within the all-encompassing *Apeiron*) are not occluded by the schematism of the favored set. But—here is the conceptual optimism—the true (read: homonomic) selection of the categories of (i) will, in the context of their use, implicate the entire system (ii) of all such concepts. There will be no "privation," because reality has a changeless structure. It cannot have such a structure, of course, unless that structure is uniquely what it is, all-encompassing, homonomic. *It would preclude incommensurabilism and relativism, therefore.* There is the point of the "agreement" between Heidegger and Davidson: insofar as it is discernible, human inquiry and science are foundational, transparentist.

The tacit claim, bridging the otherwise enormous gulf between Anglo-American pragmatists and continental existential phenomenologists, may be fixed by a line from Hans-Georg Gadamer's *Truth and Method*—a line as arbitrary to, and as ineluctable for, the archic pretensions of either as any that might be cited. It is, of course, entirely dependent on Heidegger's vision of *Dasein* and the "languaged" nature of the world:

> in language the world itself presents itself. The experience of the world in language is 'absolute'. It transcends all the relativities of the positing of being, because it embraces being-in-itself, in whatever relationships (relativities) it appears. The linguistic quality of our experience of the world is *prior*, as contrasted with everything that is [enunciatively] recognized and addressed as being. The fundamental relation of language and world does not, then, mean that world becomes the object of language. . . . The linguistic nature of the human experience of the world does not include *making* the world into an object.[62]

And, since the linkage to Heidegger entails a commitment to the essential invariances of *Dasein* (which betrays Heidegger's archic penchant), it signifies through that the pointed antirelativism of Husserl and Wilhelm Dilthey as well.[63] Given this much only, it is easy to see that the resistance to conceptual incommensurabilism and the insistence on the invariance of the "subject" or *Dasein* are merely alternative faces of one and the same foundationalism—whether in science or practical life. The economy is as welcome as it is surprising.

The archic vision, then, is committed to the myth of an intelligible plenum, the fixed system of the world. This it may obscure because, on its own assumption, there is no limit to the competence of enunciative discourse. In different ways, this is the common theme of Parmenides, Aristotle, Descartes, Leibniz, Spinoza, Kant, and Husserl. Context is only an accident of what we say here and now; ultimately, contextual indeterminacies are homonomically resolved. The opposing vision (the an-archic) treats (i) and (ii) as equivalent. There is, we may say, no difference between Thales and Anaximander. But Anaximander may be read in a way Thales cannot be, if we interpret his utterance as a glimmer of a deeper reading of the *Apeiron*—at least suggestively caught by Nietzsche and Heidegger (for their own ulterior uses).

That is why the distributed sense of the context of enunciative discourse is taken as a sign of the ineliminable openness, the inherently asystematic nature, of *both* inquiry and reality. For, *if* the intelligible world presupposes an ultimately impenetrable symbiosis (only partially suggested by the alternative schematisms of "subject" and "object" and *Dasein* and *Sein*), then *no homonomic system can be in place*, no foundationalism or transparentism is possible. (Heidegger and Davidson, we were just suggesting, are not committed to the archist's thesis, only to these parts of it that suit them opportunistically.) Conceptual analysis cannot but be radically provisional, historicized, constructivist, praxical, existential, moderately incommensurabilist, contextual—and privative. Indeterminacy is as much a feature of what *is* as of what we believe. There you have the key to Anaximander's inkling, a glimmer of an insight from which Anaximander himself may well have turned away.

Notes

1. I take the translation from Charles H. Kahn's article on Anaximander in Paul Edwards, ed., *The Encyclopedia of Philosophy*, vol. 1 (New York: Macmillan and Free Press, 1967), pp. 117–18. See, further, Charles H. Kahn, *Anaximander and the Origins of Greek Cosmology* (New York: Columbia University Press, 1960). The translation obscures, however, the sense in which the *Apeiron* lacks number.

2. Martin Heidegger, "The Anaximander Fragment," *Early Greek Thinking*, trans. David Farrell Krell and Frank A. Capuzzi (New York: Harper and Row, 1984); Friedrich Nietzsche, "Philosophy in the Tragic Age of the Greeks" (1873).

3. Kahn suggests "untraversible" in order to contrast the sense of the term with that of the mathematically infinite, which he takes not to be Anaximander's sense: *Anaximander and the Origins of Greek Cosmology*.

4. I have explored the viability of Protagoras's attack in an as yet unpublished paper, "Métaphysique radicale," *Archives de philosophie*, forthcoming.

5. Aristotle, *Metaphysics*, bk. 1, chap. 3.

6. See G. S. Kirk and J. E. Raven, *The Presocratic Philosophers* (Cambridge: Cambridge University Press, 1971), p. 122.

7. This is the judgment of Kirk and Raven, ibid., chap. 3; and of Kahn, *Anaximander and the Origins of Greek Cosmology*, app. II.

8. Kirk and Raven, *The Presocratic Philosophers*, p. 194.

9. Ibid.

10. Kathleen Freeman, *Ancilla to the Pre-Socratic Philosophers: A Complete Translation of the Fragments in Diels, Fragmente der Vorsokratiker* (Oxford: Basil Blackwell, 1952), p. 19.

11. Aristotle, *Physica*, trans. R. P. Hardie and R. K. Gaye, in Richard McKeon, ed., *The Basic Works of Aristotle* (New York: Random House, 1941), 206a.

12. Ibid., 204a. See chaps. 4–8.

13. Ibid., 203b; cf., also, *Metaphysics*, bk. XI, chap. 10.

14. See Kitaro Nishida, *Intelligibility and the Philosophy of Nothingness*, trans. Robert Schinzinger (Honolulu: East-West Centre Press, 1958).

15. Heidegger, "The Anaximander Fragment," p. 18.

16. See, for instance, Martin Heidegger, "The End of Philosophy and the Task of Thinking," *On Time and Being*, trans. Joan Stambaugh (New York: Harper and Row, 1972).

17. Jacques Derrida, "Différance," *Margins of Philosophy*, trans. Alan Bass (Chicago: University of Chicago Press, 1982).

18. Ibid., pp. 7, 27. See, also, "*Ousía* and *Grammé*: Note on a Note from *Being and Time*," *Margins of Philosophy*, which also touches on "The Anaximander Fragment"; and Walter Brogan, "The Original Difference: *Différance*," in David Wood and Robert Bernasconi, eds., *Derrida and Différance* (Evanston: Northwestern University Press, 1988).

19. P. F. Strawson, "On Referring," *Mind* 59 (1950); Bertrand Russell, "On Denoting," *Mind* 14 (1905).

20. For a useful overview cast in the style of analytic philosophy, see Keith Lehrer, *Knowledge* (Oxford: Clarendon, 1974), particularly chap. 4.

21. These terms have become general coin largely through the work of Hilary Putnam. To draw on them here is not, however, to endorse Putnam's own solution of the "internalist" question. See Hilary Putnam, *Reason, Truth and History* (Cambridge: Cambridge University Press, 1981), chap. 3. The pith of his distinction is conveniently summarized and some-

what refined in *Representation and Reality* (Cambridge: MIT Press, 1988), chap. 7.

22. This explains the rationale for Richard Rorty's now notorious attack on the presumptions of (canonical) philosophy: they are all, he believes, committed to some form or other of transparency, even if not (for instance, as in Aristotle) to some form or other of correspondence. See Richard Rorty, *Philosophy and the Mirror of Nature* (Princeton: Princeton University Press, 1979).

23. See Aristotle, *De Anima*, bk. III, chaps. 4–8.

24. On the concept "system," see Joseph Margolis, *Science without Unity: Reconciling the Human and Natural Sciences* (Oxford: Basil Blackwell, 1987), pp. 433–34.

25. René Descartes, "Meditations on First Philosophy," Meditation I, in E. S. Haldane and G. R. T. Ross, trans., *Philosophical Works of Descartes*, vol. 1 (Cambridge: Cambridge University Press, 1931), p. 147.

26. *Philosophical Works of Descartes*, vol. 2, p. 38.

27. Ibid. Cf. "Meditation V," pp. 182–83.

28. Principle LII, *Philosophical Works of Descartes*, vol. 1, p. 240.

29. *Philosophical Works of Descartes*, vol. 2, p. 53.

30. I have benefited here from Lilli Alanen, *Studies in Cartesian Epistemology and Philosophy of Mind*, Acta Philosophica Fennica 33 (Helsinki: Societas Philosophica Fennica, 1982), particularly pp. 139–44. Cf. also Jaakko Hintikka, "Cogito ergo sum: Inference or Performance," *Philosophical Review* 71 (1962).

31. See Saint Thomas Aquinas, *Summa Theologiae*, trans. Thomas Gilbey (London: Blackfriars, 1964), vol. 1, question 1.

32. Roderick M. Chisholm, *Theory of Knowledge*, 2nd ed. (Englewood Cliffs: Prentice-Hall, 1977), p. 127.

33. Ibid., chaps. 1–2. See also Roderick M. Chisholm, *The Foundations of Knowing* (Minneapolis: University of Minnesota Press, 1982), chap. 1.

34. Roderick M. Chisholm, *The First Person: An Essay on Reference and Intentionality* (Minneapolis: University of Minnesota Press, 1981), pp. 79–80.

35. Ibid., p. 89.

36. Martin Heidegger, *Being and Time*, trans. from 7th ed. John Macquarrie and Edward Robinson (New York: Harper and Row, 1962), pp. 36–37 (pp. 15–16 in the German pagination).

37. Ibid., p. 86 (p. 59 in the German pagination); cf. Introduction, chap. 1.

38. Ibid., p. 87 (p. 60 in the German pagination).

39. Ibid., pp. 40, 41 (pp. 18, 19 in the German pagination).

40. Ibid., p. 250 (p. 206 in the German pagination); cf. pp. 43–44 (pp. 22–23 in the German pagination).

41. See Edmund Husserl, *Cartesian Meditations*, trans. Dorion Cairns (The Hague: Martinus Nijhoff, 1960), Introduction and First Meditation. I have benefited here from the account in Charles B. Guignon, *Heidegger and the Problem of Knowledge* (Indianapolis: Hackett Publishing, 1983), chap. 2.

42. Heidegger, *Being and Time*, pp. 40, 41 (pp. 18, 19 in the German pagination).

43. Ibid., p. 42 (p. 20 in the German pagination). Cf. the whole of Introduction, chap. 2.

44. Ibid., pp. 33–34 (p. 13 in the German pagination). Cf. also pp. 244–45 (pp. 200–201 in the German pagination).

45. Cf. ibid., sec. 13.

46. Ibid., p. 89 (p. 60 in the German pagination).

47. See Donald Davidson, "On the Very Idea of a Conceptual Scheme," *Inquiries into Truth and Interpretation* (Oxford: Clarendon Press, 1984). Davidson is reported to be somewhat annoyed at the tendency to link him and Heidegger and other similar-minded "Continental" thinkers. But here the linkage is plausible.

48. See, for instance, Ian Hacking, "Language, Truth and Reason," in Martin Hollis and Steven Lukes, eds., *Rationality and Relativism* (Cambridge: MIT Press, 1982).

49. On Davidson's view, see, further, Joseph Margolis, *Pragmatism without Foundations: Reconciling Realism and Relativism* (Oxford: Basil Blackwell, 1986), pp. 80–81.

50. *Being and Time*, pp. 87–88 (pp. 60–61 in the German pagination).

51. Martin Heidegger, "Letter on Humanism," trans. Frank A. Capuzzi and J. Glenn Gray, in David Farrell Krell, ed., *Martin Heidegger: Basic Writings* (New York: Harper and Row, 1977), p. 199.

52. Cf. *Being and Time*, sec. 60.

53. See, for example, Martin Heidegger, *Discourse on Thinking*, trans. John Anderson and E. Hans Freund (New York: Harper and Row, 1966).

54. Cf. *Being and Time*, pp. 44–46 (pp. 22–24 in the German pagination).

55. See, for example, Martin Heidegger, "The End of Philosophy and the Task of Thinking," *On Time and Being*, trans. Joan Stambaugh (New York: Harper and Row, 1972). See, also, John D. Caputo, *Radical Hermeneutics* (Bloomington: Indiana University Press, 1987), part III.

56. "Letter on Humanism," pp. 216–17.

57. *Being and Time*, pp. 272–73 (p. 230 in the German pagination).

58. "Letter on Humanism," p. 217.

59. Ibid., pp. 219, 221.

60. Ibid., p. 193.

61. It would not be extreme, for instance, to term Davidson's attraction to homonomy Milesian. See Donald Davidson, "Mental Events," *Essays*

on Actions and Events (Oxford: Clarendon Press, 1980).

62. Hans-Georg Gadamer, *Truth and Method*, trans. from 2nd ed. Garrett Barden and John Cumming (New York: Seabury Press, 1975), p. 408; italics added.

63. Cf. Heidegger, *Being and Time*, p. 38 (pp. 16–17 in the German pagination).

Two

Foundationalism in Plato?

RONALD POLANSKY

The several forms of foundationalist theories of knowledge aim to avoid infinite regresses of justifications through locating principles that stop the regress and justify whatever else is known. Strong forms of foundationalism require that these principles be in some sense self-certifying, for example, by direct presentation through sense perception or immediate intuition of the mind. Weaker forms of foundationalism allow that principles might merely be acceptable in some sense, for example, that they be prima facie acceptable or acceptable beyond a reasonable doubt.[1]

These various versions of foundationalism are not new. They have been around as long as philosophers have worried about the possibility of knowledge. Roderick Chisholm states, "Most of the problems and issues of the 'theory of knowledge' were discussed in detail by Plato and Aristotle and by the Greek skeptics. There is some justification, I am afraid, for saying that the subject has made very little progress in the past two thousand years."[2] It should hardly be inappropriate, therefore, to reconsider the contribution to debates about foundationalism that may come from antiquity.[3] This essay focuses upon Plato's thoughts about the prospects of the positions that converge under the label "foundationalism."

It seems especially appropriate to reconsider Plato in this light because his school was closely connected with the formalization of geometry, the result of which was Euclid's work. In this enterprise and the reflection upon it, axiomatization was not only highly developed and implemented but also projected as the paradigm for all knowledge. Hence, Aristotle's treatment of knowledge in the

41

Posterior Analytics is generally supposed linked with the formalization of geometry. The ideal of knowledge grounded in pellucid principles inspired by geometry often returns in the history of philosophy; it became quite strong in our own modern period of philosophy. The Cartesian project, for example, might seem to be rather Platonic in its search for certain principles from which could be spun out all else, as if a universal mathematical understanding of the world were possible. Given the continuing fascination of the foundationalist project, particularly in its geometrical version, it may be quite useful to return to the period in which our fundamental conceptions of knowledge were formulated.

Foundationalism in Plato may enter into the *practice* of argumentation in the dialogues or the occasional discussions of the *theory* of that practice or the theory of inquiry generally. To trace Plato's views, we shall have to consider what takes place in the dialogues as well as explicit thematization of foundationalist positions. Let us start with the actual method of investigation in the dialogues.

I

Most prominent in Socratic practice in the so-called early dialogues is Socratic elenchus or cross-examination. Socrates in these dialogues first elicits an answer from an interlocutor about what some moral concept is. The underlying assumption here is that if someone knows something, such as a moral concept, he ought to be able to give an account of what he knows, even if only to state what it is that is known (see, e.g., *Laches* 190c, *Charmides* 159a). Receiving the answer, Socrates refutes it, usually by calling upon some further beliefs of the interlocutor that conflict with the initial answer. Presumably, the refutation succeeds because the interlocutor holds more strongly to the beliefs in terms of which Socrates produces the refutation than he holds to the original answer.[4] But what sort of justification is there for the beliefs Socrates uses? One possibility is that they are endoxic beliefs, that is, opinions that are reputable because held by everyone or by the wise.[5] Another is that as part of the belief set of the interlocutor they are acceptable to him and so in need of no further justification. Another is that they are also part of Socrates' belief set, built up over time through much experience of elenctic confrontations, and thus inductively established. Whichever way it is that the beliefs Socrates uses in the elenchus are supposed justified, it seems clear that they hardly have the status of self-certainty and no appeal is made to such status. Consequently, at play here could only be some weak form of foundationalism. Yet even this is suspect when Socrates' general project is considered.

The Socratic elenchus is on "the way to, not from" first principles.[6] When Socrates asks the famous "What is *x*?" question regarding some moral notion, he seeks the first principle in terms of which it could be further determined what ought to be done. The "What is *x*?" question frequently arises in a context in which the interlocutor seems sure he has a correct principle or may be presumed to know. He either relies on it to justify his actions (such as Euthyphro's relying on his understanding of piety to prosecute his father) or practices a craft that may presuppose it (such as the implied understanding of virtue of Gorgias and Protagoras). Hence, the elenchus is in the service of determining whether the interlocutor really has the firm understanding of the principle that it seems he should or thinks he does. The elenchus tests how well grounded the principle is in the set of beliefs of the interlocutor. Were the principle to resist all efforts of refutation, then it would presumably be a secure foundation for a set of doctrines or for practices. It thus may appear that the elenchus is in the service of foundationalism, but a foundationalism that hardly gets off the ground because none of the principles offered by the interlocutors resists Socratic refutation.

Yet there may be something in Socratic practice surpassing aspiration for foundations. In refuting the interlocutors' answers, Socrates may use his own well-founded beliefs. Though sometimes he seems to rely upon beliefs that the interlocutor holds though he himself does not—a notorious case in which Socrates refutes an opponent in terms of a belief he probably does not accept is the refutation of Protagoras based on the hedonist's assumption of the equation of pleasure and good (*Protagoras* 351b ff.)—more frequently Socrates resorts to beliefs he holds as well as the interlocutor. If so, and if he has many experiences of cross-examinations, then a kind of inductive assurance arises about some of these beliefs. Perhaps a typical product of this sort of induction is the belief that the soul is more valuable than the body and that the body should assist it. Such a belief could serve as principle for others. Socrates' confidence that he can always handle arguments directed against what he considers good is strongly expressed in this passage in the *Theaetetus* (177b, Fowler trans.): "Whenever they [those who contend the opposite of Socrates] have to carry on a personal argument about the doctrines to which they object, if they are willing to stand their ground for a while like men and do not run away like cowards, then, my friend, they at last become strangely dissatisfied with themselves and their arguments; their brilliant rhetoric withers away, so that they seem no better than children."[7] This indicates an inductively grounded confidence in principles, since conflicting principles have always been refuted. At most, this could be called a weak version of foundationalism because the principles are inductively grounded rather than directly evident.[8]

Let us turn to another part of the Socratic practice, beyond the standard elenctic examination of the interlocutor. When the situation demands it, Socrates himself makes suggestions to the interlocutor of principles that may contribute to the investigation. For example, in the *Euthyphro* (12d) he proposes that piety is some part of justice; in the *Meno* (87b) to determine whether virtue is teachable, he tries the hypothesis that it is knowledge; and in the *Phaedo* (100b) the forms are hypothesized to help with the consideration of immortality. The case I shall examine is the *Republic*. Socrates must defend justice under the constraints imposed by his interlocutors. To do so he introduces, without quite announcing what he is doing, fundamental premises about human nature. These premises, which will permit the defense of justice, are partially in disagreement with those in terms of which injustice had been defended. These premises are: the natural desire of humans is for self-sufficiency ([369b]; this opposes the Thrasymachean assumption that humans naturally desire to outdo each other [359c]); this desire for self-sufficiency can be satisfied only in association with fellow human beings; and humans naturally differ in ability (370a–b). Because of the inequality in ability, an association established on the principle that each does what each is best qualified to do will best provide for self-sufficiency.

The supposition that humans are unequal in ability is shared by Socrates and Thrasymachus. Only, whereas Thrasymachus combined differences in ability with the desire to surpass others, so that it was in the interest of the superior persons to take advantage of their strength to dominate the weaker people (343b–344c), Socrates secures individual and collective self-sufficiency through the employment of the different talents for different useful occupations. Since inequality is a shared assumption of Socrates and Thrasymachus, it might not need argument, and only the naturalness of the desire for self-sufficiency would. But Socrates does have to spell out the sense of the inequality, so there is much argument regarding inequality as well as about natural desire.

Socrates spells out the differences in ability by locating three different classes in the city and three parallel parts of the soul. The abilities requisite to the occupation of the ruler, soldier, and farmer or craftsman correspond to the contributions that the rational, spirited, and appetitive parts of the soul can make in a well-ordered soul. It may appear that Socrates uses the "large letters" of the city to help him read the "small letters" of the soul, but in fact he develops the account of the classes in the city with the soul in mind. For example, only with the introduction of spiritedness in the soldiers does the class of soldiers become identified as a separate part of the community (374e–375b). In the case of the different classes, Socrates seems first to foresee the need for performance of a certain task, such as the task of soldiering, and then he establishes that there is a group available with the requisite abilities for performing this task. In the case of the soul, the procedure is to consider certain experiences of conflict within the soul in the light of a principle such as the principle of noncontradiction and to conclude that the conflict is due to different principles in the soul (435b ff.).

What seems common to the delineation of the differences within souls and cities is a style of reflection upon numerous phenomena. The phenomena are one's own experiences, common opinions, statements in poetry, and so on. All of these encapsulate some of what goes on or might go on in souls and cities. From this wealth of experience various possible articulations emerge. Presumably, Socrates settles on that articulation which best characterizes the fundamental differences, has the most explicative force, and allows for the parallel of city and soul. Thus selecting principles from a wealth of data pointing toward them and tailoring the principles to the work they must do is a widely employed and most acceptable procedure. It hardly accords, however, with strong forms of foundationalism, for no appeal is made to self-evidence. It also shows how weak the weak versions must be, since it appears that the principles are not selected and justified independently of that of which they are the principles. Much of the support for the principles derives from their success in accounting for what follows from them.

That self-sufficiency is the basic human end requires different arguments from the premise about inequality, but arguments that perhaps work in rather similar ways. Socrates' first important move is to construct the so-called city of pigs. He appears to recognize that much of the plausibility of the Thrasymachean view that human desire is insatiable stems from confusion of the desires. When the love of honor becomes jumbled with the love of money, then it is especially likely that desire seems infinite. Honor love provokes people to compare their situations with respect to money and such things with other's situations. This comparison propels them to unlimited acquisition.[9] But the city of pigs has no place for concern with honor or recognition. The basic needs catered to nearly exclusively are natural needs for food, clothing, shelter. The description of the city establishes that these are easily satisfied (369d). Hence, humans do not in principle have limitless, insatiable desires for such materials necessary for life. Even when the dialogue develops more complicated communities, the basic point remains that money is strictly necessary only to the extent required for survival and that love of money and honor are separable. Kept separate, these desires need not drive toward infinity. Moreover, they can be seen to be instrumental to a further end rather than themselves true ends. As mere means they will be limited by the end.

But what is the end to which these desires are subservient? The *Republic* tries two answers. One is the good order of the soul or community, the other is philosophy. Good order exists where justice prevails and each part of the soul or city is doing its own job. Concerns for money and honor serve the whole soul or city when they are subordinated to just functioning. Where this is the case, the soul or city seems healthy and well ordered. But because of the fact that the highest part of the soul or city has two functions, ruling and seeking knowledge, money love and honor love may subserve the pursuit of wisdom (philosophy) as well as the good ordering of the soul or city. The desire of wisdom to which love of money and honor are subordinated might seem nearly as infinite or insatiable as those seemed to Thrasymachus. This is the case because humans all lack complete wisdom. Nonetheless, the situation with knowledge is quite different from that with money and honor. First, unlike those other chief objects of desire that are valuable only because scarce, knowledge may have a different source of worth. Second, knowledge may be shared without diminishing anyone's quantity of it. Third, wherever there is any perfection in knowledge, for example, in geometry, nothing is lacking to that knowledge. The sciences seem to have standards internal to themselves (see, for example, 350a). The only similar limit with respect to money or honor derives, as indicated above, from some outside principle such as good order of soul or philosophy. Fourth, even if humans are all imperfect in the highest wisdom, there is at least a limit in principle, namely, perfect wisdom. If wisdom is not a cumulative concept, that is, it is not an infinitely enlargening sum, it would be perfectible in principle. Wisdom would not be cumulative were it grounded in something like Plato's forms or ideas.

The line of argumentation supporting the view that the natural human desire is for self-sufficiency seems to start with the distinction of desires for money, honor, and knowledge and then reflects on their respective natures. The eliciting of money, honor, knowledge as the primary sorts of human objectives is a very high-level inductive generalization from much experience. It seems a permanent insight into the human condition. Even where one or the other of these is undervalued by some individuals or cultures, they remain constant human possibilities. Still, they are hardly self-certifying. In the reflection upon the natures of these different desires, they are ranked. This consideration of the natures and the ranking uses many arguments. Numerous arguments are employed to support that reading of the phenomena which has life revolving around standards or limits and to attack the opposed reading that conceives life as limitless. This variety of arguments construable as supporting the principle that humans aspire to self-sufficiency indicates that things are not really quite as foundationalism may lead us to suppose. The principles are not easily acces-

sible and readily acceptable and smoothly justifying what follows
from them. Rather, they may require considerable argumentation
even to make them seem plausible. And that argumentation develops from just that sphere that the principles were presumed to
account for.

In the fields of real philosophical interest to Plato, human conduct and ultimate reality, there seems to be a need for "rich" principles, that is, principles adequate to account for the phenomena.
Where such ample principles are sought, there is no possibility for
self-certification. The principles derive from careful consideration
of a wealth of experience and are acceptable only if through extensive argumentation they hold their own and justify the position for
which they are introduced. There is thus a kind of nascent pragmatism in Plato's assumption of principles only insofar as they lead
to viable theories.

II

We have reviewed enough of the practice of Plato's dialogues
to determine that only part of the foundationalist position appears
in them. This is the part that emphasizes that principles must
be located. The dialogues constantly resort to principles. These
principles, however, neither seem to be directly evident nor obviously based upon directly evident materials. If the foundationalist
project of justification is in evidence in the argumentation of the
dialogues, it is present only in a quite weak version. But perhaps
Plato or Socrates holds to a stronger version of foundationalism in
theory even if not successfully in practice. This possibility warrants
exploration.

Some places to check are the section of the *Republic* in which the
form of the good seems to be the ultimate principle and the *Theaetetus*, which offers the lengthiest sustained Platonic inquiry into
knowledge. It seems clear that the *Republic* formulates a foundationalist conception of knowledge in which wisdom depends upon
an unhypothesized highest principle, the good (511b–c). Given
that Socrates does not claim such insight for himself and even
reserves it for the utmost conceivable wisdom rather than for ordinary human knowledge, it seems that foundationalism in a strong
version serves as a human delineation of a divine sort of knowl-

edge. All the reservations Socrates employs regarding his account of this wisdom and all its restriction in range suggest despair at any strong sort of foundations for knowing. Perhaps the main reason he introduces his foundationalist-sounding theory is to point out the shortcomings of ordinary human arts and sciences. For him, the fact that sciences such as the mathematical sciences merely posit principles that they do not further explore indicates inadequacy in their foundations and a place for philosophical investigation. These sciences leave to philosophy the effort to ascertain just how far thought can go in justifying the principles of the sciences. That this further consideration is possible and necessary, and unlikely ever to terminate, discredits any thought of an easy foundationalist grounding of the arts and sciences. Where foundationalism might be thought best to succeed, in the arts and sciences, it will not, because none of these can justify their own principles. Geometry is a somewhat dubious paradigm for the wisdom philosophy seeks.

A most interesting point for our purposes in the *Republic* is the restriction of the objects of knowledge to kinds rather than individuals (see, e.g., 475e ff.). It may well be that the kinds are forms. Yet, if the arts and sciences are to be permitted some claim to knowledge, then it must be allowed that they study kinds, whether or not the kinds are forms. The arts may work on individual things, but insofar as they provide knowledge, they do so through comprehension of kinds. The traditional reason for restricting the possible objects of knowledge to kinds is that these do not change and are not relative. The underlying assumption here is that knowledge is infallible. What is known to be the case must truly be the case and must be true always.[10] The restriction to kinds eliminates much of what contemporary foundationalist epistemologies normally take themselves to be establishing.[11] Most antiskeptical arguments aim to support judgments about sense experiences. For example, that things generally are as they appear or that the perceiver truly exists are typical reliable propositions. Plato seems indifferent to the status of such propositions in his consideration of the theory of knowledge. As important as particulars are for practice, they do not constitute appropriate objects of knowledge.[12]

The *Theaetetus* confirms the restriction of knowledge to kinds. This is strongly emphasized in the "digression." Socrates contrasts

those practitioners of oratory who must concern themselves with
particulars with philosophical orators who seek to know what man
as such is or what justice or happiness is (175c). Though some
passages may lead commentators to suppose that Plato permits
there to be knowledge of particulars—this is especially the mistaken conclusion drawn from 201a–c—this is not really the case.
Any time he makes an argument that deals with particulars, the
point applies as well to kinds and more importantly to kinds. The
long section of the dialogue that allows that particulars, and only
particulars, may be known, the long exploration of the conception that knowledge is sense perception (151–86), ends by refusing
to grant that sense perception can be knowledge (184–86). Even
though Socrates several times acknowledges that what appears to
us through the senses undeniably does appear, and so we may be
infallible about appearances, nonetheless, he does not look toward
this self-presenting feature of appearances for any foundation of
knowledge.

Where the *Theaetetus* comes closest to views that might be lik-
ened to contemporary foundationalism is in the final section in
which the possibility that knowledge is true opinion with an account, that is, justified true belief, is considered (201c ff.).[13] What
constitutes justification of an account is the pressing issue of the
dialogue. Several different possibilities are explored, all unsuccess-
fully. It seems that Plato sets the conditions for knowledge so high
that no attempt could succeed. Whereas contemporaries seek to
determine when ordinary arts and sciences are genuine knowledge, Plato is convinced that, from a certain perspective, these
disciplines cannot be knowledge. That perspective is the one which
demands a full articulation of all principles. Modern projects of
justification either have sought subjective certainty or have recognized the need to stop with evident principles. Subjective certainty
in the Cartesian vein meant certainty about particulars, matters
of existence, and about the application of concepts to an existing
world. Plato seems willing to allow that for most purposes the
established arts and sciences provide genuine knowledge, yet he
also holds out a perspective from which they do not.[14] It is from
this perspective that all the attempts to give an account of account
in the *Theaetetus* fail.

Plato hardly doubts that the arts and sciences are excellent within their own domain. Consider the contrast of art with mere knacks for the conviction that arts have true standards rather than relative standards (see, for example, *Gorgias* 465a). In spite of excellence within their sphere, the established arts and sciences can lead to mistaken suppositions that they provide the highest knowledge. Such is the complaint about them in the *Apology* (22d). This complaint persists through all the other dialogues. Were the various sciences adequate, there would be no need for philosophy. Philosophy seeks the most embracing wisdom, that which the various arts and sciences do not provide. With an eye to such wisdom, it seems that all humans can recognize is their lack of this wisdom. The fullest completion of the project of foundationalism is for the Platonist, therefore, not possible. What remains, then, for philosophy to attempt? The *Theaetetus* seems to provide an interesting answer to this question.

The dialogue, in its attempts to give an account of knowledge, explores the most promising candidates for what knowledge might be: sense perception, true opinion, and true opinion with an account. Each of these is given a very thorough review. Inasmuch as the promising candidates are under consideration and in such a full treatment, the review in the dialogue is undertaken in a quite self-conscious way by Socrates. In spite of Socrates' insistence that he merely engages in midwifery and that his interlocutor begets all the conceptions (150c–d), he is not so passive as he suggests. Rather, he directs the path the dialogue takes. There is striking evidence of this. In the last section of the dialogue (206–9), Socrates explicitly offers the several accounts of account. These *accounts* of account correspond perfectly to the various *accounts* of knowledge developed earlier in the dialogue. If this is so, then the efforts to give an account of account amount to reflection upon the activity of account-giving in the dialogue. Thus the *Theaetetus* offers a remarkable instance of what it discusses. Theaeteus and Socrates have attempted many accounts of knowledge and then returned to reflect upon what it can mean to give an account. The dialogue thus achieves a kind of self-reflective understanding. The dialogue presents all the elements of knowledge, the various accounts of it, and in such a way that the place of these various accounts seems well understood. The theory of knowledge present in the dialogue seems to be that human knowledge requires the investigation of

all the possible candidates for what that knowledge might be and
the appreciation of their various strengths and shortcomings. With
the appreciation of the respective place of each of the candidates
in the adequate conception, there is justification provided for the
opinions about them. Full justifications may never be available,
but continuing reflection upon the strengths and weaknesses of
the various possibilities for what some concept may be goes so far
as humanly possible to justify our thoughts.

The *Theaetetus* seems to present an alternative vision of knowledge to that suggested by foundationalism. Instead of laying foundations, inquiry might be viewed as "squaring." In the dialogue
it is observed that some magnitudes become commensurable with
others only when taken to the second dimension, or squared
(147d). Opinion or thought seems similarly incommensurable with
knowledge. When we have true opinion, we still need not know.
And if we merely *add* more opinions to the original opinion in the
effort to justify it, we seem unlikely to get beyond opinion. The
best hope is to square our thinking. Such squaring would be taking
our thought through all the articulations of the field and in a way
in which our efforts are well understood by ourselves. Thus our
thought might reach a dimension beyond mere thought.

We should gather from the *Theaetetus* a greater sense of the
diversity of meanings of knowledge. There is knowledge constituted by the arts and sciences. There is also, in a sense, knowledge
of particular things and of appearances. There is knowledge of
possibilities and actualities, things, states of affairs, terms, propositions, and collections of propositions. There is knowledge that
may guide practical life other than that available in the arts. There
might be a comprehensive universal knowledge as sought in philosophy. All these different senses of knowledge emerge in the
dialogue. It is very unlikely that any single account could cover
all of these. Contemporary epistemologists should be more aware
of this. They might also recognize that the supreme knowledge
would be that sought by philosophy and presumably had by the
gods. The prominence given to arguments of the skeptics seems
to have confused the theory of knowledge about its object. It often
appears that knowledge appropriate to the gods is sought about
the most trivial propositions, for example, "the cat is on the roof."
It ought to be clearer what sort of knowledge is to be expected in

different areas. More attention to these distinctions would lead to a better appreciation of the status of the knowledge in the various areas.[15] In philosophy, until divine wisdom presents itself, the project should be like that exhibited in the *Theaetetus* and elsewhere: a self-conscious, comprehensive inquiry into the promising candidates.

The theory of knowledge presented in the *Republic* and *Theaetetus* does not seem to sustain any stronger foundationalist position than appears in the practice of the argumentation of the dialogues. Surely, heuristic forms of foundationalism guide both Plato's conception of knowledge and the practice of investigation in the dialogues. This must be the case at least to the extent that he seeks principles and principles that will account for other things. However, the status of the principles Plato seeks is unusual. They are universal though not at all abstract; they are outside the subjects of the ordinary sciences;[16] they are justified insofar as they can be by that for which they must account. This suggests an extraordinary sort of foundationalist position, if we care to call it that at all. Plato hardly supposes that we shall finally arrive at some ultimate principles fully justified. In working out his views on these matters, he has traversed the territory to which we are now returning. Reconsideration of his views may thus inform modern controversies.

Notes

1. Most contemporary versions of weaker foundationalism offer theories of justification in which the principles of justification themselves are not self-certifying. See, e.g., Roderick Chisholm, *The Theory of Knowledge*, 3rd ed. (Englewood Cliffs, N.J.: Prentice Hall, 1989), pp. 72–74.

2. Chisholm, "Theory of Knowledge in America," reprinted in *The Foundations of Knowing* (Minneapolis: University of Minnesota Press, 1982), p. 109.

3. Note this comment about Aristotle: "Aristotle, the inventor of the syllogism and of the deductive method in the philosophy of science, brought his formidable acumen to the sphere of practice as well and, with his theory of the practical syllogism, made a promising start towards rendering matters of conduct as precise and as deductively neat as the theo-

retical sciences. With his analysis of man's essence, he provided the new science with a priori first principles, to be grasped by intuition but not subject to rational argument." Martha Nussbaum says this is a prominent view about Aristotle, though she calls it into question. See her work, *Aristotle's De Motu Animalium* (Princeton: Princeton University Press, 1978), pp. 166–67.

4. Surely, since it is in conflict with them, the original answer is logically inconsistent with the other opinions to which Socrates gets the interlocutor to agree. Now, inconsistency implies that at least one member of the inconsistent set must be abandoned, but it remains indefinite which should be dropped. Socrates and the interlocutor agree that the interlocutor's original answer is what must be rejected, so it seems the other beliefs are adhered to even more strongly.

5. See the account of *endoxa* in Aristotle, *Topics* I.1. Gregory Vlastos, who has produced the most prominent account of the logic of Socratic elenchus, argues that though Socrates uses endoxic beliefs where he can, he does not always do so and does not rely on their status of being *endoxa*. See "The Socratic Elenchus," *Oxford Studies in Ancient Philosophy* 1 (1983): 41 ff., and my criticism of his claims in "Professor Vlastos's Analysis of Socratic Elenchus," *Oxford Studies in Ancient Philosophy* 3 (1985): 249–53.

6. This phrase comes from Aristotle's *Nicomachean Ethics* (I.4.1095a30–b1), where he states that Plato insisted upon the distinction of investigations to or from the principles.

7. Plato, *Theatetus and Sophist*, trans. Harold North Fowler, The Loeb Classical Library, vol. 2 (Cambridge, Mass.: Harvard University Press, 1967).

8. This inductive justification has an interesting twist. It is not a single argument that justifies some proposition, but a lifetime of arguments that does so. There is also the possibility that this inductive justification is not the only justification at play, i.e., there may also be some other more direct. What this is, is not stated. So far as Socrates relies on his experience of the elenchus to sustain his basic beliefs, he seems to have at most a weak foundationalist position.

9. It is of course possible that someone may seek unlimited acquisition of money without any care for reputation. This is relatively rare and not really what Thrasymachus has in mind. The desire to outdo others (*pleonexia*) must involve comparison of situations.

10. See Chisholm, *Theory of Knowledge*, chap. 10, for the traditional assumptions about knowledge. Cf. Aristotle *Metaphysics* VII. 16.

11. Chisholm presents a foundationalist account of "empirical knowledge" in the third edition of *Theory of Knowledge*, chap. 7. One looks in vain in this work for any consideration of the implications of restriction of knowledge to knowledge of kinds.

12. In the previous note it was indicated that Chisholm does not emphasize the reduction of appropriate objects of knowledge to kinds. Surely the Greeks speak as we do of knowing particulars, yet Plato and Aristotle insist upon kinds as the appropriate objects of knowledge. To know a kind is to grasp it in terms of its causes, where cause is understood, perhaps, in one of Aristotle's four ways (form, matter, mover, end). The comments about the division in the *Republic* of desires into that for money, honor, or knowledge should make it clear that kinds and causes of kinds are at issue. Moreover, at the level of kinds there are difficult questions regarding what would be verification or falsification of a theory. Theories involving kinds seem to require some complex understanding of possibilities. For example, were there an entire society lacking, say, lovers of honor, that would not necessarily falsify the claim to truth of Plato's scheme.

13. Myles Burnyeat provocatively denies that Plato anywhere in the *Theaetetus* considers the contemporary view that knowledge is justified true belief ("Socrates and the Jury: Paradoxes in Plato's Distinction between Knowledge and True Belief," *Proceedings of the Aristotelian Society* supp. 54 [1980], p. 180). I argue that he is seriously mistaken in my commentary on the *Theaetetus, Philosophy and Knowledge* (Lewiston, Pa.: Bucknell University Press, 1991).

14. The "dream theory" in the *Theaetetus* (201c–206b) is an interesting effort at foundationalist theory and an illustration of failure from a certain perspective. On the dream theory, the elements or principles are accessible through perception but capable of no further account, whereas what is constituted from the elements will have an account through the elements. Socrates argues that where the elements can have no account, then any account they constitute is worth little. This is true from one perspective and not from another. As a model for what occurs in the sciences, the "dream" well depicts the form of justification from scientific principles. *Within* a science this seems perfectly appropriate. But from a perspective outside that science, it seems that the principles are inadequately grounded.

15. Aristotle is very clear about these points and emphasizes that the educated person knows what precision to expect in each science. In *Nicomachean Ethics* I.3.1094b23–27, he states: "it is the mark of an educated man to look for precision in each class of things just so far as the nature of the subject admits; it is evidently equally foolish to accept probable reasoning from a mathematician and to demand from a rhetorician scientific proofs."

16. The possible exceptions to this statement are those "sciences" that have a very wide field somewhat like philosophy. For example, poetry and rhetoric speak nearly of all things, as does philosophy. This explains why these subjects are of particular concern in the dialogues.

Three

Foundationalism and Temporal Paradox: The Case of Augustine's *Confessions*

GARY CALORE

In book XI of the *Confessions* Saint Augustine introduces a series of celebrated paradoxes, a dialectical chain of impasses and resolutions concerning the nature of time. This mind-numbing sequence of contradictions constitutes an argument from which Augustine appears to draw three conclusions. These are that: the present is the whole of temporal reality (that is, past and future are not "real" and thus not per se measurable); the present is a moment of pure passage without duration; and time itself is analytically resolvable into two discontinuous, independently real aspects, one subjective, the other objective. For the most part these distinct but interwoven notions have dominated the efforts of traditional metaphysicians to frame a satisfyingly general account of time. Many thinkers, to be sure, have rejected one or another of these conclusions, but few have resisted them all. The very pervasiveness of the claims arising from the paradoxes is evident in the way in which a common commitment to them makes doctrinal allies out of philosophers who are otherwise by tradition, temperament, and outlook often radically opposed. The ontologically privileged status of the present, for example, has been maintained alike by the pragmatist George Herbert Mead,[1] the phenomenologist Maurice Merleau-Ponty,[2] and Alfred North Whitehead[3] in the name of process metaphysics. Though Mead's appropriation of the idea is certainly more radical, culminating in the insistence that the past has no integrity distinct from the present and is therefore as indeterminate or "open" as the future, both Whitehead and Merleau-Ponty adhere to the view that, in a relevant and significant sense, the present is metaphysically ultimate. Similarly, theorists such as Isaac Newton,[4] John Locke,[5] and René Descartes[6] have sought to account for generic traits of time (for example, "passage" and "duration," and so forth) in terms of irreducibly atomic knife-edged moments dividing a nonexistent future from an equally nonexistent past. Moreover, though Adolph Grünbaum[7] and Henri Bergson[8] are philosophers not often mentioned in the same breath, they are nevertheless united in their adherence to temporal dualisms that reflect a difference less of fundamental perspective than of selective emphasis.

Despite innumerable efforts from various directions to account for Augustine's paradoxes, it is my belief that their sources have yet to be adequately explained, while their theoretical results have yet to be systematically scrutinized. In this essay I will argue that the paradoxes of the *Confessions* and the claims that are derived from them are paradigmatic expressions of the consequences of rooting a conceptualization of time in foundationalist principles. The assumptions that give rise to these contradictions are deeply embedded in the fabric of Western metaphysical discourse. The Augustinian temporal dialectic is only perhaps the most vivid and dramatic example of the difficulties inherent in a commitment to the notion of privileged orders of "being" and the search for absolute termini of analysis upon which to ground philosophical query. My intention is to show that when these commitments are abandoned, the paradoxes dissolve and the conclusions warranted by them go begging for justification. Where such notions are purged, there lies the possibility of a just metaphysical account of time. Thus, by an examination of Augustine's argument I hope not only to lay bare the foundationalist machinery of the paradoxes but also to suggest the way toward a reconstruction of the concept of temporality along antifoundationalist lines.

To make the case that problems in the *Confessions* concerning time derive from foundationalist assumptions and can be transcended only from an antifoundationalist perspective is to reject at least two prevalent strains of criticism of this much discussed text.

The first of these is most notably manifest in the work of Ludwig Wittgenstein,[9] Friedrich Waismann,[10] O. K. Bouwsma,[11] and J. N. Findlay,[12] whom I shall take to be representative. It is characterized by the claim that Augustine's paradoxes do not embody real problems, that they are brought about solely by linguistic confusion and can be resolved merely by exposing the sources of that confusion. The second critical mode is expressed by thinkers such as John M. Quinn,[13] James McEvoy,[14] H. M. Lacey,[15] and W. H. Newton-Smith,[16] who maintain that the argument of the *Confessions* illuminates serious philosophical difficulties that are either "intractable" (in Newton-Smith's case), or are resolvable on Augustine's terms or by some manner of reconstruction that leaves Augustine's metaphysical commitments intact. Neither of these views is adequate: I take the paradoxes to be genuine but the claims predicated upon them incorrigible, and not some higher understanding of time redeemed by the recalcitrant mind in the crucible of contradiction.

Ordinary language philosophers assume that the eloquent expression of perplexity with which Augustine initiates the reader into the mysteries of time manifests the search for a definition:

> What then, is time? Is there any short and easy answer to that? Who can put the answer into words or even see it in his mind? Yet what commoner or more familiar word do we use in speech than time? Obviously when we use it we know what we mean, just as when we hear another use it, we know what he means. What then *is* time? If no one asks me, I know; if I want to explain it to a questioner, I do not know.[17]

The question "Quid est ergo tempus?" is said to be answered by a misguided attempt to replace ordinary language with some ideally exact discourse imitative of the sciences. Such an attempt is seen as paradigmatic of what constitutes the origin of traditional "metaphysical" problems. On this view, the apparent contradictions in our reflection about time arise, not because of any conceptual difficulty or categorial failure, but rather are the result of philosophers' wrongheaded and futile efforts at exactitude. Augustine's paradoxes, so the account goes, can be resolved at their source—linguistic confusion—by clarifying the grammar of the word 'time', and that of the temporal expressions we commonly use.

According to Findlay, it is queer that we should find time such a puzzling and paradoxical matter when we are able to deal quite competently with "temporal situations." It is "a strange disorder," he writes, "that people who have spent all their days 'in time' should suddenly elect to speak as if they were casual visitors from eternity."[18] The problem arises because the attempt to generalize our experience of temporal situations inevitably leads to the employment of language different from that "perfectly adapted to dealing with them."

Our misguided belief that ordinary language leaves us analytically ignorant of the nature of time leads us, for example, to make precise our use of the present tense and the temporal adverb 'now'. In ordinary circumstances, to say even of happenings that last a long time that they are happening "now" is unexceptionable. By discarding this everyday sense, however, we are tempted by the apparent similarities between temporal and spatial grammars to conflate the two. Thus, we might be convinced that, since a whole cannot be occurring 'now' unless all its component parts are also occurring 'now', our use of the term should be restricted only to those happenings that take no time at all. Thus, by this "disordered" habit of speech one might be inclined to accept that nothing of which a part lay in the past could properly be said to be happening now, and that anything that takes time does not happen "all at once" but in a sequence such that when one of its parts is happening, the others either have happened or will happen. It is but a short step to be forced to acknowledge that no happening that takes time can be said, strictly speaking, to be taking place, and that the only parts of it of which it *could* be said were rightly those that took no time at all. Such results, according to Findlay, have serious consequences, for they

turn a serviceable way of talking into one that has no use. For it is obvious that all the happenings that we can point to (in any ordinary sense of 'point to') take time, and that pointing itself takes time, so that if the only happenings of which we may say 'This is happening now' are happenings which take no time, there *are* no happenings which we can point to of which we may say, 'This is happening now'.[19]

The use of language in such a "pseudo-scientific" manner is, on "commonsense" terms, the source of contradiction. It turns time into a "mystery" that we must "penetrate" if we are to think that we have any understanding of it at all. 'Philosophy', in the sense discredited by ordinary language thinkers as 'metaphysics', transforms everyday patterns of speech perfectly well adapted to our experience of time into a fruitless search for something veiled, transempirical, the "really real."

I have chosen to dwell on this example at length to illustrate the central claim of the "antimetaphysical" interpreters of Augustine's text. According to Findlay and others, the origins of temporal paradox lie, not in managing our experience "in time," but in the illegitimate attempt to describe temporal situations in general terms. On this view, the mere effort to generalize *necessarily* involves a law-like application of the terms of ordinary temporal discourse, which, unlike terms in a scientific language, are not susceptible to such use.

For ordinary language thinkers, any attempt to construct an adequate "metaphysical" account of time is thus inevitably bound to fail, for it could only replace one misconceived effort at precision with some other, deemed superior until the contradictions in *its* grammar became apparent. To adopt a metaphysical attitude toward time is thus to engage in an endless round of generating insoluble problems by applying false grammars. It is like a perpetual dance in which we choose partners whose movements entice us with a promise of fulfillment only to leave us entangled in our own feet. There is no reason, on this account, why ordinary language ought to be supplanted by some ideal discourse. Philosophy (metaphysics) in this sense is a misbegotten enterprise.

The so-called commonsense analysis, for all its economy and ingenuity, falls short as a critique largely because its premise is incorrect. Few of Augustine's difficulties are linguistic in origin, and, most importantly, his account of time in the *Confessions* is not concerned with the search for a definition. The text of book XI does not support the claim that Augustine was attempting to construct an ideal language of pseudo-scientific exactness that would supersede ordinary discourse about time. In fact, as James McEvoy convincingly points out, the reverse appears to be true. Augustine continually affirms his approval of linguistic custom in an aporetically punctuated dialectical movement toward a fuller, more comprehensive understanding of time. Nowhere, moreover, does Augustine actually provide a definition. According to McEvoy,

"though starting from a question that appears to demand a definition in answer [he] does not define time; he offers, not a definition,
but a phenomenology of speaking, intending and acting, in and
over time." [20]

If not a rigorously consistent grammar of time, what was Augustine seeking by posing his much-pondered question? H. M. Lacey
argues that Augustine's bewilderment was not linguistic in origin
and that he had no difficulty at all handling ordinary usage. His
problem, according to Lacey, was that he did not know to *what* his
terms *referred*.

> He wanted to know whether time is a feature of the objective world,
> or whether time is a subjective phenomenon; whether temporal rela-
> tions are relations among physical events, or relations among private,
> mental events. Ordinary usage did not supply answers to these ques-
> tions. . . . In other words, Augustine's problems are problems central to
> the metaphysics of time. They are the traditional problems: objectivity
> vs. subjectivity; absolute vs. relational. [21]

Lacey proceeds to distinguish two strains of Augustine's account
of time in book XI; one "objective" and (unfortunately) undevel-
oped; one "subjective" and quasi-coherent, for which he provides
a masterly, if misguided, in my view, empiricist reconstruction.

Lacey's account of the paradoxes is superior to that of Findlay
for two reasons: (1) he acknowledges that Augustine's paradoxes
represent real problems, while (2) he clears for metaphysical understanding of time a path free from the tyranny of commonsense
language games. My dispute with Lacey concerns his view that a
metaphysics of time is primarily a matter of a thinker's encounter
with a specific set of problems whose origins lie in the possibility of referential free-play. That ordinary language underdeter-
mines the referential scope of temporal terms confers legitimacy
on Augustine's questioning: wanting to know what can be said of
time in cases where common linguistic practice is silent cannot be
attributed to grammatical crossover. Nevertheless, Lacey does not
explicitly render an account of the nature of the terms whose "reference" is in question, and thus, I argue, he does not capture what
I take to be the essential character of metaphysical discourse, its
genericness.

It is the striving for descriptive adequacy and the attempt to construct temporal categories of most comprehensive scope that is Augustine's task in the *Confessions* and, ultimately, the source of his problems. The questions he seeks answers to arise in the act of framing the constitutional factors (traits) of the subject matter under consideration in the most general terms possible. Is time constituted of a past and future, as well as a present? Are past, present, and future species of existence, or of some other ontological genus? Are they metrical? These are the questions that arise in the effort to discriminate temporal complexes of widest possible scope. In other words, Augustine's pursuit is the primary metaphysical goal: to identify the generic traits of time.[22] 'Metaphysics of time', as I am using the term, refers to the conceptual schematization that frames our understanding of the temporal world in the most encompassing way possible. The "traditional" problems of which Lacey speaks derive from this vital activity of categorial construction.[23] They are a secondary result of the process of generalizing about temporal features regarded by a thinker as descriptively unavoidable. Augustine seems secure in the knowledge, for example, that time is constituted of a past, present, and future; he regards tensed discourse as uneliminable in a satisfactory general account, and thus, some of the traits discriminated by ordinary understanding as among those encountered features of time that compel recognition. That he takes heed of and expresses a reverence toward ordinary ways of speaking is evident in the following passage, which occurs after he has reached the conclusion that past and future do not exist: "By all means continue to say that there are three times, past, present and future; for, though it is incorrect, custom allows it. By all means say it. I do not mind, I neither argue or object: provided you understand what you are saying and do not think future or past now exists" (*Confessions*, XI. 20).

For Augustine, descriptive adequacy demands not that ordinary ways of speaking and understanding be replaced by some ideal discourse, only that they be conceptually relocated in the light of dialectical refinement. Thus, having metaphysically abandoned all temporal determinations but the present, we do not thereby begin to talk only in the present tense. It is, rather, that when we speak of "past" and "future" we mean respectively, "a present of things past" and a "present of things future."

So conceived, the tensed traits of time discriminated by common sense become in Augustine's scheme generic traits, that is, elements categorially necessary, not because they are subject to law-like usage but simply because time would not be the discursive subject that it is without them. The fact that they so enter into his categorial perspective, however, does not mean he does them metaphysical justice. It is the attempt to coherently associate these generic traits with ontological concepts of insufficient scope that creates, in part, the Gordian dialectical knots against which Augustine struggles.

The problem engendered by the legitimate and necessary effort to seek temporal complexes of ever more comprehensive scope are only "traditionally" metaphysical if the traits discriminated are concepts of a traditional sort. This last point is significant because Findlay and his ilk would have us believe that Augustine the metaphysician was trying to "penetrate" through appearances and grasp what was "really real" about time. Augustine did seek something "really real" about time, but it was not qua metaphysician that he did so. The error of ordinary language criticism is to mistake the substance of a traditional metaphysical scheme for the form of metaphysical schematization. Augustine's metaphysics of time is paradoxical largely because the concepts with which he chooses to articulate his understanding of time are foundationalist; in practice, as I hope to show, this means that they lack suitably ontological breadth. Yet, there is nothing in the endeavor of "descriptive generalization" per se that dictates a categorial framework in which a search for ultimates and a commitment to privileged realities holds sway.

Augustine, therefore, does not attempt to establish a definition of time that would be validated in its legislation of ideally consistent usage in violation of ordinary language. Rather, as a thinker concerned to construct a metaphysics of time, he views ordinary language as an element integral to the scope of categorial discriminations and their validation.[24] (Such validation rests on the power of encompassment of the concepts discriminated, their appositeness in reconciling experience with linguistic practice in both common and special forms of discourse.) For the author of the *Confessions*, ordinary language is an ineluctable point of departure for generalized description. The cause of the paradoxes lies elsewhere than in the attempt to overthrow it.

Antifoundationalism and Metaphysics

Augustine's temporal paradoxes and their consequences arise because of a commitment to privileged orders of being and to the existence of metaphysical ultimates. These commitments embody what Justus Buchler has termed "a principle of ontological priority." Buchler's work, notably the epochal *Metaphysics of Natural Complexes*, is insufficiently appreciated for its radical critique of foundationalism and its equally radical antifoundationalist systematic metaphysics.[25] By 'antifoundationalist metaphysics' I refer to the framing of descriptive structures that do not involve dualisms, privileged representations and their ontological counterparts, privileged "entities," or "ultimates" of any sort. In what follows I draw upon Buchler's so-called Ordinal framework to illuminate what I take to be the genuine sources of the paradoxes.

A principle of ontological priority manifests itself in two distinct but related philosophical tendencies: that of claiming privileged status for some "being" and subordinate status for some other or others; and that of maintaining a belief in the reducibility of complexes to simples. Both tendencies are crucial to a full understanding of the contradictions present in Augustine's account of the temporal; each is considered in turn.

A thinker reflects a principle of ontological priority whenever he or she expresses a commitment, either by acceptance or assertion, to the idea of degrees of being or reality. Such a principle is evident, for example, in Aristotle's reduction of *ta onta*—"what there is"—to *ousía*—"primary being," or substance, in the *Metaphysics*. In this case the generic traits of 'being as such' (*on he on*) are identified with the traits of a specific being, determined as "primary." Aristotle's ontology becomes in effect an ousiology; substance is asserted to be that in relation to which its "accidents" are said "to be" while remaining self-sufficient in its "being."[26] Thus, subjects are seen to be "more real" than predicates and, as such, the foundation of their intelligibility. Similar instances of adherence to a principle of ontological priority in the Western tradition could be multiplied indefinitely. Notwithstanding the historically pervasive appeal of such principles, any claim that some "being" has, in relation to others, a privileged metaphysical status must be considered fundamentally arbitrary.

Naturalist philosophers, among them John Dewey and J. H.

Randall, as well as Justus Buchler, have justifiably insisted that 'reality' is an evaluative, not a descriptive term, and consequently has no place in metaphysics. In Randall's words,

> "Reality" means either everything whatsoever . . . or else that a distinction of relative importance has been made. In any other than an evaluative sense to say only the Good is "real," only Matter is "real," only Mind is "real," only Energy is "real," is to express a prejudice refuted by a child's first thought or by every smallest grain of sand. No, everything encountered is somehow real. The significant question is, not whether anything is "real" or not, but how and in what sense it is real, and how it is related to and functions among other reals. To take "the real" as in fundamental contrast to what appears to us . . . seems to have resulted invariably in confusions and insoluble contradictions.[27]

As Dewey reminds us, to call something "real" in relation to which something else is "less real" or "unreal" is to make a normative judgment: it is to say that the former makes a greater claim on our attention pursuant to a situation we may consider problematic; that it is urgent or satisfying in relation to our needs and purposes. Thus, to insist that something is "real" merely expresses the view that it is worth exploring or analyzing and conveys nothing meaningful about its ontological constitution. To somewhat perversely paraphrase Kant, 'reality' is thus no "real" (by which it is meant, descriptively valid) predicate. Once we accept the view that any discriminandum (what can be grasped, identified, specified by any means whatsoever), "whatever is, in whatever way," is real, we affirm that the task of metaphysics involves describing *how* it is real and how it relates to other realities.

Ontological hierarchies inevitably presuppose a standard by means of which some order of discriminanda can be considered "more real" than some other. Such standards constitute the "foundations" that function to dictate unconditional priorities. To make the judgment, for example, that "substances" are more "real" than their "accidents" is meaningful only as an expression of that desire for control over nature which values the "stable" over the "precarious." A philosophy is foundationalist if it transforms standards of contextual priority into standards of absolute, or ontological, priority. Because such "foundations" of necessity presuppose the descriptive use of the term 'real', they lack *metaphysical* justification.

To place the matter in a slightly different light, foundationalisms posit the existence of an "Archimidean point," something unconditioned in relation to which everything else is conditioned. In corollary fashion, this complex or "order," whatever it may be, is alleged to provide the conditions of intelligibility for all others at the same time it is accorded the privilege of being "intelligible in itself." Yet, no order could conceivably be thus self-determining without violating the very conditions necessary for anything whatever to "be," and to be discriminable. For, it is location in an order other than itself that ontologically determines any complex: to "be" anything whatsoever is to be limited, environed, determinate in a given respect. Absent a wider context, one distinct from that for which *it* provides limiting conditions, no complex could either be differentiated from, or connected with, others. Such a complex would necessarily be outside of nature, that is, "intrinsically unrelatable to . . . and discontinuous with any of the actualities and possibilities of the world."[28]

Because it *is* only in relation to its own limiting and determining conditions and because this is also true of all its traits, "every complex is an order of complexes and belongs to an order of complexes."[29] Among the most important theoretical consequences of this, the "principle of ordinality," is the claim that there can be no "ultimate" order, no complex that is ontologically prior to all others. If every complex is at once determined and determining in relation to others, it follows that there can be no absolute ontological context, no order or system in which all others could be located. Foundationalist thinkers, whatever their stripe, frame relations between orders of nature in contrary terms. Materialists, for example, assert that physical complexes are unconditionally "real" while phenomenal or conceptual complexes are real only in a subordinate or derivative sense, the latter orders "reducible to" or "epiphenomena of" the former. Such a claim violates the principle of ordinality, according to which the physical order in which a Greek column bulges has no intrinsic priority, is not more "real," than the optical order in which it is straight. To affirm the ordinal vision of nature is not, however, to deny priorities altogether— merely priorities that are unconditional or absolute. It is inevitable that in nature we encounter complexes that are prior *in some respect* to others, that are, say, heuristically prior, morally prior, causally prior, and so forth. However, having priority in a given respect (order) does not confer priority *kata phusin*—according to nature.

An adequate metaphysics requires commitment to an ontological principle that pays tribute to this:

> Let us contrast a principle of ontological priority—which has flourished from Parmenides to Whitehead to Heidegger, and which continues to flourish in unsuspected ways—with a principle of ontological parity. In terms of the latter, whatever is discriminated in any way (whether it is "encountered" or produced or otherwise related to) is a natural complex, and no complex is more "real," more "natural," more "genuine," or more "ultimate" than any other. There is no ground, except perhaps a short-range rhetorical one, for a distinction between the real and the "really real," between being and "true being."[30]

The principle of ontological parity is embodied in the construction of a category of unlimited scope and unrestricted generality: the 'natural complex'. Metaphysical generality demands a term univocally applicable to the possible as well as the actual, fictions as well as facts, the nontemporal as well as the temporal (and we might add—the past and future as well as the present), irrational numbers as well as integers, even the absence or negation of something. "The concept of natural complex permits the identification of all discriminanda generically, without prejudicing the pursuit and the analysis of differences, of further similarities within the differences, of further differences within these similarities."[31] 'Natural complex', the central notion of a radical antifoundationalist *metaphysica generalis*, reflects an acceptance of the burden that, in ontological matters, we avoid reducing "whatever is" to a single species thereof.

To assert that 'whatever is, in whatever way' is a natural complex is to affirm at once that nothing is unnatural, that is, relationally disconnected from every other of the innumerable complexes which are (distributively) nature, and that there are no metaphysical simples. The incoherence of the later notion plays an essential role in the foundationalist machinery of Augustine's paradoxes, and thus a brief explanation of the ordinal critique of simples is in order before discussing the paradoxes proper.

The allure of metaphysical simplicity, variously expressed in the history of philosophy in the form of Lucretian atoms, Leibnizian monads, and (more recently) Strawsonian alpha-particulars, along with the innumerable "substantial entities" that have been the mainstay of Western metaphysical discourse, lies in their providing thinkers with an element of certainty. Buchler concludes:

> The idea of ontological simples, of irreducible components of nature, implies belief in absolute termini of analysis. Its appeal is not hard to detect. It seems to yield the assurance of a "foundation" for knowledge, and a stable or reliable foundation. It seems to provide "real" or "ultimate" elements. It seems to certify that familiar things, if they do dissolve, do not dissolve into nothing and are lost.[32]

Not the least reason, historically, that thinkers have upheld the existence of metaphysical simples involves the belief that simples are necessary to constitute complexes. A convincing case for the opposite view can be made: there are no such simples, for if there were, they could not constitute complexes. To call something simple is to assert either that it has no traits or that it is constituted of a single trait. Anything lacking traits would be totally unconstituted; it would lack "being." Furthermore, were it but a single trait, it would have no relations.

Now, among the discriminanda frequently alleged to be ontologically primitive are perceptual traits, so-called sense data. Sensory properties such as the color yellow are often said to be simple, that is, "indivisible," "unanalyzable," or "indefinable." The alleged "simplicity" of such a trait is mythological: it is always a trait of some complex, be it a brush stroke, a swatch of cloth, a fleck of metal, and the like. As a trait of a complex, such a "simple" would be related to that complex. This relation would be a trait of the so-called simple, since relational traits are constituents, just as any others. It makes no sense, in other words, to assert that a trait is not related to that of which it is a trait. The notion that complexes may be constructed out of simples, thus, does not bear up to scrutiny. Ultimately, the effect (if not the purpose) of such efforts to isolate irreducible components of nature is to release us from the responsibility of scrutinizing and defining, while tolerating (in effect mandating) without good reason the termination of an instance of query. In ordinary speech the "complex-simple" opposition is a practical way to distinguish what we need or desire to explore and what we do not. But neither this usefulness nor philosophical habit can dictate to metaphysical investigation.

More seriously, metaphysical simplicity involves nothing less than "relationless freedom from all multiplicity," a condition that entails freedom from relation to any knower or investigator. Thus a trait-simple would by necessity be indescribable. Not only would it lack the possibility of being described, it would lack all possibilities, for possibilities are traits just as any others. A simple would be indescribable because it would be indiscriminable. Lacking discriminability, its "being" or "reality," its ontological status, as the case turns out, is exclusively verbal, its precious categorial primacy purchased at the price of unintelligibility.

Two elements of foundationalist metaphysics, a principle of ontological priority and the quest for simples, underly the contradictions central to Augustine's doctrine of temporality. Scrutiny of the paradoxes proper reveals this to be the case.

The Paradoxes and Their Consequences

Augustine laces his account of temporality with three paradoxes. Significantly, he prefaces them with an affirmation of common-sense understanding. Tensed discourse, he insists, is not descriptively empty: "if nothing passed, there would be no past time; if nothing were approaching, there would be no future time; if nothing were, there would be no present time." Evidence of the reality (and objectivity) of all three modes of temporal passage continually surrounds us. Skin wrinkles; rocks weather; events unfold; empires rise, persist, and perish. Further reflection, however, leads us to the first paradox:

> But the two times, past and future, how can they *be*, since the past *is* no more and the future *is* not yet? On the other hand, if the present were always present and never flowed away into the past, it would not be time at all, but eternity. But if the present is only time, because it flows away into the past, how can we say that it *is*? For it is only because it will cease to be. Thus we can affirm that time *is* only in that it tends towards not-being. (*Confessions*, XI, 14; translator's emphasis)

Augustine assumes prior to the first paradox that time is a manifold constituted of three traits, past, present, and future. He concludes that, because the past no longer exists and the future does not yet exist, only the present can be real. Through ontological analysis, the temporal manifold is reduced to a single dimension. This is accomplished through the identification of reality with existence. Augustine is committed to the claim that "*x* is real ≡ *x* exists." Thus, it follows that what does not *exist* cannot be *real*. Because nonexistence enters into the trait constitution of both past (the no-longer-existing) and future (the not-yet-existing), they are, according to him, species of nonbeing.

Similarly, the ontological status of the present is problematic. For, although the present is, it is tending not to be (*tendit non esse*); or rather, put more strongly, since the very existence of the present involves its passage towards the nonbeing of the past, *its* very being is questionable. Furthermore, Augustine assumes that the present is a species of pure passage; otherwise, "it would not be time at all, but eternity."

The second paradox builds upon the first. Since past and future do not exist and hence are not real, they cannot be the subject of any predication whatsoever. As duration and, in particular, terms indicating the degree of duration, that is, "long" or "short," are predicates, their use in the case of past and future things or events are meaningless, as attributions to the past or future per se. Such predicates may, of course, be used as a manner of speaking so long as it is understood that they do not actually refer to past and future events. Augustine, it seems, would rule out two sorts of temporal ascriptions. Those that ascribe a duration *between* the present and some future or past event, for example, (1) "Social reform is a long way off (in the future)," and those that ascribe a duration to the past or future event *itself*, for example, (2) "The earthquake, though destructive, was brief."

Augustine's ontological reduction of a complexity of temporal traits to a single trait, the present, requires that statements referring to past or future things or events in reality refer to some aspect of present existence. Thus, when we speak of the past, we mean the "present of things past," that is, memory; when we speak of the future, we mean the "present of things future," that is, anticipation. Accordingly, in applying durational predicates to past events, we will be referring either to memories that are long or short, or to memories of events that when present took more or less time to occur. In applying durational predicates to the future thus, we actually refer to either long or short anticipations, or to anticipations that events when present will be of greater or lesser duration. Augustine does not disdain the use of tenses, so long as it is understood that when we talk about the past or future, we are in fact discoursing about memory and anticipation. Consequently, (1) is permissible so long as what is meant is something like (1') "At present there is a long anticipation of social reform," whereas; (2) would be acceptable so long as it could be interpreted as (2') "At present there is memory of a destructive, albeit brief earthquake."

The first two paradoxes lead dialectically to the third. If past and future cannot be said to be, then they cannot be said to be the subject of any predication, including duration. We can say that a particular event was long while it was present, because insofar as it was present, it took a long time to occur. While present, it was still an existent and therefore capable of predication; by ceasing to be, it also ceased to be long. Yet, the question inevitably arises: how can the present, framed in the first paradox as a temporal trait of pure passage whose existence consists in "tending not to be," have a duration?

Surely, Augustine responds, the present century is long; but, can it be *present*? When the first year of the century is present, then that year is present, but the remaining ninety-nine are not, for as they are in the future, they do not exist. Now, is the year excerpted from the not-present century present? That is likewise impossible since, although the first month is present, the remaining eleven are nonexistent, being not-yet. The same analysis forbids us to call a single month, a single day, or even a single hour present:

> If we conceive of some point of time which cannot be divided into even the minutest parts of moments, that is the only point that can be called present: and that point flees at such lightning speed from being future to being past, that it has no extent or duration at all. For if it were so extended, it would be divisible into past and future: the present has no length. (*Confessions*, XI, 15)

Augustine's dialectic leads to a characterization of time in doubly reductive terms. The present is all that remains of the tensed determinations, past and future having been categorially eliminated through the identification of reality with existence. Reference to past and future is hollowed to predication of memory and anticipation, both modes of present awareness. The present is further pared to a single trait of instantaneous passage, a moving knife-edge dividing a nonexistent past from a nonexistent future. Augustine concludes the third paradox by an affirmation of the subjectivity of temporal extendedness:

> It is in you, O my mind that I measure time. Do not bring against me, do not bring against yourself the disorderly throng of your impressions. In you, I say, I measure time. What I measure is the impress produced in you by things as they pass and abiding in you when they have passed: and it is present. I do not measure the things themselves whose passage produced the impress; it is the impress that I measure when I measure time. (*Confessions*, XI, 27)

These agitated reflections finally come to rest on three principles concerning the nature of time: that the present is metaphysically ultimate; that the present consists in a single trait of dimensionless transience; and that time is measured not only *in* but *as* awareness.

Some commentators have argued that although Augustine denied the "existence" of past and future, he did not deny that they are "real."[33] It seems to me, however, that telling evidence for the claim that Augustine did indeed deny past and future traits of time any ontological status lies in his failure to answer the question that emerges in the first paradox: how can the no-longer-existing and the not-yet-existing *be*? In subsequent analysis Augustine conspicuously does not provide an alternative ontological location for past traits as defunct existents or future traits as potential existents; in other words, as traits of time they fail to obtain in any respect whatsoever (in any order of the "real"). Thus they simply *cannot* be; as no-longer-existing and not-yet-existing, they are for him species of nonbeing.

It appears, then, that any "realistic" doctrine of past and future on Augustine's part must be discounted. The ontologically privileged status of "existence" ensures that only the subjective present is real: past and future have no objective reality. In fact, it requires that they have no reality whatsoever, since qua past and future, they have no existence whatsoever, mental or otherwise; and, of traits of time, only the present could in any meaningful sense be said to "exist."

Ordinary language philosophers have analyzed Augustine's problems with temporal measurement as the result of an erroneous assumption that temporal wholes must behave like object wholes. Findlay argues that Augustine is misled to conflate temporal wholes, whose parts do not coexist, with object wholes, whose parts do coexist, and to expect that the former act in every respect like the latter. When he realizes that no two parts of time occur simultaneously, this confusion leads Augustine to declare that the present can only be that trait of temporal movement without parts, an instantaneous "now." Since duration has no basis in the world outside the mind, measurement must therefore be confined to mental activity. I reject Findlay's analysis because, although the fact that the grammar of temporal and spatial measurement can easily be confused may have abetted Augustine in asserting that the extramental present is without duration, the salient reasons for doing so lie elsewhere, in a metaphysically compelling design.

Augustine knew full well that the term 'present' has a plurality of meanings referring to an indefinite number of temporal wholes. He understood that the durational scope of any given application of the term varied according to the requirements of the context. He knew that the historian's "present" is not the same as the musician's, but it is a "present" all the same. It was not that he was offended by the sheer profusion of durational referents to which this temporal predicate applied in "ordinary" and specialized usage, which he then sought to nullify and bring into a unity by means of some fallaciously ideal discourse. It is not the nonsimultaneity of temporal wholes that leads Augustine to reject duration as an objective trait of time. Rather, his denial of the extramental reality of temporal wholes derives from a need to compress time or the present—what remains of time after the operation of his dialectical lathe—within what for him are the limits of intelligibility.

Augustine's argument through all its intricate turns represents the search for something irreducible upon which to ground the metaphysical query of time. In its stark ultimacy, the fleeting, dimensionless present is the Archimedian point, the analytical terminus of all our reflections. Within the compass of this laboriously constructed notion is articulated all that we know with certitude about the relation of time to the world, human finitude, and eternity. The theoretical outcome of the temporal dialectics of book XI

of the *Confessions*, the concept of the perishing, punctiform moment, is the crucial premise in an occult argument concerning time.
If we were to ask why Augustine decrees that the manifold of time
should be reduced to a single trait of pure passage, a dimensionless fleeting "now," the answer could only be that this existent
functions as a kind of theoretical absolute; in fact, it is for him
the apotheosis of the destabilizing forces of nature. It represents
one pole in a rigid metaphysical opposition between absolute permanence (eternity) and absolute flux (time). The instantaneous
present is framed in terms that are intrinsically contradictory to
serve as the foundation of time's subordinate ontological status in
a scheme of cosmic ranking where the permanent, as the reification of the orderly processes of the world, is conceived to be the
"really" real. This flow of indivisibly atomic moments having no
connection to what comes before or after is the conceptual icon of
all that is random, unpredictable, and catastrophic in the relations
of nature to human experience. In a sense, this theoretical function
is foreshadowed in the first paradox, where we are told that time
could not be other than a perpetually perishing present, *or else it
would be eternity*.

Thus, time could have no duration (outside the human psyche),
for any duration would be characteristic of permanence however
relative, and this would contradict time's essence by introducing an
aspect of transcendence. To a certain extent, then, time's paradoxical dispositions are the result of a failure to recognize within the
concept a duality well understood by Aristotle, Kant, and above
all Dewey;[34] that, as a pervasive feature of nature, the temporal
encompasses both (relative) invariance and change and embodies
both the stabilizing and disorganizing features of the world. .

To argue thus, however, is not quite to bring to bear the full
force of the antifoundationalist critique of Augustine's metaphysics
of temporality. It is necessary to show not only that the instantaneous present, salient concept of his account of time derives from
foundationalist principles but that it is indeed unintelligible in nonfoundationalist terms. Before examining this issue, however, we
need to concern ourselves briefly with the conclusion that results
from time's resolution into a moving knife-edge.

The effect of the third paradox is to engender a temporal dualism. Augustine affirms the durational present as a mode of con-

sciousness, while he denies that it exists in the world outside the mind from whose occurrences are drawn the impressions that enter into attention and memory. Thus, the language of objective time is written in the characters of the punctiform instant, whereas that of subjective time, whose mental dispositions are the effects of objective events, is inscribed in the alphabet of epochal unities. The question that inevitably arises in this account is one that has haunted Western metaphysics since the very invention of a substantially distinct realm of subjectivity in the writings of Augustine: how then can one language be translated into the other? For translation is at once theoretically necessary and, given the radical discontinuity between "realms," impossible. The attempt to answer this question, a central preoccupation of philosophers throughout the modern period—at least from Descartes onward—constitutes a story too long to tell here. Suffice it to say that Augustine's problematic is representative of all attempts to radically isolate specific temporal traits within a given order of nature. In this sense, the difficulties that befall Augustine's account are remarkably akin to those of the contemporary, Grünbaum, who argues that tensed traits are mind-dependent and at the same time causally related to physical states whose temporal traits are exclusively tenseless. The difference is that Augustine is willing to accept that temporal passage is continuous through the objective and subjective world, whereas Grünbaum would isolate "becoming" within a realm of human psychology. That aside, the two thinkers can be said to inhabit the same fundamental metaphysical perspective and thereby to be afflicted with the same difficulty. In nonmetaphorical terms the difficulty is this: the world is bifurcated into two discontinuous orders that are said to be related in time but whose temporal traits are completely incommensurate. The difference between the two accounts, it seems, lies primarily in *which* traits are construed to be wholly contained within or excluded from *which* dimensions of nature. Though the proximate sources of temporal dualisms—Augustine's and Grünbaum's represent only two—vary, all could be said to derive from a common foundationalist principle, a proposition whose defense belongs to a discussion that shall not be deferred any longer.

Foundationalism and the Origins of Temporal Paradox

The concepts and principles of ordinal ontology provide a powerful antifoundationalist framework for the analysis and resolution of Augustine's temporal paradoxes.

The contradictory nature of time exhibited in the first paradox arises because of a failure to construct categories of sufficient breadth to provide an ontological location for the no-longer-existing and the not-yet-existing. This failure in turn discloses a commitment to the ontological priority of 'existence', a corollary of the categorial primacy of the present. Such a principle is without metaphysical justification; its result is to efface the integrity of discriminanda nevertheless deemed worthy of description and in fact essential to a coherent account of time and the real. Past and future traits, though not present existents, can in fact be shown to be "real." At the very least, they are real as the 'once present' and the 'potentially present'. They are discriminable, if in no other way, in terms of their relations to, and relevance for, the present. This, by the same token, confers determinateness and ontological status upon past and future as distinct temporal orders. 'Having-been-present' (having been made actual through temporal passage) is not less distinguishable than 'being-now-present'. Consider the case of a man, one of whose traits (in an order of political morality) is that presently he is a believer in the moral justifiability of private property. Suppose, further, that at one time he was a socialist. We would say, then, that in the given order his no longer being socialist is a trait ascribable to him at present. Clearly, the fact of his having been a socialist in the past is a condition for his location in an order of apostate socialists; it determines him in a particular way. It is by virtue of this past trait that his inclusion in that order is a possibility. As an actuality, moreover, the trait in question functions for that temporal span to exclude the possibility of others, for example, the said individual's being an anarchist. Such a trait is thus both distinctly discriminable as past and efficacious in the present, though in this case the efficacy in question need not be seen as strictly causal.

Similarly, though unlike the past and present, the future is in no sense actual; it is imminently actual. "Imminent actuality," the potentiality for actualization of present possibilities, consists in a determinate order of possibilities that obtain for a complex, the alternatives "open" to it, in contradistinction to those that are not. Of its possibilities, actualization of some may preclude actualization of others. In ordinal terms, the 'future' of a complex denotes an order of possibilities—as opposed to actualities—that are efficacious in excluding other possibilities. Strictly speaking, a given complex may have more than one possible future, each excluding actualizations of the others. Future traits are "real," for however slight a difference they make, they make a difference to the identity of a complex by limiting the range of further actualizations of that complex. To deny the reality of future traits simply because as "mere" possibilities they cannot be said to "exist" is absurd; such is, in fact, a part of the contradiction underlying the first paradox, inherent in the principle of the ontological priority of the present.[35]

If the first of Augustine's paradoxes dissolves in the light of ordinal analysis, so, a fortiori, must the second. Since past and future are legitimate traits of temporal complexes, terms, including those designating duration, may be predicated of them. To say otherwise would be to imply that, to take the previous example, a brief flirtation with socialism in the past had the same temporal scope and significance as a deathbed conversion to capitalism after a lifetime spent in the revolutionary underground. That is, if "long" and "short" were not "real" as traits of past and future *as* past and future, then it would be because they made no difference; but then they would not be discriminable, for what is discriminable is, to whatever extent, efficacious; and if efficacious, "real."

If the first paradox, and by extension, the second reveal the crippling difficulties associated with struggling to maintain ontological hierarchies, the third underscores the pitfalls inherent in a search for ultimates. It takes but a moment's reflection to realize that Augustine's durationless "now" is an expression of the myth of simplicity in temporal guise. A knife-edged present could not "be," and if it could, it could not constitute passage. Such a present would have no traits but the indivisible, unanalyzable trait of fugitiveness in which it supposedly consists. Having no trait other than this, it could not even be a trait of passage, for passage involves a "movement" from, through, and to, that is, relation to what comes before and after. Yet, being related to other moments would violate its simplicity, since relational traits are traits no less than any others.[36] Without complexity, without relations to an order of the past or future, the durationless "now" is unlocated, and without locations it has no trait constitution, no ontological integrity. Possessing no traits, it violates the very conditions necessary for anything whatsoever to "be." Such a traitless, totally self-contained, transitory atom is an impossibility, its reality "exclusively verbal." The third paradox arises because the reality of time, reduced by Augustine to the present, is asserted by theoretical means that, as we have just seen, are contradictory and untenable.

It is in light of the above critique of temporal simples that the ordinary language critique reveals (if further evidence is needed!) an added measure of impoverishment. Findlay argues that linguistic confusion leads Augustine to erroneously compare "the familiar sense in which a pile of money is built up out of coins, with the new sense in which a happening which takes time may be built up of happenings which take no time. Because one couldn't amass a fortune out of zero contributions, one tends to think one couldn't make a measurable duration out of parts with no duration."[37] Once we realize that the grammars of space and time are distinct and we rid ourselves of "misleading pictures," Findlay concludes, "if we wish to speak of 'happenings which take no time' we are quite free to fix what may be said of them, and this means that we may simply rule that events which take time *are* made up of events which take no time."[38]

Of course, "happenings which take no time" cannot be happenings at all, since they have all the integrity of metaphysical simples. Findlay would deny that the issue is resolvable as a matter of metaphysics; but if not, we have cause to ask, in what sense are the term 'happening' and the phrase 'tak[ing] no time' being used? If they are being employed as terms descriptive of the most general features of time, then their function is metaphysical and their theoretical collusion incoherent. If not, then we might well ask, what meaning do they have in a philosophical account of the subject?

The notion of temporal simples (instantaneous moments) is metaphysically dubious, whatever its incarnation. As a characterization of the generic traits of time it is empty, regardless of its parochial utility in other orders of discourse. That the idea of instantaneous rates of change is integral to a theory of dynamics of great explanatory power and elegance is no warrant to claim for

such an idea ontological generality. If, for the purposes of pre-
diction and control, physical scientists find it useful to treat time
as a continuous independent variable in framing their theoretical
judgments, this is no more evidence for the existence of temporal
simples than a statistical analysis of the population is evidence of
the existence of a household in which there are two and one-half
children.

A consequence of Augustine's third paradox, as we have seen, is
a dualistic conception of time in which duration is said to occur exclusively within subjective awareness, while such states of awareness are seen to be effects of durationless objective events. This
"bifurcation of nature" into two domains, one durational, the other
not, disconnects duration from its causal conditions, in violation
of the principle of ordinality.

If, in Augustine's or Grünbaum's case, duration or tense is a trait
of states of mind that are themselves effects of causal conditions
that are instantaneous or untensed, how can it meaningfully be
said that the former are not likewise traits of the latter? A cause is
a cause of an effect; their effects are relational traits of the causes,
constituents of their being the causes—the complexes—that they
are. To deny that duration or tense is a trait of the objective event,
as Augustine or Grünbaum does, would be, in the final analysis, to deny any relation between the world of such events and
subjectivity altogether.

Conclusion

It is the plan of this essay to reveal the foundationalist substrate
beneath the paradoxes and paradoxically wrought conclusions of
Augustine's dialectic of temporality. Significantly, the theoretical
elements that conspire in the metaphysical dramaturgy of *Confessions* XI to create this doctrine of time constitute a core of assumptions, principles, and categories shared by many traditional
accounts. The quest for ultimacy and an adherence to ontological
hierarchies are the source of Augustine's paradoxes; wherever they
are found, they lead to the distortion, exclusion, or annihilation of
legitimately specifiable features of temporality.

A metaphysics of time without foundations would enshrine the
principle of the ontological parity of past, present, and future.

It would attempt to answer the question "in what sense are the past and future real?" rather than the fruitless one "are they real?" It would embody the effort to construct temporal categories of widest possible scope. In such a metaphysics, absolutes such as the Augustinian moment-without-duration would not be found, nor would dualisms that fractured the world of time into radically incommensurable realms. So much the task of criticism has affirmed. The task of reconstruction remains.

Notes

1. G. H. Mead, *The Philosophy of the Present* (LaSalle: Open Court, 1959), pp. 1–31.

2. Maurice Merleau-Ponty, *The Phenomenology of Perception*, trans. Colin Smith (London: Routledge & Kegan Paul, 1962), p. 424.

3. Alfred North Whitehead, *Process and Reality: An Essay in Cosmology* (New York: Macmillan, 1929), p. 31.

4. Sir Isaac Newton, *Mathematical Principles of Natural Philosophy and System of the World*, trans. Florian Cajori after Motte, 1729 (Berkeley. University of California Press, 1934), pp. 38–39.

5. John Locke, *An Essay Concerning Human Understanding*, ed. A. C. Fraser, 2 vols. (New York: Dover Publications, 1959), 1: 238–59.

6. René Descartes, *Meditation III*, from *Philosophical Works of Descartes*, trans. E. S. Haldane and G. R. T. Ross (New York: Dover Publications, 1955), p. 168.

7. Adolph Grünbaum, "The Status of Temporal Becoming," in Richard Gale, *The Philosophy of Time: A Collection of Essays* (New Jersey: Humanities Press, 1968), pp. 322–54.

8. Henri Bergson, *Time and Free Will: An Essay on the Immediate Data of Consciousness*, trans. F. L. Pogson (New York: Humanities Press, 1971), pp. 226–27.

9. Ludwig Wittgenstein, *Philosophical Investigations*, 2nd ed., trans. G. E. M. Anscombe (New York: Macmillan, 1958), p. 42. Also see Wittgenstein, *The Blue and Brown Books* (New York: Harper & Row, 1960), pp. 6, 26–28.

10. Friedrich Waismann, "Analytic-Synthetic," in Gale, *Philosophy of Time*, pp. 55–63.

11. O. K. Bouwsma, "The Mystery of Time," in *Philosophical Papers* (Lincoln: University of Nebraska Press, 1967).

12. J. N. Findlay, "Time, A Treatment of Some Problems," in Gale, *Philosophy of Time*, p. 154.

13. John M. Quinn, "The Concept of Time in Saint Augustine," *Studies in Philosophy and the History of Philosophy* 4 (1969): 75–127.

14. James McEvoy, "St. Augustine's Account of Time and Wittgenstein's Criticisms," *Review of Metaphysics* 38 (March 1984): 547–77.

15. H. M. Lacey, "Empiricism and Augustine's Problems about Time," *Review of Metaphysics* 22 (December 1968): 219–45.

16. W. H. Newton-Smith, *The Structure of Time* (London: Routledge & Kegan Paul, 1984), pp. 3–5.

17. Saint Augustine, *The Confessions of Saint Augustine*, trans. F. J. Sheed (New York: Sheed & Ward, 1943), p. 271 (XI, 14).

18. Findlay, "Time," p. 144.

19. Ibid., p. 150.

20. McEvoy, "St. Augustine's Account of Time," p. 568.

21. Lacey, "Empiricism," pp. 219–20.

22. Justus Buchler, *Metaphysics of Natural Complexes* (New York: Columbia University Press, 1966), p. 38. Hereafter cited as *MNC*.

23. Douglas Greenlee, "The Problem of Exhibitive Judgment in Philosophy," *Southern Journal of Philosophy: Special Issue on the Philosophy of Justus Buchler* 14, no. 1 (Spring 1976): 129.

24. See Beth J. Singer, "On Some Differences between Metaphysical and Scientific Discourse," *Journal of Speculative Philosophy* 1, no. 1 (1987): 38–54.

25. For an excellent general analysis of Buchler's antifoundationalism see Robert Corrington, "Justus Buchler's Ordinal Metaphysics and the Collapse of Foundationalism," *International Philosophical Quarterly* 25, no. 3 (September 1985): 290–98.

26. Aristotle, *Metaphysics*, Book Gamma, trans. Richard Hope (Ann Arbor: University of Michigan Press, 1960), p. 61.

27. J. H. Randall, Jr., *Nature and Historical Experience* (New York, 1958), p. 131. Quoted by Buchler in *MNC*, p. 30.

28. Justus Buchler, "On the Concept of the 'World'," *Review of Metaphysics* 31 (June 1978): 562.

29. Buchler, *MNC*, p. 93.

30. Ibid., p. 31.

31. Ibid., p. 2.

32. Ibid., p. 17.

33. I have argued that by declaring only the present exists, Augustine affirmed the unreality of past and future. This analysis is central to the claim that I will subsequently make, namely, that such a move on Augustine's part betrays a commitment to foundationalist principles. This claim,

however, might not seem self-evidently true: did he in fact imply, by saying that past and future are nonexistent, that they are therefore not real? Lacey, for one, disagrees with this assessment of Augustine's doctrine. He argues that although Augustine denied the existence of the past and future, he held them "real enough," since "they once existed and they have causal repercussions now." Lacey, "Empiricism," p. 224. He allowed, according to Lacey, that we can make true statements about the past, even in cases where we have no memory of the events in question. This attitude toward the past is essential for Augustine to hold; otherwise, his conclusion concerning the nature of time could not be stated, since this conclusion, "It is this impression [of things in their passage] that I measure when I measure time," requires the truth of past-tense statements such as 'things in their passage, caused the impressions in the memory.' As a result, in Lacey's view, past events must have a certain reality since we surely do not remember these things causing such impressions. Lacey concludes that Augustine's theory does indeed require that he consider past (if not future) to be objectively real, but that his categorial equipment was inadequate to develop the objective side of his temporal metaphysics. Augustine's failure was in not realizing or making explicit the fact that reality is wider than existence.

Lacey is correct, I believe, in identifying the source of Augustine's difficulty as a failure to employ complexes of sufficiently wide scope in seeking to discriminate the generic traits of time. Yet, since, as Lacey himself admits, this categorial inadequacy is "self-imposed," it seems reasonable to conclude that this failure reflects the result of Augustine's self-conscious metaphysical commitments. At any rate, it is sufficient for my purposes to show that the impoverished ontological vocabulary of the *Confessions* harbors foundationalist assumptions and that it is the source of a serious incoherence.

34. John Dewey, *Experience and Nature* (La Salle: Open Court, 1971), pp. 37–66. See also Gary Calore, "Towards a Naturalistic Metaphysics of Temporality: A Synthesis of Dewey's Later Thought," *Journal of Speculative Philosophy* 3, no. 1 (1989): 12–25.

35. Augustine's metaphysics of time exemplifies only one principle of the ontological priority of the present. Ordinal analysis demonstrates that all assertions to the effect that the present is "really real," or "more real" than the past and future, are fundamentally arbitrary and thus descriptively illegitimate. They are the source of metaphysical injustices wherever they occur. A case in point is Whitehead's "epochal theory" of time. The central category of Whitehead's account of temporality is the so-called actual occasion. Unrepeatably experient events, actual occasions are said to be the "ultimate" cosmological facts and to embody the reasons for all

other discriminanda. The actual occasion is (both in the tenseless logical sense and in the sense of being temporally present) its act of becoming. Thus, what is uniquely individual, subjective, radically emergent, and wholly present is said to be "more real" than that which is social and objective, repeatable, enduring, stable, and past, future, or atemporal. The person-at-one-moment is the "really real," whereas the person's life history and prospects are derivatively real. The fallacy of this vision is evident once we realize that it is a person's life history, the society of all that person's acts, that enables us to understand the person-at-one-moment; that, if the acts of an order of the present are what define the person, so the facts of an order of the past prescribe limits to the possibilities of definition. To insist on the metaphysical ultimacy of the present is, paradoxically, to declare that that which is least explicable is most real. The way out of this anomalous result, of course, is to accept the view that neither the society of past acts nor the acts of present individuation are in any sense ontologically prior.

36. One could argue that the Augustinian moment is not a simple in that it enters into relation with all the complexes with which it is simultaneous. The question becomes, then, one of the intelligibility of "nature at an instant." As the order of all simultaneous complexes, the present is still metaphysically simple because, as a temporal trait, it is isolated within that order and disconnected from all other orders of time.

37. Findlay, "Time," p. 153–54.

38. Ibid., p. 154. In all fairness to Findlay, he does state in a prefatory remark to Gale's reprint of his article that he considers the metaphysical issues to be of greater importance than (presumably) he did when it was first written.

Four

Hierarchy and Early Empiricism

FRED S. MICHAEL AND EMILY MICHAEL

*F*oundationalism is a term of art, and one of recent vintage. It is also a term of criticism; those who espouse foundationalism seem to be rather defensive about it. The main target of the critics of foundationalism appears to be the views of logical empiricists and sense datum theorists. But these views are seen as being new incarnations of very old ideas, found articulated in a work as early as Aristotle's *Posterior Analytics*. Foundational theories are said to have the following kind of structure. Any such theory has a set of basic theses that are self-evident or self-justified, or at any rate that cannot be justified by any other theses of the theory. This set of theses is the foundation of the theory, providing it with its fundamental premises. Theses that are not foundational are all derivative from those that are. However, the foundational theories upon which present-day controversy principally focuses are based upon the classical empiricist theories of John Locke, George Berkeley, and David Hume; and these theories do not very easily fit the pattern described above. For the foundation of the classical empiricist theories consists not of theses, statements, or other propositional units, but of ideas, sense impressions, items of experience; and what is not in the foundation is not so much derived from as composed of, or constructed from, elements of the foundation. Of course, there is a common pattern; both are kinds of epistemic hierarchy, and foundational theories of both kinds are problematic. Most discussions of foundationalism do not give separate treatment to idea-based theories, but treat them as if they were statement based. Latter-day empiricists, of course, do as-

85

similate items of experience to statements, some to sense datum statements, others to observation statements, and others still to protocol statements. But there is no reason to think that comments applicable to such statement-based theories will apply mutatis mutandis, or with little modification, to idea-based theories as well. Foundational theories of justification are often contrasted with coherence theories, but what a coherence theory of ideas would amount to is not easy to see. So it seems that we should recognize two kinds of foundational theory: we should distinguish between statement-based theories with inferential hierarchy and element-based theories with compositional hierarchy.

The purpose of this essay is to examine two theories of the early empiricist, Pierre Gassendi, in the light of the controversy over foundationalism. Gassendi has a theory of ideas; it is in fact the first full-scale theory of ideas and one very largely incorporated into Locke's theory. But unlike Locke's theory of ideas, Gassendi's is not foundational. There are, in Gassendi's theory, no compositionally simple ideas. It is not that Gassendi's theory is incomplete in this respect, but that it is in this respect significantly different from that of Locke. There are no ideas in Gassendi's theory whose nature can be intuitively and immediately grasped. What Locke calls simple ideas are for Gassendi general ideas and, like all such ideas, arise from the perception of likeness in what has been directly experienced. Gassendi also has a theory of how truth is recognized and knowledge acquired. But although Gassendi holds that we can acquire a knowledge of truth, all our knowledge is provisional (except possibly that of conceptual truths, including the truths of mathematics). Gassendi's theory, although like a foundational theory in structure, denies that there are any foundational truths. It can be considered a form of foundational theory whose foundation can be changed.

I

According to Aristotle, all true knowledge must be derived from first principles. First principles themselves are discovered by induction from experience and by inferring causes from their effects. Proceeding in this way, we reach the most general explanatory principles. Though reached by experience, they are nonetheless not empirical principles. If they were merely empirical, they could conceivably be false, and no true or scientific knowledge could be based upon them. What happens is that once they have been reached, they are intuitively recognized as self-evidently, necessarily true. These are first principles; all of our knowledge is derived from them. Moreover, every subject has first principles of its own. Only that which is derived from first principles is demonstratively known, and we truly know something only when we know it demonstratively.[1] For René Descartes also, knowledge comes from first principles. But, for Descartes, first principles do not have their source in experience. Experience is the source only of prejudice and inadequately justified beliefs. To distinguish beliefs that are first principles from those that are not, we must clear our mind of all beliefs acquired by experience, for these obscure first principles from our view. There will remain certain clear and distinct perceptions and, as clear and distinct perception is the Cartesian criterion of truth, these perceptions, underived from experience, are true. Such are Descartes's first principles. From these first principles, not derived from experience, all of our knowledge must be derived.

Gassendi recognizes no first principles, whether derived from experience or not. How, then, are we to obtain knowledge in his view? How are we to determine what beliefs are true and what false? What criterion of truth does he propose? It will help to answer such questions if we first look at the source of his views in the *Syntagma Philosophiae Epicuri*, the work in which Gassendi seeks to reconstruct the philosophy of Epicurus. Epicurus's philosophy is based on certain principles of cognition and action known as the Canonic. In Gassendi's reconstruction, there are eight canons (or rules) of cognition, four of cognition by the senses, four of cognition by means of images. The canons of sense concern us here. They are:

Canon I: Sense is never mistaken; and so every sensation or appearance is true.

Canon II: Opinion is something added to sense and is capable of truth or falsity.

Canon III: An opinion supported or not contradicted by the evidence of sense is true.

Canon IV: An opinion contradicted or not supported by the evidence of sense is false.[2]

The first two canons express a view that is by no means peculiar to the theories of Epicurus and Gassendi. Versions of that same position are found in Aristotle, Descartes, and in many others. It was in fact a commonplace of seventeenth- and eighteenth-century philosophy that there is a class of cognitions, known as simple apprehensions, that are just what they seem to be inasmuch as they involve no claim that can be either true or false. Only where there is belief, opinion, or judgment can there be truth or falsity, and only then can there be error. This is just the view involved in the first two of the canons of sense. Canons III and IV, however, are more significant. Before we comment on the content of these canons, there is a difficulty in their formulation of which we should take note. As canons III and IV are formulated, an opinion neither opposed nor supported by the evidence of sense would be both true and false. But it is easy to avoid this embarrassing consequence. The reason why an opinion not opposed by the evidence of sense is said to be true is to allow for truths known not by direct sense perception but only by inference. For instance, perspiration indicates the existence of pores and from the behavior of objects accessible to our senses we infer the existence of atoms.[3] But the grounds for claiming these things to be true is that they are indirectly supported, not merely that they are not opposed, by the evidence of sense. Thus, canon III should be changed to read: An opinion supported, directly or indirectly, by the evidence of sense is true. And a similar change should be made in canon IV.

These two canons, in effect, make sense perception the criterion of truth and falsity. It is important to recognize that a criterion of truth is not a definition. Gassendi defines truth as correspondence with the facts. Supposing this to be so, the question remains: how do we know what the facts are? According to canons III and IV, we know this by experience. A definition says what truth is; a criterion of truth says how we are to recognize what is true and distinguish it from what is false.

Canons III and IV articulate an empiricist criterion of truth and falsity. It also furnishes what may be considered a criterion of empiricism, since it seems clear that the criterion of truth of an empiricist ought to be an empiricist criterion of truth. In this sense Aristotle, although he claims that all knowledge originates in the senses, is not in the full sense an empiricist, since he holds that there are nonempirical self-evident truths on which all true or scientific knowledge is founded. For a true empiricist, there are no nonempirical self-evident first principles, no intuitively known truths. What we claim to know intuitively are really just generalizations from experience.

In this respect, Gassendi is a true empiricist. Even such principles as "the whole is greater than the part" are held to be mere empirical generalizations. Gassendi explains the derivation of this principle as follows:

> When we first hear this principle and understand what 'whole,' 'part,' and 'greater than' mean, there occur to us instantaneously, as it were, several examples of this sort, the house is greater than the roof, the man than his head, the tree than the branch, the book than the page; and at once it comes into the mind confusedly that all that we ever have seen, or ever could see, is like this, as a result of which without delay we admit the principle to be true.[4]

Although it would be consistent with empiricism to admit that there are some truths that depend simply on the meanings of words and that "the whole is greater than the part" is just such a truth, Gassendi sees the principle as derived by a process of empirical generalization. This would appear to be as far as one could plausibly go in making all truths empirical.[5]

Since all knowledge of what is true or false derives from experience, on Gassendi's view, what is not revealed to us by experience we cannot know. Thus, we can know things only as they reveal themselves in experience; we cannot know the nature of things as they are in themselves. In this respect, Gassendi is in full agreement with the Pyrrhonian skeptics. Gassendi was also a fierce opponent of what he considered dogmatism. For these reasons and because of his sympathetic treatment of the Pyrrhonian position, Gassendi himself was considered to be a Pyrrhonian skeptic. Although he did deny that certainty could be attained, he thought that knowledge was possible; and in this respect his position differs from that of the skeptics. But he was quite adamant about the impossibility of obtaining any knowledge of the intimate nature or essence of things.

But what is it to know the intimate nature of a thing, as Gassendi understands this? It will help us see how Gassendi views this matter, if we look at what he says in an early work, the *Exercitationes Paradoxicae Adversus Aristoteleos*, when he is criticizing the view that to know the essence of a natural thing, we have only to know that it is composed of form and matter. Gassendi denies this, arguing that we do not know the essence of even the least of natural things, such as a flea, unless we can answer such questions as

> just what sort of matter this was, what dispositions it required to receive that form, for what reason it was distributed so that this part of it went into the proboscis, that part into its feet, another into its hair and scales, and the others into the remainder of its body, what was the active force and how was it brought to bear when it formed both the entire body and its very different parts in this order, this shape, this texture, this size, this colour.
>
> Again, just what would the nature of this form be, what its origin, by what force is it stimulated to action, how is its perceptive and sentient faculty forged, how does it penetrate such tiny body tissues, which of the organs does it use, how does it make use of such organs? By what power does the flea bite you so sharply to ingest his nourishment from you, how does he digest it and assimilate part of it in various passages, and transform part of it into spirits which conserve him and impart life to his entire body, and eliminate its superfluous parts through his different winding intestines? Where does the power to jump so swiftly dwell in him? . . . What does he think when he does not want to be caught? What qualities result from that form deep within him and how? When his little body is crushed, what becomes of that form? And a hundred other questions like that.[6]

Suppose we switch from a form-matter ontology to an ontology of atoms and the void, of the sort Gassendi favors. Nothing changes. To say that a flea is composed of atoms and void space, or even to give a complete account of the atomic structure of the flea, if that can be done, reveals little about the nature of the flea, as Gassendi understands it, for it does little to enable us to answer questions of the sort Gassendi proposes. Given Gassendi's conception of what it is to know the nature or essence of a flea, we think it would have to be conceded that we have no hope of ever having complete knowledge of this kind.

Still, we do have knowledge of many things that are not immediately evident to sense. According to Gassendi, we have knowledge by signs; we can acquire knowledge of what is unperceived or imperceptible by means of perceptible signs. Among the examples of knowledge by signs that Gassendi offers are the following: perspiration is a sign of the existence of pores in the skin; motion is a sign of the existence of void space; our awareness of mental operations are a sign of the existence of the soul or mind; the phases of the moon are a sign that the moon is a sphere.[7] In each case, from something present to the senses, we derive truths that the senses themselves do not directly reveal. We do this, in each case, by reasoning. This allows Gassendi to say that two criteria are involved: the senses and reason. He says:

> We may distinguish two criteria in ourselves: one by which we perceive the sign, namely the senses, and the second by which we understand something hidden by means of reasoning, namely the mind, intellect or reason. And although it is admitted that the senses are sometimes misleading and that therefore the sign may not be reliable, still reason, which is superior to the senses, can correct the perception of the senses so that it will not accept a sign from the senses unless it has been corrected and then at last it deliberates or reaches its judgment of the thing.[8]

This is not a departure from the criteria of truth and falsity of canons III and IV. Reasoning just connects what is evident to sense with what is not, so that what is evident to sense is shown indirectly to support beliefs about things that are not evident to sense. Reasoning is not really a separate criterion; it never operates except on the basis of information from the senses. Moreover, it never corrects sense perceptions except on the basis of other perceptions of the senses. How this is done, we examine below.

It is plain from the examples given of knowledge by signs that such knowledge falls short of theoretical certainty. Gassendi is perfectly well aware of this. Although Gassendi does call the reasoning involved in knowledge by signs 'proof', he concedes that such a proof is "not one such as Aristotle requires or one which insists upon a previous inquiry of a most exact sort into the sign."[9] It is, rather, "one that all well-endowed, wise, and intelligent men will accept as reasonable and which cannot be denied except for contradiction's sake."[10] These proofs then do not afford certainty; they are not conclusive. They are, however, reasonable, and if they can be disputed, it is not with good reason. A proposition, such as that pores exist, is said to be "firmly established upon propositions which are known in their own right and which the intellect cannot reject."[11] The propositions in question are not "known in their own right" in being self-evident; they are propositions such as "perspiration exudes from the skin," supported directly by the evidence of sense, and are thus asserted "on the basis of the proof of experience itself, which requires no proof."[12] The intellect further cannot, that is, has no reason to, reject them.

If Gassendi expresses himself very obliquely here, it is because he wants to create as much distance as possible between his views and that of the skeptics, to counter the impression that he himself is a skeptic. There is, however, a large measure of agreement between Gassendi and the skeptics. Gassendi is as much against dogmatism as the skeptics are. What he has said amounts to this: there is knowledge but not certainty, convincing but not conclusive arguments. The possibility that inference from perceptual signs may in some cases result in error and not knowledge is conceded, but deemphasized.

Error can also occur in perception. We are sometimes misled by the senses; Gassendi acknowledges this. But he maintains that perceptual error can be avoided. We learn by experience that a straight oar when immersed in water is apt to look bent, that a square tower at a distance looks round, and so forth. This being so, we can avoid being misled, if we refrain from judging whether an oar in water that appears to be bent is in fact bent, until we have taken it from the water; and if we restrain ourselves from forming the opinion that a tower seen at a distance is round rather than square, until we have seen it from close at hand.[13] By precautions such as these learned from experience, we can avoid being misled by the senses. Experience is our guide throughout: if experience can mislead, then it is by experience also that we learn how to avoid being misled and by experience that we correct our errors when we have been misled. To avoid being misled, we have to be vigilant. Of course, it is not always possible to avoid being misled. But at least we can correct the errors we make.

Such is Gassendi's view of the acquisition of knowledge. Is it foundational? There is a degree of hierarchy. Some truths are derived, some underived, being directly supported by sense experience. This is not just a matter of congruence between propositions. Propositions directly supported by sense perception are the foundation for the rest. However, coherence does play a role in this theory. Propositions directly supported by experience have the sort of coherence that makes experience a suitable foundation for the acquisition of knowledge. Also, individual perceptions are accepted as veridical or rejected according as they cohere or do not cohere with the body of our experience. There is another important point. The distinction between propositions directly and derivatively supported or opposed by sense experience is not absolute. For instance, a theory about the effect of distance on perception can lead us to reject as nonveridical the perception of a tower at a distance that represents it as being round.[14] A derivatively supported proposition can justify us in rejecting something that direct sense perception had led us to believe.

A theory may be said to be foundational just so long as it has a structure in which there are some propositions that have a direct claim to truth and all other propositions derive their truth from them. Since Gassendi's theory has this structure, his theory can be considered foundational. But it is not strictly foundational, since, as already noted, nonfoundational propositions may justify us in rejecting certain propositions directly supported by sense or may lend such propositions additional support. It is not clear why a foundational structure should be seen as being per se questionable or why it should be denied that knowledge acquisition should have this structure.

It is a fact that a number of important theories of knowledge acquisition about which there is serious question have this structure.[15] They are questionable, however, not because they use this structure, but because they are dogmatic. There is unfortunately a common tendency to confuse foundationalism with dogmatism and to see an attack on a dogmatic foundational theory as an attack on foundationalism itself. This confusion is apparent when a foundational theory is said to be one in which the propositions constituting its foundation have some guarantee of truth and these guarantee the truth of all nonfoundational or derived propositions. A theory of this sort is not only foundational but dogmatic as well. Claims such as that the acquisition of knowledge has its basis in unassailable first principles, which are self-evident, infallible, indubitable, or incorrigible, are just dogmatic. Reasons to reject such a dogmatic foundation are not reasons to reject foundational theories per se.

Yet why not take this further step, rejecting not only first principles and the like, but even a fallibilist foundation such as that proposed by Gassendi? The problem is this: if we are not prepared to allow even propositions directly supported by sense any claim to truth, not even provisionally, then how can we ever begin to acquire knowledge? Any proposition that is believed must be deemed acceptable on its own account, or it must be derived from propositions that are themselves considered acceptable. But in either case, there must be some proposition that has been granted at least provisional acceptance. Considerations of coherence, as already stated, support taking sense experience as providing such a stock of provisionally accepted propositions. If even a fallibilist foundation for knowledge is ruled out, there does not seem any alternative to skepticism. It is difficult to see how, if knowledge is to be possible at all, we could reject such a foundation.

II

Although ideas play a very significant role in Descartes's reasoning, Descartes says little about the nature of ideas. He does offer a threefold classification of ideas in order to establish the existence of innate ideas; and clear and distinct ideas are, for him, the criterion of truth. Yet ideas are not the focus of his attention; they play an important role in establishing what, for Descartes, are fundamental truths, but they receive little attention in their own right. Descartes provides the basis for a theory of ideas but does not develop such a theory himself. A full-scale presentation of a Cartesian theory of ideas first appeared in the *Port Royal Logic*, first published in 1662. But Gassendi's theory of ideas had appeared four years earlier. Unlike Descartes, Gassendi does examine ideas in their own right, and he treats ideas in a systematic manner.

Gassendi adopts the term 'idea' from Descartes, but little else. Gassendi's theory of ideas, like his theory of knowledge acquisition, derives from Epicurus.

The theory of ideas, like the theory of the acquisition of knowledge, has its source in the reconstruction of Epicurus's Canonic in Gassendi's *Syntagma Philosopiae Epicuri*. The theory of ideas is based on the canons concerned with cognition by means of images, or the canons of the *anticipatio*, as Gassendi calls them. In these canons, images are understood to be anticipations of perception. Images, derived from previous perceptions, serve as anticipations of perception in that they determine how what is presently perceived will be apprehended. Thus, when you perceive a horse, what you perceive is something that resembles the image of a horse, an image you have formed on the basis of previous perceptions. This is what is meant when it is said that images are anticipations of perception. There are four canons of the *anticipatio*:

> *Canon I:* An anticipation of sense or prenotion comes into the mind directly from sense or is formed by increase or diminution, similitude, or composition.
> *Canon II:* The anticipation is the very notion and (as it were) definition of a thing, without which we cannot inquire about, doubt, think about, or even name any thing.
> *Canon III:* Anticipation is the principle of all reasoning. It is what we consider when we infer that one thing is the same as another or different, joined with another or separated from it.
> *Canon IV:* That which is not evident must be demonstrated from the anticipation of a thing which is evident.[16]

The fourth canon concerns the acquisition of knowledge by inference and was a basic feature of Gassendi's theory of knowledge acquisition considered in the previous section. Canon III represents the anticipation or image as being the source of logic, and indeed Gassendi's view that logic is based on the theory of ideas has its source in this canon. Canons I and II are the source of his theory of ideas.

Gassendi's theory of ideas is found in his logic, the *Institutio Logica*.[17] The *Institutio Logica* is part of logic section of the *Syntagma Philosophicum*, Gassendi's main work. This work is divided into three parts: logic, physics, and ethics. Included in the physics are four books on psychology, which have to be considered if we are to understand the theory of ideas in the *Institutio Logica*. We begin therefore with an account of cognition derived largely from the psychology of the *Syntagma*.[18]

Ideas, according to Gassendi, are just images.[19] This means that they are in the imagination and are distinct from cognitions of sense, or sensations. Some ideas are also images in the sense of being copies, copied from sensations and resembling them to some extent. Whether they are copies or not, all ideas originate in the senses.

Sensations, however, are not copies of things. We know things only as we sense them and not as they are in themselves. It should be noted that when we speak this way, we are not thinking of sensation as simple apprehension, which cannot be mistaken because it involves no judgment, but as the perception of external things. Although Gassendi says that the dispute as to whether sensation is simple apprehension or the perception of external things is merely verbal,[20] when a sensation is said to be the sensible sign of some hidden or nonsensible reality (as perspiration is of pores), then sensations are being conceived as perceptions caused by external things. Sensation so conceived involves judgment as well as simple apprehension. Error is possible in two ways when sensation is conceived in this manner, for it can be the case that the simple apprehension we suppose to have been caused by some external object had no such cause (it might have been a hallucination), or supposing it has been caused by something external, our judgment of the nature of the thing causing it can be mistaken (as when we perceive a square tower as round). Since we perceive external things only by sensation and do not perceive, but can only infer the existence of, what we do not sense, the only kind of perception there is, is perception by means of the senses.

Sensation causes an impression to be left in the brain, called by Gassendi a *species impressa*. This, says Gassendi, has the form of a fold. The same view of brain impressions is also found in Descartes. The awareness of the *species impressa* is called by Gassendi a *species expressa*, and it is this that is an image or idea.[21] Ideas or images, then, derive from sensations. All apprehension of absent objects, whether in memory or in thought, takes place by means of images of these objects in the imagination.

As for things not perceived, whose reality can only be inferred, these make use of images as well, images that serve as signs of the unperceived reality. This is the way we apprehend not only unperceived entities but also universals. For there are no universal sensations or images; everything we sense and everything in the imagination is singular. There are things that we can apprehend but that cannot be framed in any image; universals, the size of the sun or of an atom, are examples of this.[22] What is thus unimaginable is apprehended by means of the intellect. It is by the intellect that we obtain inferential knowledge of the unperceived; and to apprehend what cannot be perceived and cannot be imagined, the intellect uses images as signs.[23] We might say that knowledge by the intellect is knowledge by means of signs and that images are the signs by means of which this knowledge is obtained.

In the *Institutio Logica* logic is defined as the art of thinking well (*ars bene cognitandi*). Thinking well is said to involve four powers: imagining well, proposing well (that is, forming correct propositions), inferring well, and ordering well. Logic, accordingly, has four parts: the first part is concerned with simple apprehensions, the second with judgment, the third with reasoning, and the fourth with method.[24] "On the Simple Imagination of Things," the first part of Gassendi's logic, is his theory of ideas.

Part I of the *Institutio Logica* consists of eighteen canons, which can be conveniently divided into five groups. The first three concern the nature and formation of ideas; canons four through six concern the formation of general ideas; canons seven through ten concern the perfection of ideas, that is, the accuracy with which ideas represent sensations or general notions; canons eleven through fourteen concern ways in which ideas may mislead; and finally canons fifteen through eighteen concern such matters as how the idea we have of a thing is expressed in its definition. It is with the first six canons that we will be principally concerned.

The first canon asserts that the simple imagination of a thing is the same as the idea we have of it. A clear and distinct idea Gassendi describes as a strong and vivacious image, such as we have of a man we have seen often and recently, and to whom we have paid particular attention as compared with the image of a man we have seen once only, in passing.[25] This makes it plain that clearness and distinctness is not for Gassendi, as it is for Cartesians, a criterion of truth. An idea or image that is clear and distinct simply is one likely to represent its object more adequately than one that is not.

The second canon, which can be seen to derive from the first canon of the *anticipatio*, formulates a fundamental empiricist principle: *Every idea in the mind derives its origin from the senses*. Gassendi elaborates as follows:

> This indeed is the reason why a man born blind has no idea of colour. He lacks the sense of vision by which he might obtain it. It is also why a man born deaf has no idea of sound, for he is without the sense of hearing, the power by which he might acquire it. So therefore, supposing this were possible, a man who lived without any senses . . . would have no idea of anything and therefore would imagine nothing.
>
> It is this then that the celebrated saying, *There is nothing in the intellect which was not first in sense*, means. This is also what is meant by the claim that the intellect, or mind, is a *tabula rasa*, on which nothing has been engraved or depicted.[26]

Gassendi then holds that mind is a tabula rasa. This was a commonly held view, as Gassendi points out. But though the view itself is certainly not original, the argument Gassendi uses to support it appears to be.

Concerning innate ideas, Gassendi remarks only that those who claim that there are ideas that are naturally imprinted, or innate, not acquired by sense, say what they do not at all prove. Although Gassendi denies that there are any innate ideas or principles at all, he does not attempt to provide any general argument to show this. Rather, he endeavors to show how ideas and principles claimed to be innate have in fact been derived from experience. Thus, Gassendi tries to show that ideas claimed by Descartes to be innate (for example, the idea of 'thing') could not have been acquired without the assistance of sensation.[27] In addition, as we have already mentioned, Gassendi holds that it is by induction from experience that we discover the truth of even the most general and indubitable principles, such as *the whole is greater than the part*.

The third canon of *Institutio Logica*, Part I, asserts that every idea either passes through sense or is formed from those that pass through sense. In addition to the ideas we have of the things we sense, as in the first canon of the *Anticipatio*, there are said to be ideas formed by increase and diminution, as when from the idea of a person of normal size we form the idea of a pygmy or giant; by composition, as when from the ideas of gold and a mountain, we form the idea of a golden mountain; and by comparison or analogy, as when by analogy with a city we have seen, we form the idea of one we have not. Ideas of incorporeals, such as God, according to Gassendi, are always analogical. Thus, we form the idea of God from the image of some such thing as a grand old man or a blinding light.[28]

In fact, most of the ideas we have we form by comparison and composition. For the idea we have of man is, typically, not the image of some one particular man; rather, the image we form that might originally have been derived from the experience of one individual is gradually adjusted to accommodate the experiences we have of other men. Perceiving something as a man is accomplished by comparing it with the image we have of man and apprehending that it resembles this image. In order for resemblance to an image be the basis on which we perceive something as a man, this image must have a greater resemblance to men than it has to anything that is not a man. Even animals, according to Gassendi, have this power of forming images: "When a dog sees an unknown man coming towards him from a distance, for no other reason does he judge it to be a man rather than a hare, or a horse, than because in comparing it with the vestiges imprinted (in his imagination), he notices that it is of the sort that is represented by the vestiges of men, and not of the others."[29] In brief, most images we have, we have by comparison, and when we use such images in perception, comparison is involved again. Although the example used concerns visual recognition, the views expressed are meant to apply to any form of sensation.

There now follow a group of three canons concerned with the formation of general ideas.[30] Everything that exists and all that we sense is singular, Gassendi holds; it is the mind that out of similar singular ideas forms general ones (canon IV). The mind can form general ideas in two ways. One way is by joining similar singular ideas together and forming the idea of the collection to which each of these singular ideas belong. Thus, from the ideas of Socrates, Plato, Aristotle, and like individuals, we can form the idea 'man', a general or universal idea, since it applies to all of the individuals in the collection. Something is then seen as a man if it is seen to have enough resemblance to members of this collection to make it a member itself. The second way is by abstraction: we determine what features a group of similar singular ideas have in common and, disregarding differences between them, form a separate idea of the common features. This idea is general, since it represents the features that a group of singular ideas share. Thus, when the mind notes that ideas such as those of Socrates, Plato, and Aristotle have in common that they all represent two-legged animals with head erect, capable of reason, laughter, discipline, and so forth, it forms the idea of a creature with these features, disregarding features that do not apply to all, such as that one (Socrates) is the son of Sophroniscus, while another (Plato) is the son of Ariston, that one is tall, another short; the idea of a creature with the common features is the general idea of man, obtained by abstraction. By collection and abstraction from general ideas, we can proceed in the same manner to form more and more general ideas, ascending the tree of Porphyry, from the idea of 'man' to the idea of 'animal' and then successively to the ideas of 'living thing', 'corporeal thing', 'substance', and finally 'being'. Irrational animals, Gassendi believes, can form ideas of collections of things; they cannot, however, form general ideas by abstraction.

That there are two ways of forming general ideas, by collection and abstraction, implies, although Gassendi does not say this explicitly, that general ideas have a double signification. A general idea signifies the collection of objects represented by the idea and also the collection of all the properties these objects have in common, considered in abstraction; the former comes to be called in the *Port Royal Logic* (part I, chap. VI) the extension; the latter, the comprehension of ideas or terms. Although the *Port Royal Logic* is generally credited with introducing the distinction between extension and comprehension, it is quite clearly implied in what Gassendi says about the two ways of forming general ideas.

There is a problem with what Gassendi says about general ideas, however. All images, like sensations and external things, according to Gassendi are singular. An idea that is general, therefore, cannot be an image. What is general can, however, be represented by an image, and this is just the way Gassendi views the matter: an image, which is itself singular, is a sign of something general.

Gassendi in his logic ought to have distinguished more carefully between the sign and what it signifies. The sign is properly an idea or image but what is signified is not; it is something we might more properly call a notion or conception. Elsewhere Gassendi recognizes this distinction and speaks not of general ideas but of general notions (*notiones universales*).[31] Whether we speak of God, the void, general notions or relations, Gassendi says: "We imagine something corporeal; we apprehend however at the same time something beyond the corporeal species, which is as it were something hidden by it. Now this is beyond the bounds of the phantasy and is proper to the intellect alone; and indeed the apprehension is of such a kind that it can be called not imagination, but intelligence or intellection."[32] Gassendi here clearly distinguishes between the image and the hidden reality it represents. What Gassendi in his logic perhaps inaccurately calls general ideas are not images, but are hidden realities of this sort.

Locke accepts virtually the whole of the theory of ideas in Gassendi's logic.[33] There are, however, two important innovations in Locke's theory. The first is in Locke's view that there are, in addition to ideas of sensation, also ideas of reflection. Now, this is not simply adding something that Gassendi had left out. Gassendi speaks of reflection as well. He, however, sees reflection as a function of the intellect.[34] Reflection is not a separate source of ideas from sensation. If there were no sensation, there could be no reflection either. Reflection, in this sense, has its source in sensation. Also, if ideas are images and there are ideas of reflection, then a reflection on an idea would be an image of an image. Plainly, a reflection on an idea is something other than an image of it. It is not likely that Locke would have denied any of this. What it indicates is that, despite Locke's saying repeatedly, certainly in the 1671 drafts of his *Essay*, that ideas are images,[35] his conception of ideas is broader, corresponding to the Cartesian conception of ideas as "whatever is immediately present to the mind when it thinks."[36] When ideas are understood in this manner, then it makes sense to speak of ideas of reflection. But not if we hold, as Gassendi does, that ideas are just images.

The second major innovation of Locke is his distinction between simple and complex ideas. Here it is very likely that Locke considered Gassendi's theory incomplete and that in his view he was simply supplying something Gassendi had left out. Of course, when this is added, we have a compositional hierarchy with simple ideas intuitively grasped and all other ideas composed from simple ones. If we see Gassendi's theory as Locke probably did, then it is just a foundational theory of ideas that is incomplete.

For Locke, the distinction between simple and complex ideas was of the greatest importance. In Locke's view many of the most bitter disputes between people are merely verbal, due to the fact that though the same words may be used, these words mean different things to different people, that is, the ideas signified or represented by these words are not the same.[37] Such disputes could be resolved if it could be shown that they are disputes about what ideas certain words signify.[38] To do this, we have to compare the ideas of one person with those of another. What it means for two ideas to be the same is that they have the same composition; and ideas are different when one has some component that the other does not have. Ideas compared are seen as complexes, and they are compared by examining their simple components, that is, the simple ideas of which they are composed. A distinction between simple and complex ideas is plainly necessary for implementing such a project.

Without denying the usefulness of such a distinction, it is important to notice that the way in which Locke makes this distinction is inconsistent with Gassendi's views on the nature of ideas. According to Locke's conception, simple ideas are simple not only in that they are not composed of any other ideas, but also, more generally, in that they are not derived from any other ideas. Other ideas are known derivatively; simple ideas, and they alone, are intuitively known. On Gassendi's view, however, only ideas that directly reflect sensation are underived, and these ideas are like uninterpreted symbols; for any interpretation involves comparing some sensation or idea with others previously acquired and the result is not an intuitive cognition, but a cognition derived, by accommodation or abstraction, from previous experience. For Gassendi, essentially, there is no intuitive cognition. In all cognition, what is experienced is known or understood by comparing it with what has been previously experienced. Even what Locke calls simple ideas are acquired in this way; we get the idea of 'red' in the same way exactly as we get ideas such as 'man' or 'horse'. The principle way in which most of our ideas is formed is by accommodation or abstraction, and what Locke calls simple ideas are formed in the same way. There is no fundamental difference between what Locke calls simple ideas and other ideas. Such is Gassendi's view. He derived it from Epicurus. Thomas Reid would take a similar position; it would be subsequently defended by Charles Sanders Peirce and William James as well.

The principal mode of idea formation according to Locke is composition; for Gassendi, it is comparison and abstraction. Locke's theory of ideas is a compositional hierarchy, with simple ideas as its foundation; Gassendi's theory of ideas has no such foundation. Locke's simple ideas are intuitively apprehended and all other ideas are composed from them; there are no intuitive cognitions in Gassendi's theory. Gassendi's theory of cognition is hierarchical; its foundation is, however, not in cognitions intuitively apprehended, but on uninterpreted data from the senses. Locke's theory of ideas is foundational; Gassendi's is not.

Notes

1. See Aristotle, *Posterior Analytics*, particularly bk. II, chap. 19.
2. From P. Gassendi, *Opera Omnia* (Lyons, 1658), vol. III, pp. 5–7. In this case, and whenever the Latin text is cited, the translation is our own.
3. Ibid., p. 7b (page 7, column b).
4. Ibid., II, 458a.
5. Gassendi's views are clearly a precursor of the radical empiricist views of mathematics and necessary truths found in J. S. Mill's *System of Logic*.
6. Craig B. Brush, ed. and trans., *The Selected Works of Pierre Gassendi* (New York: Oxford University Press, 1972), pp. 98–99.
7. See ibid., pp. 333–39. This is translated from bk. II (De Logicae Fine) of the logic section of Gassendi's *Syntagma Philosophicum* in *Opera Omnia*, I, 67–90.
8. Brush, *Selected Works of Gassendi*, p. 333.
9. Ibid., p. 346.
10. Ibid.
11. Ibid., p. 347.
12. Ibid.
13. See ibid., p. 346.
14. See ibid., pp. 344–45.

15. For example, those of Aristotle and Descartes.

16. From Gassendi, *Opera Omnia*, III, 8–9.

17. The text of the *Institutio Logica*, part I, is in ibid., I, 92–99. A new edition of the *Institutio Logica* together with an English translation is in Howard Jones, *Pierre Gassendi's Institutio Logica (1658)* (Assen, The Netherlands: Van Gorcum, 1981). The text of part I occupies pp. 3–20, with translation on pp. 83–101. The translation of all passages cited in this paper is ours.

18. The relevant material is in sec. III, part II, bks. VI–IX, of the *Physics*. See Gassendi's *Opera Omnia*, II, 328–468.

19. *Opera Omnia*, I, 92b.

20. Brush, *Selected Works of Gassendi*, p. 345.

21. For this distinction, see *Opera Omnia*, II, 405b.

22. Ibid., pp. 451–52.

23. Ibid., p. 450.

24. Ibid., I, 91.

25. Ibid., p. 92b.

26. Ibid.

27. See ibid., III, 318–20.

28. Ibid., I, 92b–93a.

29. Ibid., II, 410b.

30. Ibid., I, 93–94.

31. Ibid., II, 441a.

32. Ibid., p. 451b.

33. See our "The Theory of Ideas in Gassendi and Locke," *Journal of the History of Ideas* 51, no. 3 (1990): 379–99.

34. See Gassendi's discussion of reflection in his *Opera Omnia*, III, 441a.

35. See, for instance, *An Early Draft of Locke's Essay* (Draft A), ed. R. I. Aaron and Jocelyn Gibb (Oxford: Oxford University Press, 1936), p. 3. The very first sentence of this work speaks of "simple ideas or images of things."

36. Descartes, from a letter to Mersenne in July 1641, in response to an unknown correspondent. This letter is translated, in part, in Descartes, *Philosophical Letters*, trans. and ed. Anthony Kenney (Oxford: Oxford University Press, 1970). See p. 105.

37. See *An Early Draft*, pp. 4–6.

38. Actually, Locke describes the problem as being due to "imperfect ideas" and "wrong definitions"; ibid., p. 4.

Five

Hegel, German Idealism, and Antifoundationalism

TOM ROCKMORE

This essay concerns the foundations of knowledge in German idealism, with particular attention to G. W. F. Hegel's ambiguous interest in antifoundationalism. We can begin with a comment on the meaning of "German idealism." There is an unfortunate tendency to consider this period as beginning with Johann Gottlieb Fichte and ending with Hegel. In my view this tendency should be resisted since it eliminates from consideration two of the most interesting thinkers of this or any other period: Immanuel Kant and Karl Marx. For present purposes, I shall understand German idealism as the wider period including both Kant and Marx. I will take seriously Kant's claim that his critical philosophy is empirically real and transcendentally ideal, and hence a form of idealism. And I will disregard Marxist efforts to refute idealism, either by driving a wedge between Marx and philosophy or by classifying his view as materialism, where this term is understood to mean "nonidealist philosophy."[1] Marx will be understood as belonging to the movement of thought that originates in Kant's position and continues in the writings of Fichte, Friedrich Schelling, and Hegel, each of whom, with the possible exception of Schelling, directly influenced his thought. This essay falls naturally into two parts, including a general description of some forms of foundationalism in German idealism, followed by a more specific account of Hegel's position as an attempt to come to grips with this epistemological strategy in his own account of knowledge.

I

From Kant onward, the entire German idealist tradition is centrally concerned with the problem of knowledge. Hence, it is not surprising that an interest in foundationalism and antifoundationalism runs throughout the thought of this period. Certainly it is not the case, despite claims to the contrary, that epistemology disappears in the period after the critical philosophy.[2] The opposite is closer to the mark. The continued importance of the epistemological impulse in the post-Kantian German discussion is due mainly to the continued influence of the critical philosophy. Even the well-known focus in Marx's position on the relation of theory and practice is directed at least as much against the critical philosophy as against what others, but not Hegel, call absolute idealism.

The present task is not to sketch idealist epistemology, which has only rarely been studied as a whole, perhaps because of the mistaken view that it ends with Kant.[3] It will be sufficient to call attention to forms of foundationalism and antifoundationalism in the positions of the main German idealists. Here we can begin with Kant. According to Kant, philosophy is knowledge derived from concepts,[4] and his view of philosophy as composing an a priori system is obviously related to Cartesian foundationalism, or a theory of knowledge based on an initial principle or principles known to be true and from which the remainder of the theory can be strictly deduced. Now, in Kant's concept of a system as "the unity of the manifold modes of knowledge under one idea"[5] there is an ambiguity concerning the status of that idea, in his own terminology, as either regulative or constitutive, that is, as an idea toward which one strives or as a principle that is in fact instantiated and serves within the theory as its ground in a Cartesian sense. Kant's position is ambiguous on this point, perhaps because he was not fully aware of the need to choose between foundationalist and antifoundationalist approaches to knowledge.

Kant's position is both antifoundationalist and foundationalist. It is antifoundationalist since he holds that philosophy is a mere idea of a possible science that nowhere exists[6] and since he further holds that philosophical systems in fact arise by *generatio aequivoca*,[7] in other words, through mere accretion. It is foundationalist in other, perhaps more important senses: in the idea of system as the a priori realization of an idea constitutive of philosophy,[8] perhaps in the appeal to the transcendental unity of apperception as the highest principle of the understanding, of logic, and of transcendental philosophy,[9] and above all in the assertion that the Copernican Revolution, introduced as a mere hypothesis, will be proved apodictically in the book.[10] What he initially regarded as a mere hypothesis is, rather, treated by Kant as a ground in a fully Cartesian sense since, as he grandly states, a change in even the smallest part of the critical philosophy based on the Copernican turn would cause all of human reason to totter.[11]

In the philosophical tradition, above all in modern philosophy, there is a general movement from foundationalism to antifoundationalism. Fichte cuts a curious figure in this respect, since there is an evolution in his position from an early antifoundationalism to a later foundationalist view. In his early writings he clearly supports a circular, hence antifoundationalist, form of knowledge. This support is visible on several levels. One is his rejection of the traditional view, widely followed in the tradition since Aristotle, by Kant as well, that circularity undermines a theory. In his claim that theory is necessarily and inevitably circular Fichte rehabilitates a form of argument that had been much neglected since early Greek thought. Another instance is his insistence that logic initially must be presupposed but later "verified." This application of his concept of circularity to logic means that even logic cannot be assumed as true as the basis of a theory. A further example is the remark in the beginning of the *Science of Knowledge* (*Grundlage der gesamten Wissenschaftslehre*, 1794), the initial, main formulation of his major treatise, where Fichte insists that the task of philosophy is to determine an initial principle that, since it is first in the chain of reasoning, cannot be proven within the theory.[12] The result is, as he indicates in a metaphilosophical text of the same period, a view of philosophy as merely hypothetical,[13] in a word, as ungrounded. But Fichte rapidly changed his mind. In a later version of his theory, perhaps in part brought about by the celebrated *Atheismusstreit*, he invoked the concept of intellectual intuition,[14] not present in the original, to my mind most impressive form of the position. This concept was intended to justify claims for knowledge based in a quasi-Cartesian sense as an initial principle known to be true, which makes of the revised Fichtean position a form of foundationalism.

Schelling's position contains both intuitionist and foundational-ist aspects. His foundationalism is apparent, for instance, in his early, much misunderstood discussion of transcendental idealism, which in turn led to significant misreadings of Fichte's and Hegel's theories. In an important passage, obviously influenced by the Kantian approach to a categorial framework, Schelling proposed a deduction of history leading to the proof of the final ground of the harmony between the subjectivity and the objectivity of activity in a point of absolute identity. According to Schelling, his concept of the absolute should be understood neither as substantial or personal, nor as a pure abstraction.[15] From this perspective, Hegel's celebrated critique of Schelling's concept as a featureless absolute, in his words as the night in which all cows are black, misses the mark.[16] We see that this idea is indeed foundationalist since Schelling's intention is to deduce both the objective and subjective dimensions of reality, as revealed in experience, from his so-called indifference point (*Indifferenzpunkt*).

Marx's position is antifoundationalist. His antifoundationalism is visible in his methodological reflections.[17] He insists on the categorial approach to the interpretation of experience and develops an interesting view of the category. In the wake of Kant, German idealism is deeply concerned to find an acceptable deduction of the categories, in a word to surpass what Kant, in a famous reference to Aristotle, called a mere rhapsody.[18] On the contrary, Marx insists, correctly I believe, that categories which apply to experience emerge from it and must be altered as the experiential object to which they refer changes. It follows that there can be no final ground to knowledge in a foundationalist sense.

II

This brief sketch of the role of foundationalism and antifoundationalism in the thought of the main figures of German idealism is incomplete in several ways. Although we have indicated a continuing concern with the foundations of knowledge from Kant to Marx, so far only minimal effort has been made to supply the reasoning that led various idealist thinkers to support or to reject a foundationalist approach to knowledge. Now, it is at least as interesting to scrutinize the reasoning that supports the adoption of foundationalist or antifoundationalist epistemological strategies as it is to note their adoption. In the remainder of the essay I study in somewhat more detail the epistemological reasoning in Hegel's position.[19] Now, like Kant's, Hegel's position is both foundationalist and anti-foundationalist. It is foundationalist in its continuation of the effort begun by Kant, and prolonged by Fichte and Hegel, to provide an a priori deduction of the categories. In that sense, Hegel's position carries forward an enterprise that comes into the German philo-sophical tradition in the critical philosophy. But, pursuing a hint from Fichte, Hegel offers an antifoundationalist analysis of knowl-edge based on an interesting rehabilitation of the circular form of argument condemned by Aristotle. In this sense, he breaks sharply or at least innovates with respect to preceding thought.

My account of Hegel's contribution to the foundations of knowl-edge differs from the usual discussion in the literature in a number of ways. First, and most obviously, my interest here is revisionary, that is, to revise what has often been said about Hegel. It has often been claimed that Hegel did not have a theory of knowledge, or that in some unexplained sense he went beyond epistemology. On the contrary, Hegel not only was interested in this topic but made an often unsuspected, indeed fundamental, contribution to it. In that sense, I am concerned to call attention to an aspect of Hegel's thought that, I believe, has been unjustly neglected. Second, I shall not be concerned with the study of a single book or the interpreta-tion of a single text in isolation from others. My concern is, rather, with a particular problem, that is, the problem of knowledge and Hegel's contribution to it, not in a single book but throughout his thought. Third, there is a pronounced tendency to approach Hegel, who was deeply versed in the history of the philosophical tradi-tion, in ahistorical terms, through the internal study of his writings and in terms of various manuscripts. Although this approach is useful, it has its limits. Aristotle is the first thinker in the tradition who is concerned to take into account all previous thought in the formulation of his own. More than any other thinker since Aris-totle, Hegel attempted to elaborate his own position as the result of a detailed consideration of the earlier philosophic tradition. I concentrate on the reconstruction of the problem of knowledge as Hegel understood it. In this manner I think it will be possible to gain a basic clue as to the nature of Hegel's epistemological view.

Fourth, the articulation of the works in Hegel's corpus is a matter of much scholarly debate. Considerable stress has been placed on the possible discontinuity of these writings. The relation between them, in particular between the *Phenomenology of Spirit*, the *Encyclopedia of the Philosophical Sciences*, and the *Science of Logic*, is not well understood. But every thinker's position develops against a background of continuity. This is above all the case for Hegel, whose thought develops and deepens but does not, if I am correct, undergo fundamental alteration after its initial formulation in his text on *The Difference between Fichte's and Schelling's System of Philosophy*, the so-called *Differenzschrift*. I shall accordingly stress the continuity in the understanding of knowledge as a circular enterprise in the early *Differenzschrift* and the mature *Encyclopedia*.

If we are to understand Hegel's form of antifoundationalism, it is useful to begin with a comment on the available strategies for knowledge. If we look at the history of philosophy, we can discern different epistemological strategies, that is, procedures that, when correctly applied, are supposed to yield knowledge as their result. For present purposes, it is sufficient to distinguish three broad strategies, which we can relate to Greek thought and to modern philosophy. In the former, the claim to know in some sense rested on the direct intuition of being itself. This approach continues in the modern philosophical tradition in various forms of intuitionism, for example, in Husserlian and in some types of post-Husserlian phenomenology. But it becomes difficult to defend if, as came to be the case, Greek ontology is no longer assumed as valid.

A second strategy, that employed by René Descartes, is to argue for an initial point, or foundation, that can be known with certainty, in the Cartesian view the *cogito*, from which the remainder of the theory can supposedly be rigorously deduced. The argument for this strategy is twofold. On the one hand, properly applied, this approach can be held to yield incorrigible knowledge, knowledge in the full, or traditional sense, knowledge that is apodictic. On the other hand, in the wake of the rejection of intuitionism, this approach can be held to be the only available road to knowledge. If it fails, it has often been suggested that no other avenue to knowledge in the full sense is available and knowledge as such becomes impossible. The view that this is the only possible road to knowledge explains the almost existential despair that some have voiced about its evident failure.[20]

Hegel's own argument can be understood as representative of a third form of epistemological strategy, intended as a viable alternative to the other two approaches. It displays neither the Greek intuition of reality—in fact, Hegel rejects all claims for a direct, intuitive form of knowledge on the grounds that knowledge is not immediate but necessarily mediated—nor the foundationalist approach of Descartes. Hegel advances his circular theory of knowledge as an alternative epistemological strategy since, as he sees it, the foundationalist approach cannot succeed. In terminology that has only recently become fashionable, we can describe Hegel's theory of knowledge as "antifoundationalist," since it does not rely upon the known truth of its starting point. Strange as it may seem, the genius of Hegel's argument consists in the attempt to acquire knowledge if there is in fact no starting point in the usual sense, if there is no privileged place to initiate the inquiry, in other words, if the proper way to begin is just to begin.

Hegel's antifoundationalism is not the product of an isolated systematic insight. It is, rather, the result of his grasp of the discussion of the problem of knowledge in the history of philosophy. I am not unaware of the important relation between Hegel's position and ancient Greek thought. But as concerns the general constitution of Hegel's wider position, and in particular his own theory of knowledge, the main background against which his view is to be understood does not lie in ancient philosophy, to which he only later extended his gaze. More precisely, Hegel's circular view of knowledge is the result of the continuing epistemological discussion set in motion by the appearance of *Critique of Pure Reason*. For a grasp of Hegel's reaction to that debate, it is useful now to retrospectively reconstruct some of its main points.

It is difficult today to imagine the impact of the publication of Kant's book.[21] To say that it had a profound effect is certainly to understate the impression it made. Although Kant had his philosophical enemies, thinkers such as Johann Georg Hamann, Johann Gottfried von Herder, and Friedrich Heinrich Jacobi, who rejected the critical approach as such, numerous thinkers of the most diverse persuasions were united by the belief that Kant's conclusions were fundamentally correct. But nearly as many held that, although the results were sound, and despite Kant's insistence on system, the systematic formulation needed to complete the critical philosophy was not contained within the *Critique of Pure Reason*.

Now, in an important passage we have already noted toward the end of the book, Kant insists that philosophy must form a scientific system, which requires unity of the different forms of knowledge under a single leading idea. If system is the requirement for scientific philosophy, it is fair to ask if the critical philosophy adequately meets the criterion it officially adopts. For our purposes, it is important to note that Kant's contemporaries mainly held that the idea of system functions in the critical philosophy as a regulative idea, but it is not constitutive of the theory. Indeed, it was widely felt that Kant's views represented no more than his opinions, since they lacked systematic form. If these views were to be accorded full philosophic weight, they needed to be restated in the form of a scientific system. In other words, those interested in the task of the critical philosophy were convinced on the basis of Kant's own standard, that to carry out the effort at a truly critical philosophy, one needed to restate Kant's results in systematic form.

This felt need provides an important clue to the later development of German idealism. The post-Kantian moment in the German philosophic tradition can be regarded from various perspectives; but a central thread, which runs throughout the discussion at least until Hegel, is a related series of efforts to provide a systematic restatement of the critical philosophy, that is, a restatement of it in the form of a scientific system. Now, it is obvious that different models of systematicity are available. Not surprisingly, since system is an important concept in the rationalist moment of the modern tradition, the effort in Kant's wake to provide a systematic formulation of the results of the critical philosophy turned on the proposed constitution of a quasi-rationalist form of system, that is, an interrelated, presuppositionless conceptual matrix.

It often occurs in such debates that its nature changes over time. The complex nature of the debate concerning the reconstruction of the critical philosophy as system can be described as beginning with an attempt at foundationalism, which, in the course of the discussion, is transformed into an argument for antifoundationalism. More precisely, the initial argument for foundationalist system is altered during the debate, as a result of basic criticism directed against the concept of the foundationalist form of system, into an alternative, antifoundationalist form. The key event in this discussion, which leads from a concern with foundationalist system to an interest in antifoundationalist system, is a basic change in the understanding of epistemological circularity. It is through this revised understanding of epistemological circularity that, in spite of the decisive criticism advanced against the foundationalist type of system, a way was found to argue for an antifoundationalist approach to knowledge.

In the present context, it will suffice to mention only four thinkers who played a significant role in the discussion of systematic knowledge following the appearance of the critical philosophy. Each of these writers had a significant role in the transition from Kant to Hegel. Karl Leonhard Reinhold, a minor philosopher, the author of the so-called Elementary Philosophy, is today nearly forgotten. His significance is that he was the first writer to concern himself with the systematic reformulation of the Kantian results. Because he was a neorationalist, his approach was dominated by the concern to provide a foundationalist form of system, whose claim to truth rested on an initial principle, which he named the Principle of Presentation. According to Reinhold, this principle was indemonstrable but could nevertheless be known to be true.

Reinhold's views were criticized by two contemporaries, both skeptics, Salomon Maimon and Gottlob Ernst Schulze. Of the two, Maimon was the better philosopher. Although the claim to provide the only correct interpretation of the critical philosophy was routinely made by many writers, it is significant that Kant thought that Maimon's reading of his view was unrivaled for its grasp of the main problem. Maimon's criticism of Reinhold is important for three reasons. First, he denied that the critical philosophy required reformulation, or that it could be otherwise improved. Second, he rejected Reinhold's attempted proof of an indubitable first principle of thought on the grounds that a fact of consciousness is not valid as the basis on which to found a system. Finally, he suggested, on good Kantian grounds, that principles could be justified, although not demonstrated, in terms of the use to which they were put, that is, in terms of their utility.

Schulze's critique, which is also skeptically motivated, was essentially more narrow, and less interesting philosophically; it is mainly focused on Reinhold's Principle of Presentation. Schulze's importance for the present discussion is that his critique influenced Fichte, as did Maimon's criticism of Reinhold. In Fichte's thought,

these different strands of the post-Kantian effort to reformulate
the critical philosophy in fully systematic form come together in
a highly original manner. Although Fichte is a major philosopher,
he is also a neglected thinker. But his influence on other, better
known thinkers, in particular on Schelling, Hegel, and Marx, is
also of decisive importance.[22] A widespread failure to comprehend
his important role in the constitution of Hegel's position is certainly one reason why Hegel's circular view of knowledge has
so far mainly been overlooked.[23] In the present context, Fichte is
memorable because he provides both a stunning critique of foundationalism and an initial hint, later developed by Hegel, of how
to argue for knowledge in the absence of foundations.

In both cases, Fichte owes much to Maimon. His own critique
of foundationalism lies in the argument, which we have already
remarked, that in order for a principle to be first in a chain of
reasoning, it cannot, in virtue of that fact, be established as true.
In a word, if the principle is first, it is unlimited and its truth is
therefore unknown. This criticism effectively removes the possibility of basing a system on an initial proposition known to be true.
It lays the ghost of the linear form of epistemology, exemplified
in the quasi-rationalist attempt to derive a system from an initial
principle whose truth can be demonstrated. In the context of the
post-Kantian discussion, it undercuts the efforts begun by Reinhold to provide a reconstruction of the critical philosophy modeled
on the rationalist approach.

Fichte's other contribution, which we have also noted, is equally
startling; it lies in the reinterpretation of the circular approach to
epistemology. Ever since Aristotle's criticism of circular reasoning,
with rare exceptions most thinkers interested in the problem of
knowledge have tried to avoid any appearance of circularity.[24] In
Kant's writings and in those of the later philosophers just mentioned, the claim of circularity is routinely raised as a crushing
objection. Fichte's contribution is to realize that all epistemology
is ineluctably and necessarily circular. The result is to suggest
another, nonrationalist form of system, a form of system based
not on linearity but on circularity. In sum, with respect to the ongoing effort to reconstruct the critical philosophy in appropriately
systematic form in order to make good on the Kantian concept
of rigorous theory, Fichte's two insights respectively undercut the

possibility of a rationalist approach but suggest a viable nonrationalist alternative.

In the examination of Hegel's thought against the contemporary
background discussion, we can focus on his position at two crucial
points: in the *Differenzschrift*, his initial philosophical publication;
and in the *Encyclopedia*, his mature, twice-revised statement of his
sytem of philosophy. Although there is change and development
in Hegel's thought over time, the mature version of the position,
especially as concerns epistemology, reveals an astonishing degree
of continuity, often unperceived, with its initial form.

If philosophy must take shape as a scientific system, then by
inference there cannot be more than a single true system. The *Differenzschrift*, as its full title indicates, is meant to consider the difference between the single system of philosophy supposedly found in
the thought of Fichte and his disciple at the time, Schelling. Here
and in letters written prior to the publication of this text, Hegel
makes it clear that he regards the basic philosophical task as the
completion of the philosophical revolution begun by Kant, which
has its only correct extension in the thought of Fichte. This point
is important, since there is a marked tendency in the secondary
literature, especially in virtue of Hegel's later, often summary criticism of Kant, to regard his own position as the antithesis of the
critical philosophy. But this is a mistake since, to use Kant's own
distinction between the spirit and the letter of a position, although
he was indeed highly critical of the letter of Kant's thought, Hegel
never wavered from his appreciation of what he interpreted as its
genuinely critical impulse. His criticism was not that the critical
philosophy was critical, despite his belief that it ended in skepticism. Rather, he objected to the fact that it was not critical enough.
And his own thought can be legitimately regarded as an effort to
extend Kant's interest in criticism to self-criticism.

The *Differenzschrift* is composed of three parts: a statement of
the basic ideas of his own view of philosophy; a study of the relation of the positions of Kant, Fichte, and Schelling, whom Hegel
regarded here and later as the only modern philosophers worthy
of the name; and a critical account of Reinhold's thought, which
Hegel considered as a leading form of nonphilosophy. This somewhat neglected text rewards its reader. For our purposes, it is
sufficient to focus on Hegel's account of the fundamental prin-

ciple of philosophy and his critique of Reinhold's effort to provide such a principle. Here, Hegel responds to the idea of reformulating the critical project in fully systematic form. His response, which is clearly influenced by Fichte, constitutes an argument for knowledge as the result of a circular process; the only other possible strategy, namely, the linear attempt based on knowledge of an initial principle, must necessarily fail.

Hegel's argument against a foundationalist form of system sought in the attempted return to the rationalist approach is obviously based on Fichte's thought. He maintains that a philosophical theory cannot possess a basic proposition, in his word a "principle of a philosophy in the form of an absolute axiom" (*Grundsatz*). His argument, which here follows Fichte's own objection even in its choice of terminology, is that a fundamental principle cannot be established as true since the attempt to do so degenerates into an infinite regress.

Hegel further applies this reasoning to Reinhold's effort to establish a first principle in the latest form of his position, here influenced by Christoph Gottfried Bardili. In the course of a searching critique, Hegel supplements his previous rejection of the idea of a fundamental principle by a positive view of circularity. Knowledge, he argues, does not require a foundation, since the beginning of a theory is related to the fully constituted whole as the center of a circle to the circumference; for it is only when the circle is complete that the center point is fully constituted. The theory to which its beginning gives rise is the justification of the initial principle and not conversely.

The result of this line of reasoning is a clear, indeed brilliant, inversion of the linear form of argumentation, which is replaced by a circular alternative. For whereas in the former epistemological strategy the beginning is held to justify the claim to knowledge, in Hegel's view the end justifies the beginning. The claim to know does not rest on an a priori justification arrived at prior to the confrontation with experience; knowledge and its justification, rather, are a joint consequence that follows from the elaboration of the theory and its confrontation with experience. As Hegel further notes in an obvious allusion to Kant, the entire theory as little requires a foundation as the earth needs a handle to attach it to the force that leads it around the sun.

Although this argument has rarely been addressed, its importance should not be underestimated. In a sense, Hegel performs
a revolution in epistemology. Through a circular relation between
the initial part of the theory, its full elaboration, and experience,
he makes it possible to avoid skepticism as a consequence of foundationalism. The beginning of the theory, which gives rise to it as
the real condition of the knowledge of experience, is not justified
initially, but only progressively as the result of the knowledge to
which it gives rise in the application of the theory to experience.
What we have, then, is a form of circularity that is not an epistemological error but the only acceptable approach to knowledge.[25]
To refuse this point, to insist on the need to found philosophy,
as Hegel notes, is to imply that "Making the run-up becomes its
true work; its very principle makes it impossible for it to arrive at
knowledge and philosophy."[26]

I illustrate this point with a familiar example. If we think of
Euclidean geometry, there is an obvious relation of dependency of
the theorems that derive from prior theorems on the axioms and
postulates that underlie this science. Now, in geometry the truth
of the axioms and postulates is not known and cannot be established. Hegel's suggestion, which shows the limits of this analogy,
is that the theory that can be elaborated on the basis of the initial
assumptions in turn establishes their truth. It is as if the geometrical theorems were a proof of the initial axioms and postulates from
which they derive. Obviously, the plausibility of Hegel's argument
cannot lie in the claim that a circular procedure in fact establishes
the truth of the initial axioms. Although the concern to do just that
has been mentioned by a number of writers, including Edmund
Husserl, Karl Popper, and Hans-Georg Gadamer in recent discussion, I believe there is no way to prove the truth of a presupposition
from within the theory that follows from it; rather, in terms of the
utility of a given analysis following from a presupposition or set
of presuppositions, that presupposition or set of presuppositions
can be "demonstrated."

The circular approach to epistemology that Hegel adumbrates
in the *Differenzschrift* is further elaborated in the *Encyclopedia of the
Philosophical Sciences,* his mature statement of his system of philosophy. It has been suggested that for his mature thought we must
turn to the *Science of Logic,* but I believe that we need to take Hegel

at his word in looking rather to the *Encyclopedia*. Since the *Logic* is mainly an expansion of the first portion of that work, to accept it as the source of the position would inevitably be to take the part for the whole.

The doctrine of circularity as it figures throughout the entire *Encyclopedia* is never "thematized." But it occurs in numerous, often surprising contexts, in this book, in more than 20 of the 577 numbered paragraphs. It is present, to begin with, in the title. It is not irrelevant that the word *Enzyklopädie*, like its French and English equivalents, means not only "the totality of knowledge," but also "in the circle of education of the children," from the Greek term *kyklos*.

The doctrine of circularity is further present in the first paragraph of the Introduction, at a strategic point in the book, where Hegel sets out the main lines of the position he will expound in general in the remainder of the Introduction, and will further expound in greater detail in the work that follows. I would like now to comment on this paragraph in order to clarify the central role of circularity in Hegel's mature thought.

This short paragraph is composed of three conceptual parts, or moments: a comparison between philosophy and the other sciences, a comparison between philosophy and religion, and a description of philosophy as such. As we shall see, this paragraph presents at least two reasons to introduce the concept of epistemological circularity: the first has to do with Hegel's definition of philosophy, following Plato, as a science among the sciences, and the second has to do with the problem of the beginning of science.

In order to understand Hegel's concept of circularity here in relation to his earlier writing, we will find it convenient to approach these problems in inverse order. Regarding the problem of the beginning of science, Hegel notes that any beginning, since it is immediate, presents itself as a presupposition. His point, which restates a lesson already advanced in the *Differenzschrift*, is twofold: philosophy cannot be linear in form, since it cannot justify itself in terms of its beginning; that beginning necessarily functions as a presupposition whose veracity is only progressively demonstrated in the constitution and application of the theory to experience. Philosophy is circular, since the justification of its claim to know is based on the double relation of the theory to its presupposition and to experience.

The claim that philosophy must justify itself in the course of its elaboration leads directly back to a definition that Hegel advances in the initial sentence of this, the first paragraph of the mature account of his system of philosophy, which accordingly sets the stage for the entire discussion to follow. He says that philosophy differs from the other sciences in that it lacks the advantage of being able to presuppose either its objects or its method as directly given. He writes: "Philosophy lacks the advantage enjoyed by the other sciences of being able to presuppose [*voraussetzen zu können*] its objects as directly given from representation [*von der Vorstellung*] as well as the cognitive method for its beginning and continuation." [27]

This statement demands attention. In situating philosophy as one science among others, from which it however significantly differs, Hegel alludes to the entire philosophical tradition. At least since Plato and until most recently in Husserl's thought, a number of distinguished thinkers have held that philosophy in the full sense must in fact be science—indeed, the science of science, which justifies both its own and all other claims to know. In this way Hegel rejoins the ancient Platonic conception of philosophy, which dominates the entire later tradition. The difference is that he realizes, as Plato does not, that if philosophy is necessarily presuppositionless, a demand that Plato makes and Hegel accepts, then the claim to know must make of it a circular theory. [28]

Here, then, is the continuity as well as the elaboration of the doctrine of circularity in Hegel's early and mature thought. There is no question that in the *Encyclopedia* Hegel maintains the early doctrine of circularity. In the mature statement of his position he develops the original doctrine of circularity in at least three ways. First, he makes circularity, which was merely an eccentric concern in the early thought, into a central preoccupation, as indicated in his definition of philosophy itself. Philosophy is devoid of presuppositions, is necessarily circular, and is, in Hegel's words, "the circle of circles." Second, he extends his discussion to include the ancient tradition, in particular Plato's view of philosophy as a presuppositionless science. Third, Hegel realizes, as Plato does not, that if philosophy is to be presuppositionless, it must then be circular.

To summarize the discussion: my analysis of Hegel's view depends on a distinction between two approaches to knowledge: a

linear, foundationalist strategy, in which the claim to know is based
on the fact that the entire theory follows from an initial principle
known to be true; and a circular, antifoundationalist strategy, in
which the claim to know is based on the progressive elaboration
and application of the theory, which in turn "justifies" its beginning point.

I maintain that Hegel's own circular view of epistemology derives from his reading of the attempt to reformulate the critical philosophy in fully systematic form. In particular, I think that Hegel
accepts both the Fichtean rejection of linearity and his rehabilitation of circular reasoning. From this perspective, Hegel's specific
contribution is to go beyond Fichte's early view that in virtue of its
circularity any claim to knowledge is hypothetical. Hegel argues
that circularity leads to knowledge in the full sense. He proposes,
in this way, to make good on the traditional understanding of philosophy as the presuppositionless science of sciences, which, in
virtue of its circularity, is able to justify the claims to know.

I have emphasized the historical context of Hegel's circular epistemology because I am convinced that if Hegel's thought is not
viewed against the historical background, it can be neither understood nor evaluated. Now I have some final comments about the
evaluation of Hegel's doctrine of circular epistemology and the
implications of this discussion.

Under the heading of the usefulness of the history of philosophy, we can note the dependence of Hegel's systematic approach
to epistemology upon his particular reading of the tradition. This
point must be stressed. Ever since Kant distinguished between a
posteriori and a priori forms of knowledge, it has been custom-
ary to argue for a solely systematic approach to philosophy, to the
detriment of historical considerations. But even Kant's distinction
has a historical context, which tends to undermine the concern to
separate, in his language, *cognitio ex datis* and *cognitio ex principiis*
in order to consider only the latter.[29] This relation is even more
evident in Hegel's thought. It follows that the concern to isolate
philosophy from the history of philosophy is mistaken, since, at
the limit, philosophy and its history are two aspects of a single
process.

It should further be noted that there is an intrinsic relation,
which comes to light in Hegel's thought, between idealism and a

form of pragmatism. Idealists in general and Hegel in particular have routinely been accused of making claims for absolute, a priori knowledge, in ignorance of and apart from the external world. But when we inspect Hegel's thought more closely, we can perceive, in the shift to a circular theory of knowledge, an awareness that the claim to know necessarily requires the reciprocal interaction between thought and objectivity, as given in experience, so remarkably described in the Introduction to the *Phenomenology*. If the beginning point is to be justified only in terms of the fully elaborated theory, which is further to be tested in the application to experience, then idealism, in an unsuspected sense, is by no means isolated from experience, since it is basically pragmatic.[30]

Hegel's interesting approach to knowledge as following from an intrinsically circular process represents an enormous advance through a qualified return to the circular form of reasoning discredited for some two thousand years after Aristotle's criticism. With respect to the argument for a circular theory of knowledge, let me state my belief that there is no way around the criticisms addressed to foundationalism, both in the discussion after Kant and, more recently, by contemporary writers. Hegel's enormous merit is to have clearly seen that, despite the inadequacy of foundationalism, another, antifoundationalist, circular approach to knowledge is possible. In this sense, Hegel's analysis has, I think, no real rival in the more recent discussion, which, for the most part, is concerned less with the conditions of knowledge in general from a critical perspective than the veracity of the claim to know a given object indubitably. The error, to my mind, is that Hegel evidently holds that he can in this way provide knowledge in the full sense. Manifestly, such knowledge cannot come from a pragmatic approach. Although a circular approach does indeed produce a kind of knowledge of experience, indeed, the only kind we can have, the result cannot be apodictic and hence must fall below the classical standard.

Next, I would like to note that although Hegel's argument is obviously directed against foundationalism, it may be, although this is not certain, that he did not always adhere to that standard in his own thought. In this sense he was like many thinkers, whose views, on close inspection, appear to be not wholly consistent. Although Hegel was certainly more consistent than most, there are instances when he would appear to argue in ways incompatible with the spirit of his own thought, and in particular with the circular view of epistemology. An example occurs in the *Science of Logic*, where he suggests that one can begin only with being, which is in effect to employ that concept as a foundation for his thought.[31]

My final point concerns the problem of the relation of thought and being. Hegel holds that this problem must be resolved through a demonstration of the unity of the two relata, which has in previous thinkers only been claimed. But this unity is indemonstrable in terms of the doctrine of circularity. For it is only on the indemonstrable assumption that thought can know being, although on the contrary philosophy cannot admit any presuppositions, that in any given instance thought and being can be held to be identical. It follows that Hegel cannot resolve the problem of knowledge as he understands it.

The relation of this point to Kant's thought should be noted. Hegel's position is, in a way, an effort to rehabilitate the claims of reason against the strictures introduced by the critical philosophy. According to Hegel, modern philosophy issues from the transposition into philosophy of Martin Luther's revolt against dogmatic theology.[32] From this perspective, Kant's view is insufficiently critical since it fails to demonstrate its claims to know. But Hegel's result, although this is not his intention, is closely Kantian, more so than has usually been seen in at least two senses. On the one hand, we have already noted that at least initially Hegel desired to bring to a close the philosophical revolution initiated by the critical philosophy in a manner that is faithful to its spirit. The circular approach to knowledge that Hegel sketches does that. It can be regarded as the result of a generalization of the concept of the Kantian view of the principle (*das Prinzip*), which justifies itself, not a priori, but in practice.[33] On the other hand, Hegel demonstrates the familiar Kantian point of the intrinsic limits of reason. For he unwittingly shows that reason's claim to know being cannot be demonstrated. Although modern thought arose out of the effort to distinguish between reason and faith, this distinction is ultimately untenable; for philosophy and indeed all forms of the search for knowledge require faith, that is, faith in reason.

III

It has often been incorrectly held that the interest in foundationalism is limited to recent analytic philosophy. The burden of this essay has been to correct this misapprehension by identifying some main forms of the widespread concern in the thought of this period with foundationalism and antifoundationalism within German idealism, with particular attention to Hegel's position. This essay will be useful if it succeeds in calling attention to three points concerning the thought of this period: First, an interest in foundationalism and antifoundationalism is widespread in German idealism. Second, antifoundationalism receives extensive critical attention in this period, above all, in Hegel's thought. Third, Hegel's little-known but profound antifoundationalist theory of knowledge is worthy of further attention. I would like to conclude with a remark about the utility of the idealist approach to knowledge. Idealism is often held to be naive, yet Hegel's doctrine of circularity is valuable both in itself and as a profound form of the antifoundationalist approach to knowledge.

Notes

1. Both of these tactics were originated by Engels, the founder of Marxism. See Friedrich Engels, *Ludwig Feuerbach and the Outcome of Classical German Philosophy*, ed. C. P. Dutt (New York: International Publishers, 1941).

2. For this view, see Jürgen Habermas, *Knowledge and Human Interests*, trans. Jeremy J. Shapiro (Boston: Beacon Press, 1971).

3. See, e.g., Ernst Cassirer, *Das Erkenntnisproblem in der Philosophie der neueren Zeit*, 3 vols. (Berlin: Verlag B. Cassirer, 1906, 1907, 1920).

4. See Immanuel Kant, *Immanuel Kant's Critique of Pure Reason*, trans. Norman Kemp Smith (London and New York: Macmillan and St. Martin's Press, 1961), B 865, p. 656.

5. Ibid., B 860, p. 653.

6. Ibid., B 866, p. 657.

7. Ibid., B 863, p. 655.

8. Ibid., B 861, pp. 653–54.

9. See ibid., paragraph 16, B 131–36, pp. 152–55.

10. See ibid., B xxiii, p. 20.

11. See ibid., B xxxviii, p. 34.

12. See Johann Gottlieb Fichte, *Fichte: Science of Knowledge (Wissenschaftslehre) with the First and Second Introductions*, ed. and trans. Peter Heath and John Lachs (New York: Appleton-Century-Crofts, 1970), p. 93.

13. See Johann Gottlieb Fichte, "Concerning the Concept of the Wissenschaftslehre," in *Fichte: Early Philosophical Writings*, trans. and ed. Daniel Breazeale (Ithaca, N.Y.: Cornell University Press, 1988).

14. See Fichte, *Fichte: Science of Knowledge*, secs. 5 and 6, pp. 38–62.

15. See F. W. J. Schelling, *System of Transcendental Idealism*, trans. Peter Heath (Charlottesville: University Press of Virginia, 1978), p. 4.

16. See G. W. F. Hegel, *Hegel's Phenomenology of Spirit*, trans. A. V. Miller (Oxford: Oxford University Press, 1977), p. 9.

17. See discussion of "The Method of Political Economy," in introduction to Karl Marx, *Grundrisse: Foundations of the Critique of Political Economy*, trans. Martin Nicolaus (Middlesex, England: Penguin, 1973), pp. 100–108.

18. See Immanuel Kant, *Prolegomena to Any Future Metaphysics*, introduction by Lewis White Beck (Indianapolis: Library of the Liberal Arts, 1950), p. 70.

19. This part of the discussion draws on my book, *Hegel's Circular Epistemology* (Bloomington: Indiana University Press, 1986), and on my paper "Hegel's Circular Epistemology as Antifoundationalism," *History of Philosophy Quarterly* 6, no. 1 (Jan. 1989): 101–14. In the book and in the paper based upon it, I did not bring out the residual foundationalist side of Hegel's thought. For an initial effort to address the unresolved tension in his position between foundationalism and antifoundationalism, see my "Foundationalism and Hegelian Logic," *The Owl of Minerva* 20 (Fall 1989).

20. See, e.g., Richard Rorty, *Philosophy and the Mirror of Nature* (Princeton: Princeton University Press, 1979).

21. For an excellent discussion of the reaction to the first edition of Kant's book, see Frederick C. Beiser, *The Fate of Reason: German Philosophy from Kant to Fichte* (Cambridge: Harvard University Press, 1987).

22. For an effort to call attention to his impact on Marx's view of subjectivity, see my *Fichte, Marx, and German Philosophy* (Carbondale: Southern Illinois University Press, 1980).

23. See Denise Souche-Dagues, *Le cercle hégélien* (Paris: Presses universitaires de France, 1986).

24. For Aristotle's critique of circular reasoning, see *Prior Analytics*, 57b18, and *Posterior Analytics*, I, 72b-25 to 73a-20.

25. On this point, see my "Hegel et la révolution épistémologique," *Hegel-Jahrbuch*, forthcoming.

26. G. W. F. Hegel, *The Difference between Fichte's and Schelling's System of Philosophy* (Albany: State University of New York Press, 1977), p. 180.

27. G. W. F. Hegel, *The Logic of Philosophy, Translated from the Encyclopedia of the Philosophical Sciences*, trans. William Wallace (Oxford: Oxford University Press, 1968), p. 3 (translation modified—T. R.).

28. It is highly significant that in his use of the term *Voraussetzung*, built on the verb *setzen*, meaning "to place" or "to posit," in order to claim that philosophy must be presuppositionless, Hegel provides an exact equivalent to Plato's word, *hypotheteon*, from the verb *tithemi*, which has the same sense as *setzen*. Wallace's rendering of Hegel's precise term *Voraussetzen*, meaning "to presuppose," as "to rest the existence of" and "to assume" is so misleading as to conceal the problem.

29. See Kant, *Critique of Pure Reason*, B 864, p. 655.

30. One of the few writers to have clearly seen this point is Nicholas Rescher. See his *Cognitive Systematization: A Systems-theoretic Approach to a Coherentist Theory of Knowledge* (Oxford: Blackwell, 1979).

31. See *Hegel's Science of Logic*, trans. A. V. Miller (Atlantic Highlands, N.J.: Humanities Press, 1989), "With What Must Science Begin?" pp. 67–78.

32. For an important statement of this argument by a great German poet, who was one of Hegel's students, see Heinrich Heine, *Religion and Philosophy in Germany*, trans. John Snodgrass (Albany: State University of New York Press, 1986).

33. See Kant, *Critique of Pure Reason*, B 765, p. 592.

Six

Nietzsche and the Problem of Ground

WILHELM S. WURZER

The history of metaphysics has largely been guided by what Leibniz calls "the grand principle" of ground whose concise formula states, "*Nihil est sine ratione.*" Nothing is without reason or ground, without ultimate explanation, without the certitude of dialectic presence. Moreover, the principle of ground signifies a system of concepts, a totality of connected ideas in a unique dialectic terrain that consolidates reason and ground. This peculiar but certain oneness is first and foremost radically questioned by Friedrich Nietzsche. Indeed, one of the important aims of his philosophy is the undoing of the metaphysical identity of *Vernunft* and *Grund*. Thus, his inscription of difference in aesthetic configurations marks a significant attempt at dismantling the principle of sufficient reason.

Accordingly, in what follows I first outline Nietzsche's attempts at transforming the principle of sufficient reason set in motion in *The Birth of Tragedy* and *Thus Spoke Zarathustra*. I then direct my attention to the very process of Nietzsche's subversion of ground as it culminates in the *Genealogy of Morals* and in *The Twilight of the Idols*, particularly in relation to his observations on the political. In retrospect, I ask whether Nietzsche's withdrawal from ground unveils an antifoundationalist mode of thought or whether it is merely a digression that serves the traditional principle of ground anew.

Reason's Dionysian Site

Early in his philosophy Nietzsche recognizes that the problem of ground is intimately connected with the question of reason. His aesthetic projection of the primal One (*das Ureine*) shows that ground and cause have been mistakenly aligned in the history of metaphysics. He claims that one can conceive *das Ureine* as ground of all things without granting pertinence to the idea of ground as *causa*, or even as *causa rationis*. In effect, the very idea of cause, at least in its conventional cause-effect connection, becomes problematic in *The Birth of Tragedy*. Ground as primal One is too dynamic, complex, and conflictual to be the simple, absolute cause of appearances. Initially, therefore, Nietzsche sees the problem of ground not merely as one of separating cause from ground, but, more importantly, as one of reason's withdrawal from ground. Thus, Nietzsche's aesthetic genealogy radically transforms the principle of sufficient reason by dissolving the logocentric identity of reason and ground. *The Birth of Tragedy* begins this process by granting imagination the Apollonian freedom of standing outside reason's estranged dialectical self-presence. It sets up a new world for reason, a different ground sustained by a Dionysian perspective of suffering. This transformative view of ground seeks to express reason's tragic spacings in relation to reality rather than to "pure" reason. Nietzsche, therefore, accounts for reason-in-reality, reason-in-nature, reason as Dionysian phenomenon. The idea of ground is reinscribed, but not as pure cause or reason. Ground is now *other* than reason as "reason." This radical other is the aesthetic phenomenon of reason turning to difference, to imagination, far from the metaphysical region where reason and ground are one and the same.

A closer look at the matter of reason in *The Birth of Tragedy* shows that reason is aesthetically grounded in the metaphysical abyss of the primal One, *das Ureine*, the absolute imaginal space of pain and contradiction. Torn between the Apollonian desire to be free from primordiality and the ironic Dionysian impulse expressive of the primal One, reason, in a new face that Nietzsche calls "a discursive image" (*eine Bilderrede*),[1] reveals the aesthetic tensions of the beautiful and the sublime. This "discursive image" marks a dissemination of ground whose perspective of imaginal identity signifies an aesthetic, albeit metaphysical, opening for difference. The difference of ground and reason becomes particularly operative in the Apollonian-Dionysian interplay of image and power. In turn, reason's *Bilderrede* is more than a discourse on the image of the Apollonian-Dionysian constellation; it is a discourse on primal desire conceived as reason desiring to exceed the appearances of the primal One. On this view, a tragic showing begins to challenge the Socratic dialectic seductively aligned with morality. Reason is seen as *das Ureine* extending its power over a terrain of thought that exceeds the moral and political boundaries of Socrates' search for truth. This tragic movement of reason about the center of an aesthetic ground points to a Dionysian revolution of reason, a disclosive art of thinking beyond the haunting terrain of consciousness. Still, consciousness plays a role in this drama of reason. While the Dionysian impulse encumbers the dialectic spirit of consciousness, in the Apollonian instance of individuation, consciousness turns its probing eyes toward images of the beautiful.

Accordingly, *The Birth of Tragedy* reveals a dehiscence of reason, an aesthetic difference within the primal territory of imaginal identity. Dislodged from the Socratic dialectic for which it had existed only as a pure object of reflection, reason is now free to discern its falling. Nietzsche's early philosophy, therefore, betokens the event of reason's fall from the proprietary essence of ground to the aesthetic abyss of imagination. In *Oedipus Rex* Creon's advice to Oedipus may serve to show this paradoxical turn: "Crave not to be master of all things: for the mastery which you had won, has not followed you through life."[2]

The Birth of Tragedy takes up the challenge of Sophocles' notion of reason as a displaced, abandoned phenomenon in search of truth. It tells the uncanny tale of reason's new adventure. No longer master of being, reason unfolds slowly, ironically, from one mode of reflection to the next, without yielding to the dialectical desire for an illusory repose. For Nietzsche, reason, disengaged from its former dreams, emerges as *parodos* (*paradein*—"to sing more") of truth, the first appearance of the chorus of tragic reflection. As *parodos*, reason, in a powerful aesthetic extension of the primal One, plays out the parody of imaginal identity. Entering the stage of Dionysian *lethe* or primordial forgetfulness, reason sings of a new ground, an aesthetic chaos, far from the Hegelian retreat of *Geist*. Gliding over

Hegelian transitions without falling to the ground, reason strikes out against the scowling, teleologocentric eyes of "consciousness." An aesthetic approximation of the tragic act of Oedipus grants free space for reason. Its discourse penetrates the parodic Dionysian site of imagination: "Why was I to see, when sight could show me nothing sweet?"[3] The mirror of dialectical reflection had merely shown a hermeneutic process of subduing the natural, of controlling what is real, of linking being to a logical goal "by the shortest route and with the smallest expenditure of force"[4] at the expense of imagination.

Reason's Imaginal Dehiscence

The tragic, aesthetic displeasure with metaphysics' seeing, with the historic unfolding of a logocentric ground, is enhanced by Nietzsche's revolutionary invitation to disharmonize the Socratic dialectic. Apollo's image of reason's flight from ground projects a new mode of seeing, a filming in the manner of a "parodic" Dionysian turn to the aesthetic abyss of the primal One. Granted, reason is not yet free from *arche*. The Dionysian turn to art's origin, which makes possible the birth of tragic thought, is still committed to a principle of ground. Nevertheless, for a brief moment in the Apollonian spacing of *The Birth of Tragedy*, reason is free for the imaginal production of appearances receding from ground. Attaining a certain moment (*Augenblick*) of freedom in *Thus Spoke Zarathustra*, reason, in general, however, is either preceded by a tragic Dionysian sense of oneness in the early works, or by the will to power as essential principle in the later works. This does not mean that there are no traces of withdrawal from ground in Nietzsche's works. There are, indeed, signs of radical attempts to overturn the principle of ground in *Thus Spoke Zarathustra*. One might even argue that Nietzsche is often creatively engaged in deconstructing a metaphysics of presence.[5] But as we shall see, his genealogy, which is still caught up in the *language* of metaphysics, is primarily a critique of classical ontology and does not exceed the aesthetic-political essence of ground. At most, his genealogy anticipates a radically different space of reason, imagination's post-dialectic dehiscence.

Such anticipation can be discerned in the form of a metaphysical play in *Thus Spoke Zarathustra*. There, the event of "the death of God" is initially reason's decisive attempt to recapture the Apollonian moment of freedom. The image of Dionysos is significant but only in relation to Zarathustra's subversive (Apollonian) discourse. The idea of an Apollonian-Dionysian constellation with its differentiated amplitude is no longer determined by a primal ground. Instead, it is framed in an ontotheologic absence of ground. Zarathustra appears as "moving image" of reason, as the "fluid element" of tragic reflection.[6] What concerns us here is precisely a discourse in which reason is engaged in a certain play of imagination free of the absolute.[7] *Thus Spoke Zarathustra* advances a new kind of identity between imagination and reason, one in which reason is no longer granted an ontologic privilege over imagination. Nevertheless, in spite of reason's imaginal dehiscence, it is still sheltered by the eternal wills to power. Though there may be infinite interpretations, they are invariably interpretations of power.

This framing of power leads to the central question concerning Nietzsche's text: Is power as will radically different from the principle of ground? That it varies from the aesthetic ground of *The Birth of Tragedy* can be seen from Nietzsche's consideration of the ultimate fall of the absolute in *Thus Spoke Zarathustra*. But how else does will to power as principle of the revaluation of all values differ from the traditional principle of ground? For one, will to power recedes from the absolute ontology of the principle of sufficient reason. This operation illustrates that ground is no longer conceived as being. And yet, Nietzsche still thinks of ground as *Wesen*; indeed, the will to power is the *essence* of truth. Nietzsche's compulsion toward the thought of the eternal return of the wills to power indicates an epistemic betrayal of an earlier subversive mode of thought. The Apollonian desire to be free from ground, which for a brief moment outwits all manner of dialectics, is now entirely repressed by a new metaphysical play of power revealed in *Thus Spoke Zarathustra*. Dionysos, who signifies the unity of humanity and the primal One, is faintly present in this play. He no longer resembles the image of *The Birth of Tragedy* with its "gospel of universal harmony." Exceeding the aesthetic, metaphysical dimension of the primal One, the new principle of power disengages reason from tragic unity. What emerges now is a genealogical play of forces, the wills to power sub specie aeternitatis. This exclusive

Apollonian orientation is clearly evident throughout *Thus Spoke Zarathustra*. From the moment that Zarathustra fails to communicate his thought on a sociometaphysical level, the image of ground appears as power of individuation. An intriguing transition occurs in the text. Zarathustra's discourse exhibits an aesthetic *Kehre:* the image of Dionysos becomes the face of Apollo beyond the primal One and the emancipatory concerns of *The Birth of Tragedy*. Whence it is not surprising that in *Thus Spoke Zarathustra* the story of the "death of God" is no more than a fable of Apollo's beautiful "metaphysical" illusion—the eternal wills to power.

A New Economy of Presence

The *Genealogy of Morals* calls for an active forgetting of being, for an opening of reason that will enable it to break away from a consciousness with a moral complicity of contrary values. One may think of Nietzsche's genealogy as an art of enactment, a strategy of dissension that critically dismantles morality's "sense-less" indebtedness to dialectic. Its critique of subjectivity radically questions the value of a dialectic ground operative in moral ontology. But even as an art of critique, genealogy is not entirely free from a substantive creditor. Ironically, this creditor will surface in the pluralized spaces of reason's genealogy so that the configurations of reason and imagination are not able to assert themselves outside the digressive but solid space of the wills to power. Nietzsche's principle of power, therefore, announces essence without essence-appearance distinctions. This means, of course, that there is still a metaphysical eye inspecting the spacings of reason. Imagination and reason are still in commerce with a power whose very presence constitutes a new debt for reason. Genealogy's slippage into the open simultaneously limits reason's "free play" to the "latest and noblest form" of the ascetic ideal, the wills to power. Guided by this nonderivative concept, Nietzsche's genealogy assigns limitations to a deconstruction of presence. Reflection is reduced to the plane of power-quanta that do not appear to be empirical or transcendental signifieds but are still inscribed under the rubric of essence. It is true that the postdialectical wills to power emerge as detours of a radically new presence, as moments in the interval of essence and appearance, as forces of an uncanny space somewhere between individuation and ground, between Apollo and Dionysos, between reason and imagination. Nevertheless, the process of reason's emancipation from philosophical essentiality is halted by a new essence, a new economy of higher principles, the political ontology of the wills to power. No doubt, Nietzsche's text challenges reason's confinement to dialectical presence, but can it account for reason's occlusion, its "final spacing,"[8] its seemingly indemnifying debt to the eternal return of the wills to power? Despite its polythematic positions, Nietzsche's critical genealogy always seems to circle back to the principle of power. Indeed, the text consistently asks, how far can reason reach into the essence of power? Thus, the problem of ground begins anew with this text. And the *Genealogy of Morals* fails to think without a nostalgia for ground.

The Aesthetic Ambiguity of Great Politics

The essentialist mood of Nietzsche's philosophy of the will to power is enhanced by frequent allusions to such cultural master concepts as "the strongest souls of today," "men of great creativity," "higher men," "dominating and Caesarian spirits," "masters of the earth," and so forth. These utterances evoke a renewed interest in extending the principle of ground toward individuation, toward an Apollonian image of a new political order. Even though Nietzsche takes into account the twilight of truth, his critique of metaphysics paves the way for a new grounding, an anchoring of "great politics." The "beautiful illusion" of the Apollonian image develops into Nietzsche's own illusion of the "beautiful form" of "great human beings." It should therefore be asked: Do we encounter something new in Nietzsche's *Kehre* to the political terrain?

What is philosophically fruitful about his unique ontological elevation of the individual—this creative, rational human being who invariably stands above and against the ordinary person? What are we to make of his attempts to lodge the political order of rank in the sphere of Apollonian imagination? How are we to understand Nietzsche's "new, tremendous aristocracy, based on the severest self-legislation, in which the will of philosophical men of power and artist-tyrants will be made to endure for millennia?"[9] It is quite clear that the *Kehre* from the twilight of truth to a "new enlightenment" of reason announces a time whose politics will have a different meaning.[10] This meaning, however, is not clarified by Nietzsche. Indeed, there is no explanatory social theory in Nietzsche's philosophy. This apparent lack of theoretical clarity does not diminish Nietzsche's emphasis on a new economy of political ontology. The will to power is advanced as a historical concept, indeed, as a sociopolitical category. In the summer of 1888 Nietzsche writes: "The will to power as life: high point of historical self-consciousness."[11] It is not our purpose here to reinscribe a hermeneutic gesture in Nietzsche's text. It is there already, notably, in the very irony of his formidable *Kehre*, in the political image of *Gestaltlosigkeit* ("formlessness"), in his final indelible image of exclusivity. Despite the genealogical dehiscence of reason, the image of the political order becomes thematically distinct: "great human beings," "breeding," "order of rank," "the strong of the future," "the masters of the earth." Is Nietzsche's irrepressible desire for political presence an attempt to assimilate G. W. F. Hegel's and Johann Gottlieb Fichte's construction of history? Can we speak here of Nietzsche's classic (Dionysian) political metaphysics?

No doubt, Nietzsche radicalizes the metaphysical concept of ground in his corpus as a whole. He profoundly changes the direction of philosophical thought up to his time. But, notwithstanding all the productive instances of his thought, we must ask why a great portion of his thought, particularly the last phase, is so concerned with activating a new political diction of breeding and cultivating "order of rank." If "will to power" is really the "high point of historical self-consciousness," does this signify the completion of the Western teleological ideal? Like metaphysicians before him, Nietzsche is still preoccupied with the last and highest totality of things. His principle of the will to power does not provide us with theme-effects capable of disengaging thought from all dialecticity; rather, it provides us with a thematic nucleus that merely interrupts or suspends the classical equation of reason and ground. In turn, the image of the overman does not undo metaphysics in any radical sense; it rejuvenates the history of thought in "the grand style" of *gaya scienza*, the blithe science of a new political order. In *Ecce Homo* Nietzsche writes: "It is only beginning with me that the earth knows *grosse Politik*."[12] Metaphysics is now conceived as an all-embracing historical science. Of course, Nietzsche's compulsion to large-scale politics does not reflect the petty political situation of Bismarckian Germany, but rather a genuine spiritual confrontation (*Auseinandersetzung*) with the governments of his time. *Great politics* entails the science of "new philosophers," "legislators of the future." As such, its metaphysics is a science of the "wills to power," which is neither a transcendental nor a deconstructive theory of the political order. Still, as a new system of values it is committed to the principle of ground. The image of individuation, which culminates in Zarathustra's philosophy of the overman, is a mere "photograph" of the concept of the will to power. To that end, Nietzsche's image of "great politics" does not seem to move outside of a metaphysical terrain. Enframed in the "beautiful illusion" of power, the seemingly new political image remains frozen. The irony of Nietzsche's political judgment lies in his own admission: "My consolation is that everything that has been is eternal."[13]

Does this thought invite the possibility of a new political theory of ground? Undoubtedly, Nietzsche's preoccupation with the question of a new economy of "higher culture" does not advance his "radical hermeneutics" of infinite interpretations. Attempts to "assassinate two millennia of antinature" seem to fail in light of his strong Apollonian desire to legitimate "great politics." Even his renunciation of the concept of being becomes problematic with his new "will to power" conception of the world. Thus, the political turn to "the masters of the earth" is merely an elegant reconstitution of the ideal Renaissance man. Elements of Nietzsche's intense adherence to an *Übermensch* society can be discerned in Jakob Burckhardt's study of the Italian Renaissance. Accordingly, at least two questions arise: Are the future masters of the earth slaves of the past? Is Nietzsche's philosophy of power merely the eternal return of monumental history?

Imaginal Constellations

In order to respond to these questions, we must clarify some critical aspects of Nietzsche's aesthetic transformation of the principle of ground. For one, the principle of ground as reason is transformed into a principle of ground as will to power. This radical displacement of reason reveals ground as image, more adequately, as "world of images" (*Welt der Bilder*),[14] that is, as constellation of the aesthetic and the political. Thinking, therefore, no longer signifies the power of rationality, but rather "an aesthetic state" of political imaging. While deconstructing the dialectic essence of ground for an exclusive imaging of power and history that cancels metaphysics' debt to morality, Nietzsche's aesthetic *Kehre* retains a problematic metaphysical disposition, particularly a tendency to make demands on appearances. Although his work in general tends to free imagination from the dominance of teleologic rationality, it incorporates a sense of that very dominance into the "faculty" of imagination. So, in the end, Nietzsche succeeds in espousing an *aesthetic* imperative. Let us briefly focus on this question.

For Nietzsche, the dialectic of subject and object is now conceived within the horizon of "an aesthetic condition" of power. World and human are interwoven in the very "phenomenon" (*phainesthai*) of the work of art. This "phenomenon," however, is still conceived from the epistemic perspective of appearances that pervades the Kantian-Schopenhauerian philosophy. Even though ground has fallen from the power of noumenal rationality in Nietzsche's genealogy, presence (of ground) is nonetheless affirmed in the terrain of imagination's play of the wills to power.

Nietzsche's "new conception of world"[15] is that of the will to power of imagination (*Einbildungskraft*). An antinomy thus haunts his imaging of the political: imagination is not free of the will to power. The reader will have noted that Nietzsche's principle of ground, *der Wille zur Macht*, determines the spacings of imagination. Although it is clear that Nietzsche's genealogy seeks to free imagination from the dominance of the dialectic, it is just as clear that imagination is still in the service of the wills to power. Indeed, the intrametaphysical constellation of the political and the aesthetic serves to show the epistemic dependence of imagination upon the principle of the wills to power. Consequently, thinking as imaging, that is, as "filming," is conceived as mirroring the appearance structure of modern subjectivity. This in turn means that the will, which is decentered from reason to imagination, takes on new prominence in determining appearances within a domain of "filming" still muted by aesthetic presumptions of power. In effect, imagination as *Einbildungskraft* emerges as *Einbildungs-wille der Macht*. This priority of will in Nietzsche's transformation of the principle of ground maintains a mode of imaging whose thinking is in the service of a willing. Indeed, imaging is primarily willing for Nietzsche.[16] And imagination's own power is curtailed by the wills to power, by a language of presence that dominates the terrain of imagination. Imagination's enclosure in an aesthetic play of forces does not call into question the value of the wills to power, that is, Nietzsche's phenomenalism, which some prefer to call postmodernism. His radical questioning of metaphysics does not seem to demand an "aletheic" dismantling of the wills to power. It seems that power is a necessary condition for Nietzsche's own spacing at the limit of metaphysics.[17] While a disseminative laughter, signifying strength and courage, marks an epistemic undoing of metaphysics in his text, it mimes a political tradition reinscribed by imagination in the aesthetic economy of the wills to power.

Hovering between phantasy (*Einbildung*) and power (*Kraft*), the Nietzschean image of ground emerges as "the phantom in the center," from which the reader fascinates as it skids on the surface of an ontological order of rank. A new schema for imagination's play of genealogy becomes possible. It serves to unite fantasy and power in an aesthetic discourse attentive only to a distinctive imaginal sighting of ground. Within the unique spacing of fantasy and power, images of the wills to power break free of imagination's exclusive Apollonian demands of individuality. An anticipatory imaging reveals Nietzsche's genealogical deepening of aesthetic phenomenalism, a subversive counterextension of the Kantian *episteme*. Neither cause nor ground determines Nietzsche's aesthetic interpretation of judgment unless ground is conceived as archetype (*Urbild*) of imagination. The connection of representations that concern world and human is not predecided by an a priori category but by imagination's plurality of the wills to power.

It follows that will to power surges as image of power (*Kraft*) for the *will* in imagination. Nietzsche's emphasis on the concept of "a new power" does not surpass the limitations of imagination that his genealogy projects as imagination-in-the-will. A genealogical mode of judging is here conceived as an imaginal willing, indeed, as a "filming" that "wills" a certain dehiscence for imagination within the aesthetic plurality of the wills to power. Neither the will nor imagination, however, are free of power in Nietzsche's philosophy: "In every act of the will there is a ruling thought. The will is not only a complex of sensations and thinking, but it is

above all an *affect*, and specifically the affect of the command."[18]
Exceeding Nietzsche's texts, philosophy takes up the question of
imagination's freedom from the wills to power. This "final spacing
of metaphysics" awakens the principle of ground to a new text,
one that announces imagination's withdrawal from its debt to an
aesthetic economy of power.

Irony of Political Imaging

The privilege of ground is by no means undone in Nietzsche's
philosophy. On the contrary, this privilege is solidified by his
monumental theory of power and history. Perhaps, a particular metaphysical sense of ground such as the dialectic-noumenal
dimension is weakened in his philosophy in general. Still, the aesthetic *Kehre* or turn from the tragic constellation of an Apollonian-
Dionysian ground to an exclusive image of individuation or "great
politics" remodels the principle of ground. Thus, in the later phase
of Nietzsche's philosophy, ground is understood historically *and*
superhistorically. It emerges as eternal play of forces, that "dark,
driving, insatiably self-desiring power."[19] Which amounts to saying
that history and power become conjoined, eternal superhistorical
forces in Nietzsche's monumental theory of ground. His view of
power and history according to aesthetic-cultural criteria brings
the sociopolitical reality closer to fiction. At times, it becomes impossible to distinguish between Nietzsche's serious remarks about
the monumental past and future and his seemingly ironic, mytho-
poetic references to "great politics." In general, however, one can
say that Nietzsche's play of deconstructing and constructing the
essence of ground occasions an indelible conflict. This conflict lies
between the "first" and "second nature" of his thought: the "first"
being the disruptive, critical genealogy of reason with an Apollonian desire to seek infinite "imaginal" positions of interpretation;
the "second" being determined by a pervasive Dionysian faith in
humanity that is expressed in the demand for a *monumental* history, a theory of the will to power that is eternal. The first nature
of thought implants a new instinct and habit into philosophical
reflection by attempting to free reason from "reason" (or ground)
for imagination. In striving to understand this Apollonian withdrawal, the second nature of thought misunderstands the Dio-

nysian principle by cultivating an exclusive image of ground and subsuming imagination under the aegis of historical magnanimity called will to power. Precisely this demand for what is great, for an unlimiting power, occasions as Nietzsche himself admits "the most terrible conflict."[20] An Hegelian after all, Nietzsche in his monumental conception of power serves an unhistorical truth whose ground is simply essence or "life alone, that dark, driving, insatiably self-desiring power." No astonishment at Nietzsche's radical hermeneutics, at his deconstructive instances of new meaning, should make us forget that the will-to-power concept, in spite of its interpretive amplitude, its defraction of epistemology, becomes a master-word with the eventual cultural irony of a "higher politics." Hence, Nietzsche's philosophical eccentricity turns out to be a brilliant momentary suspension of metaphysics in the hopeful, monumental "filming" of a seemingly antifoundationalist political *Ereignis*.

Turning from a dialectical self-understanding of reason, Nietzsche's mode of "filming" stages an Apollonian play of illusion in which the aesthetic engagement of imagination and judgment accommodates the language of the wills to power. Initially wedded to a radicality of thought that outstrips inherited frames of "filming," Nietzsche's *skepsis* turns against itself in experiments that may be variously described as *films* of power, deeply entangled in an unjustifiable expansion of the concept of will. Entrapped within the aesthetic paradigm of a genealogy of willing, the Nietzschean manner of "filming," while providing "a continuous sign-chain of ever new interpretations,"[21] fails to attain philosophy's release from the taint of alternatives within the metaphysical enterprise.

Notes

1. Friedrich Nietzsche, *Die Gebürt der Tragodie*, in *Werke in Drei Bänden* (Stuttgart: Europaeischer Buchklub, 1966), p. 37. An earlier version of my paper on Nietzsche has been published in my book *Filming and Judgment: Between Heidegger and Adorno* (Atlantic Highlands, N.J.: Humanities Press International, 1990), pp. 10–20. This book radically questions foundationalist claims in contemporary Continental thought.
2. *Seven Famous Greek Plays*, ed. Whitney J. Oates and Eugene O'Neill

(New York: Random House, 1950), p. 182.

3. Ibid., p. 175.

4. Friedrich Nietzsche, *On the Genealogy of Morals*, trans. Walter Kaufmann (New York: Vintage Books, 1969), p. 78.

5. "With every real growth in the whole, the 'meaning' of the individual organs also changes; in certain circumstances their partial destruction, a reduction in their numbers (for example, through the disappearance of intermediary numbers) can be a sign of increasing strength and perfection. It is not too much to say that even a partial *diminution of utility*, an atrophying and degeneration, a loss of meaning and purposiveness, in short, death—is among the conditions of an actual *progressus*, which always appears in the shape of a will and way to *greater power* and is always carried through at the expense of numerous smaller powers" (ibid., p. 78). Also compare "Eine neue Denkweise—welche immer eine neue Messweise ist . . ." in *Werke, Kritische Gesamtausgabe*, ed. G. Colli and M. Montinari (Berlin: Walter de Gruyter, 1974), vol. 8, p. 227.

6. "Being new, nameless, hard to understand, we premature births of an as yet unproven future need for a new goal also a new means—namely, a new health, stronger, more seasoned, tougher, more audacious, and gayer than any previous health" (Friedrich Nietzsche, *The Gay Science*, trans. Walter Kaufmann [New York: Vintage Books, 1974], p. 346). "The involuntariness of image and metaphor is strangest of all; one no longer has any notion of what is an image or a metaphor: everything offers itself as the nearest, most obvious, simplest expression. It actually seems, to allude to something Zarathustra says, as if the things themselves approached and offered themselves as metaphors" (*Ecce Homo* in *Genealogy of Morals*, p. 301).

7. Compare "Zarathustra's Prologue" in *The Portable Nietzsche*, trans. Walter Kaufmann (New York: Viking Press, 1968), p. 121.

8. John Sallis, *Spacings—of Reason and Imagination* (Chicago: University of Chicago Press, 1987), p. xiii.

9. Friedrich Nietzsche, *The Will to Power*, trans. Walter Kaufmann (New York: Vintage Books, 1968), p. 504.

10. Friedrich Nietzsche, "Multum in parvo. Eine Philosophie im Auszug," *Werke: Kritische Gesamtausgabe*, vol. 3, p. 344.

11. "Der Wille zur Macht als Leben: Höhepunkt des historischen *Selbstbewusstseins*," ibid., vol. 3, p. 299.

12. Friedrich Nietzsche, *On the Genealogy of Morals and Ecce Homo*, trans. Walter Kaufmann (New York: Vintage Books, 1969), p. 327.

13. "Mein Trost ist, dass alles, was war, ewig ist," in *The Will to Power*, p. 548.

14. Ibid., p. 422.

15. *Werke: Kritische Gesamtausgabe*, vol. 3, p. 166.

16. *Gelassenheit* of imagination does not occur until Martin Heidegger radically questions the principle of ground.

17. Compare Sallis, *Spacings—of Reason and Imagination*, p. xiv.

18. Friedrich Nietzsche, *Beyond Good and Evil*, trans. Walter Kaufmann (New York: Vintage Books, 1966), p. 25.

19. Friedrich Nietzsche, *On the Advantage and Disadvantage of History for Life*, trans. Peter Preuss (Indianapolis: Hackett Publishing, 1980), p. 22.

20. Ibid., p. 15.

21. *Genealogy of Morals*, p. 77.

Seven

Like Bridges without Piers: Beyond the Foundationalist Metaphor

CHARLENE HADDOCK SEIGFRIED

Foundational metaphors have long been privileged in philosophical writing. They have seduced even pragmatists. Charles Hartshorne and Paul Weiss, for instance, selected the following sentence from Charles Sanders Peirce as a fitting opening for their multivolume collection of his writings: "To erect a philosophical edifice that shall outlast the vicissitudes of time, my care must be, not so much to set each brick with nicest accuracy, as to lay the foundations deep and massive."[1] No false modesty mars Peirce's ambition to provide the basis for the human and physical sciences: "The undertaking which this volume inaugurates is to . . . outline a theory so comprehensive that, for a long time to come, the entire work of human reason" in all the various disciplines "shall appear as the filling up of its details." Even William James, who is best remembered for his iconoclastic outbursts, was not immune to such foundationalist ambitions. He states emphatically in *The Principles of Psychology*, for instance, that "conceptual systems which neither began nor left off in sensations would be like bridges without piers."[2] He literally speaks of grounding knowledge by plunging explanatory systems "into sensation as bridges plunge their piers into the rock."

This reads like the traditional empiricist belief that thought is incomplete until resolved into the "stable rock" of sensations.[3]

Furthermore, on a realist pragmatic reading, the truth is found when hypotheses are confirmed by attaining their anticipated sensible outcomes, if not in every case, then in the long run. But something happens to foundationalism as the pragmatists develop their insights. The context from which the James fragment is taken, for instance, precludes interpreting sensation as a bit of positivistic sense data, just as 'truth' does not mean a univocal relation or refer to 'the truth' as such. Why, then, the solid appeals to a rock-bottom grounding?

Like Nietzsche, pragmatists often continue to use terms bequeathed to them by the philosophical tradition after having radically reinterpreted and revalued their meanings. The undertow of the original meanings, however, sometimes pull them beneath the surface. James recognized this danger: "Since the days of the greek [sic] sophists these dialectic puzzles have lain beneath the surface of all our thinking like the shoals and snags in the Mississippi river."[4] However, he himself did not altogether escape the seduction of foundationalism. He developed the tools needed to see through the siren attractiveness of foundationalist promises and even built a pragmatic raft by means of which we could stay afloat, but he still dangled his feet below the water. Like Peirce, he hoped some day to stand on solid ground.

As long as we remain on the surface and reflect on phenomenal appearances, the distinction between appearance and reality does not even arise. But as soon as we seek to relate these appearances to their underlying reality, then we enter into the endless and unproductive disputes that have characterized the philosophic tradition. Competing criteria are given for separating appearances from reality and for grounding legitimate claims in the reality so designated. The originality of pragmatism consists in bypassing this unproductive move by staying on the phenomenal level and demonstrating that true appearances can be distinguished from false ones without one's ever appealing to a reality hidden beneath the appearances. Pragmatic analyses are therefore not foundational. But since pragmatists also developed criteria to validate experiential claims, they were not exactly antifoundationalist either. John Dewey clearly signaled the original pragmatic approach by replacing terminology parasitic on a worldview that seeks to ground appearances in reality with the terminology of warranted assertions. As a pioneering figure, James was more ambivalent.

James both developed many cogent criticisms of foundationalist claims grounded in an independent reality and held out the hope that when the false moves were recognized and rejected, then a true account could at last be given. What distinguishes James from many other participants in the long foundationalist debate was that his criticisms of previous formulations were so devastating and his pragmatic method developed in lieu of the finally true grasp of reality was so persuasive that his own yearning for an eventual closure in a fully apprehended reality can be discounted and the radical core developed further.

The appeal of foundationalist realism is still so great that some people are attracted to pragmatism precisely because it is taken to be a version of realism that strongly opposes idealism and mere speculation and rejects both skepticism and the linguistic turn. It is therefore worthwhile pointing out that in undermining traditional appeals to rationality, idealism, and skepticism, pragmatists also undermine a traditional understanding of empiricism, realism, and foundationalism. Pragmatic contextualism does not fall into any of the traditional categories. It is neither realist nor antirealist, foundationalist nor antifoundationalist. These categories are based on metaphysical outlooks that pragmatists reject, and they are therefore no longer applicable.[5] Pragmatism does, however, seek to respond to the interests that led to the long search for foundations. Chief among these interests is a concern to have a secure warrant for our beliefs, and it is this interest that was side-tracked long ago into a misconceived search for foundations.

In this essay I first argue that James's appeals to realism are misleading because his new starting point for reflection is a concrete or phenomenological analysis of experience understood as reality-for-us. The pragmatist theory of truth is shown to be a plausible development of the antifoundationalist implications of James's analysis of concrete, lived experience. The explanation that sensations can only be functionally distinguished from perceptions undercuts the foundationalist building-block theory of sensations. Finally, a pragmatist alternative to foundationalism is developed that draws on an ecological worldview to draw out the implications of James's model of a noncoercive ordering of manyness-in-one.

1. Reality-for-Us

For James, phenomena do not mean the visible appearances of an underlying noumenal reality, but the very reality itself as grasped in our interactions. "Realism is eternal and invincible in this phenomenal sense."[6] We can retrospectively designate some of our experiences as real and some as illusory, for instance, but this means that we can enter into different relations to them. Since "every manner of conceiving a fact is relative to some interest, . . . there are no absolutely essential attributes" (*EPH*, p. 52, n.21). Only "the phenomenon in its entirety," that is, as related to all possible interests, can legitimately be designated as 'real,' but our relations are always limited by the finite nature of our needs and interests (*EPH*, p. 51). The only claims he makes for getting beyond the appearances are for mystic experiences of oneness with the ineffable and for the Peircean belief in the truth that is fated to be achieved at the end of time. But against the mystic claim, James insists that philosophy is a rational enterprise, according to his own redefinition of rationality, to be sure, but this still requires giving shape to the shapeless or misshapen by unifying the manifold. Philosophers as philosophers cannot rest in an ineffable communion.[7] Likewise, the final outcome does not function in James's own analyses, which are explicitly finitist and temporally bound.

James's analysis of substance illustrates his position on foundationalism.[8] He defends the historically interesting appeal to substance because it answers characteristically human needs, not because substances exist in reality. He says that philosophers who deny the existence of substances that hold together sensible appearances will run up against "the general mind" that seeks for more reassuring solutions. Philosophers likewise seek to have expectancy defined; their criteria are simply more demanding than that required for everyday life. No explanation will continue to be accepted that does not define the future congruously to our active powers. These powers are both aesthetic and practical and include our emotional reactions (*WB*, p. 66). Philosophers overprivilege the aesthetic demands of simplicity and clarity. But these cannot be finally determinate or satisfactory without also answering to our practical demands. Like Immanuel Kant, James argues that humans are bound by the postulates of both rational and practical reason (*WB*, p. 71). Taken separately, demands for congruency between the universe and the knower and between the universe and the doer are "monstrously lopsided," but when harmonized they are maximally satisfactory. James appeals to his unique analysis of "concrete acts of living reasoning" throughout his writings as a method of deciding between competing positions, but since he never explicitly developed the model, the procedure has been missed.[9]

As an object of consciousness, "the cosmos in its totality," or reality as such, must fulfill these same criteria of satisfying our aesthetic and practical reason. The demands of theoretic reason, that is, for simplicity and clarity, can be fully satisfied only by fulfilling the demands of practical reason. The closure achieved in a finally satisfactory explanation—meaning one not subject to further revision—cannot be attained on aesthetically rational grounds alone. "Cognition, in short, is incomplete until discharged in act" (*WB*, p. 72). Acquaintance with a thing means knowing how to act in regard to it; it does not mean 'derived from a foundation in reality.' "The ultimate universal datum," as well as each particular datum, are known to the extent to which we can adopt an emotional or active attitude toward them (p. 73). Philosophies will therefore succeed only if they can "legitimate . . . the more powerful of our emotional and practical tendencies" (p. 74).

A most important consequence of James's position, unlike Kant's, is that what will satisfy our tendencies will differ from person to person. We can say in advance that claims about "the nature of things" must not be "radically alien to human nature" (*WB*, p. 75). However, since the active impulses that legitimate our conclusions about the nature of the universe are so mixed and various in different persons, they do not uniquely designate any one universe, but vary according to personal temperaments. Idealism and materialism, for instance, can equally well satisfy both our aesthetic or theoretic demands of clearness and simplicity and our practical demands that our expectations be satisfactorily resolved. But since we, as individual persons, may combine and emphasize these demands differently, neither idealism nor empiricism will be universally recognized as the most rational and the most attractive or energizing (*WB*, p. 75).

James rejects the accusation that his position is subjectivistic because such a criticism supposes there is some other, more legitimate, way to arrive at our conclusions about the universe. The satisfaction of some purely rational (aesthetic) set of rules has been suggested as an alternative account, for instance, but this can be seriously entertained only in ignorance of the fact that we are not calculating machines. We come to philosophic and scientific positions as whole persons, not as disembodied spirits, and in our theoretic deliberations "intellect, will, taste, and passion cooperate just as they do in practical affairs" (*WB*, p. 77). It does not therefore follow that philosophers and scientists give the same weight to experimental verification or to emotional solace as does someone not primarily engaged in theory construction. But to deny that such passions as that of surpassing a fellow researcher also inform our theoretical conclusions is to lose touch with "the living facts of human nature."

We accept scientific methodology because it has helped us accomplish our ends. But if other approaches do so better in a particular case, then we are justified in not waiting for scientific verification. Evaluation of the actual outcome will determine whether we have guessed well or poorly. The demand for access to unproven drugs by AIDS victims illustrates the point. Without the scientific process, there would be no drugs developed. But the careful experimental methods require withholding them from the public until they have been found to be both effective and safe. Presently terminal cases of AIDS will not benefit if these protocols are scrupulously adhered to. But if the drug should in the future turn out to be effective, then for presently terminally ill patients the direct result of these properly cautious procedures is an unnecessary because avoidable death. On the other hand, if the drug turns out to be ineffective or even harmful, the outcome will still be death. Only the person whose life is at stake can legitimately assess the risks he or she is willing to assume. "In the total game of life we stake our persons all the while" (*WB*, p. 78). But in the larger questions of life we also have only our life with which to gamble. To subordinate the living individual to a fictitious whole or to a predetermined good or to an unquestioned truth is to substitute a myth like the folk, the nation, the good, or the real for the ambiguities of the human condition.

To return for a moment to the earlier example, the appeal to a hidden substrate or substance was accepted as a cogent philosophical explanation for so long because it fulfilled the criterion of satisfying expectations. It gave an explanation, for instance, for why we can reidentify objects of which we have only fleeting and disconnected sensations. It will not do to simply abandon substance, as David Hume proposed, unless its function is replaced by a more satisfactory explanation. If not substance, then what accounts for the continuation of objects over time? They are continuous for us, and James shows how this relation to ourselves is a necessary condition for knowledge of, and truth claims about, the world. The basis for our claims is not a privileged foundation in reality as such but a satisfactory fulfillment of those conditions on which we have come to rely for attaining our ends. Philosophers try to make explicit these implicit conditions.

All the pragmatists attack free-floating speculation and want to ground their analyses in the real world. But as Lewis Hahn points out, for John Dewey it is the meaning of existence, rather than the fact of it, that should concern philosophy.[10] Dewey does not appeal to preexisting facts to ground his analyses, for instance, but to the factual outcomes of investigations. Such experimental contexts are distinguished by a particular structure of meaning but are not reducible either to meaning or to sensational immediacy. Contexts are not foundations, which is why they cannot generate certainty. But they are not reducible to mere interpretations, either, but can generate warranted grounds for action.

James insists, for instance, that he is a 'realist,' and that he grounds his analyses in the real world, that is, one that exists apart from us. But he also says that for something to be recognized and designated 'real,' it must stand in a certain relation to ourselves. It is knit in a fringe of relations. In fact, "the word 'real' itself is, in short, a fringe" (*PP*, II, 947). Once again, James recognizes a deeply puzzling issue behind something so familiar that we take it for granted: "Strange mutual dependence this, in which the appearance needs the reality in order to exist, but the reality needs the appearance in order to be known!" (*PP*, II, 930).[11]

Problems "arise from the vain attempt to reconvert the manifold into which our conception has resolved things, back into the continuum out of which it came" (*SPP*, p. 51). When the strange mutual dependence of existent object and known object is conceptually broken apart, then those who focus on the independent existence are designated realists whereas those who focus on the object as it appears to us are designated antirealists. Likewise, those who ground their analyses in the existent object supposedly accessible and describable as it is in itself are foundationalists, and those who emphasize that we have access to things only as they are for us are antifoundationalists.

But James calls into question the distinction itself as profoundly misleading. It is a "vain attempt" to take distinctions that are useful for handling the flux of experience as though they were revelatory of something 'behind' experience. Once it is recognized that all reality is reality-for-us, even though it is assumed to exist apart from us, it no longer makes sense to oppose reality as known and as it is in itself. "A pure sensation [is] . . . an abstraction, never realized in adult life" (*PP*, II, 722). It is always fringed in a network of relations from which it derives its meaning.

Since "each of us literally *chooses*, by his ways of attending to things, what sort of a universe he shall appear to himself to inhabit," then there can be no appeal to an independent, shared universe to ground our assertions (*PP*, I, 401). By calling attention to James's use of the masculine pronoun, for instance, I can corroborate his assertion in a way that he himself did not, namely, by pointing out that women's choices, objects of attention, and lived worlds are not necessarily identical to men's. We can, however, appeal to the outcome that follows from acting as though the universe were of a certain sort rather than another. If we enter into the scientific game, as James calls it, then we can reap both the benefits and the liabilities of such an organization of experience. If our universe is instead primarily religious, then a different series of results become authoritative.

2. Concrete, Lived Experience

A Jamesian radical empiricist privileges experience, but only after having thoroughly reconstructed it. Although James sometimes uses the foundational metaphors of experiential grounding, he first replaces Humean and mechanistic atomistic sensationalism with a concrete analysis of 'seeing-as.' He also consistently criticizes the foundationalist building-block metaphor: "Out of no amount of discreteness can you manufacture the concrete."[12] This applies both to sensations and to concepts: "When you have broken the reality into concepts you never can reconstruct it in its wholeness" (*PU*, p. 116).

James explicitly links his interpretation of experience with Dewey's explanation of 'situation.'[13] Dewey reformulates a situated experience as a transaction between individuals and what constitutes their environment at the time. Environment is reconstructed into the broadest possible horizon of all that contributes to the meaningfulness of an event. It encompasses such conditions as the person spoken to and the subject of conversation, as well as the implements that are handled. These "interact with personal needs, desires, purposes, and capacities to create the experience which is had."[14]

The pragmatic methodological appeal is neither to the isolated sense data of the empiricists nor to the textuality of texts of the poststructuralists, but to concrete experience.[15] Experience is a protean term, but pragmatists emphasize the two dialectically related aspects of novel eruption and historically conditioned actual situations. On the one hand, experience refers to the big blooming buzzing confusion signifying the indeterminacy of experience, always lying in wait to undermine not only formal organizational systems like science and national politics, but also the commonsensical, everyday world. On the other hand, experience also refers to the individually and socially constructed organizations of experience that misleadingly appear as ready made. The pragmatic appeal to experience has the same subversive intent as the poststructuralist appeal to the indeterminacy of the text. But it also allows and provides for something more, namely, a legitimate means of closure, albeit one that is always finite and particular and in principle revisable.

James's intent to begin with experience, as the only hope of overcoming both nihilism and skepticism, leads him to methodically employ the findings and viewpoint of both psychology and common sense insofar as they remain on the phenomenal level of experience. He calls his procedure of adopting a "practical and psychological point of view" a radically concrete analysis (*MT*, pp. 23, n.6; 115–16; 36, n.5). But the analysis itself is never merely psychological or commonsensical because he systematically questions each particular explanation from the viewpoint of a more complete reconstruction of experience that explicitly raises the question of value for life.

James insists that he is a realist but unfortunately is ambivalent as to just what this encompasses. Although he sometimes falls back into claims for the reality of universals and for unmediated, direct access to being, he more often emphasizes that such universals are subordinate to our individual organizations of experience and develops the perspectival character of all metaphysical claims. I emphasize his reconstruction of realism into an interpretive, experimental praxis as both more definitively pragmatic and as a more promising contemporary approach.

Pragmatic realism is primarily an injunction to begin philosophical reflection with a careful examination of lived experience and to test one's findings rather than just asserting them as rationally coherent. It also reminds us of the perspectival character of our appropriations of experience. Through developing the riotous abundance of life-enhancing organizations of experience, pragmatic perspectivism resists premature closure. The pragmatic move is therefore not from foundationalism to antifoundationalism, but to a reflective appropriation of the ways we make ourselves at home in the world. James replaces traditional rationalism with the rationality of concrete acts of thinking.[16] In doing so, he shows that metaphysical programs of abstracting essences and building up the house of being with them brick by brick were historically influential but ultimately barren ways of weaving chaos into order.

Although some distortion is inevitable in every conceptualization of our interactions in the world, it is far worse not to even attempt formulating such an admittedly provisional starting point. Discussions of meaning and truth that ignore the context of experience are operating with unexamined assumptions that will inevitably render the models developed irrelevant or ultimately unworkable, as the proliferation of seemingly unsolvable epistemological and metaphysical disputes amply demonstrates. (The search through uncounted numbers of journal articles for an adequate explanation of Hume's "missing shade of blue" comes to mind.) Both the empiricist and idealist traditions are rationalist insofar as they speculatively determine meanings and develop systematic explanations without first examining the unique mode of our active being in the world, of which philosophic inquiry is just one development. It was only after the fact, however, that James realized that he had, at last, "reflectively justified our instinctive feeling about immediate experience" (*SPP*, p. 59).

James is encouraged by the examples of F.C.S. Schiller and Dewey to expand the germ of pragmatic methodology into a broader epistemology and metaphysics.[17] They reflected on how scientists over time changed their understanding of their activities. Instead of assuming that the clearness, beauty, and simplicity of scientific laws mirrored a divine handiwork in nature, scientists were coming to believe that such formulations were only approximations, tolerating "much choice of expression and many dialects" (*PM*, p. 33). The realization that human ways of organizing the world to answer to our needs may or may not reflect the structure of the world as it is in itself was a fundamental insight derived by the pragmatists from reflections on Darwinian evolution. In linking his view of truth with the instrumentalism of Dewey and the humanism of Schiller, James means to emphasize that scientific theories are signs, that is, conceptual shortcuts replacing particular phenomena, which satisfactorily link one part of our experience with another (*PM*, p. 34). The linkages are as various as the aims in view.

New truth is always a "go-between" and smooths over new facts with old beliefs with a minimum of disturbance and a maximum of continuity. In fact, success is just this smooth transition and therefore always an approximation. One theory is said to be more satisfactory than another, but this means satisfactory to ourselves, and different individuals emphasize different points of satisfaction. "To a certain degree, therefore, everything here is plastic" (*PM*, p. 35)—but only to a certain degree. Such subjective satisfactions, though sufficient as personal guides to action, must also take account of the wider array of funded truths held by the relevant community and whatever counterindicating experiences arise over time, if they are to acquire the status of pragmatic truth.

Although pragmatists do criticize the standard accounts of truth, they do not thereby undermine the whole range of particular truths that are presently held. On the contrary, they provide arguments why these truths cannot be rejected all at once. But although this insistence on continuity might placate those who hold a coherentist theory of truth, it cannot reassure those realists who subscribe to a traditional correspondence theory of truth. James reconstructs the correspondence theory by arguing that older beliefs or truths, which play an indispensable role in the determination of new truths, do not occupy some privileged relationship to things as they are. They are held with such tenacity because they answer our needs so well. And these needs, expressed by us as interests of various sorts, are said by James to be the only a priori element in experience.[18]

A new opinion counts for true insofar as it can gratify the desire to graft new experiences onto the old stock of beliefs and thereby illuminate both. Those opinions are thought by us to be most true that work best at satisfying our double urgency of grasping new facts and utilizing our store of knowledge, "for 'to be true' *means* only to perform this marriage-function" (*PM*, p. 37). Purely objective truth, in the sense of true apart from any human contribution, is therefore a chimera. Pragmatically objective truth is not such an illusion because it means maximally satisfactory.

This pragmatic theory of truth relegates the notions of already verified truth, of cumulative truth, of truth as gradually closing the gap between the known and the unknown, to the status of place holders, that is, regulative ideas. Such beliefs may regulate our search for the truth and may allow us to put some truths out of reach of our skeptical attitude and the need to corroborate them. However, they do so only by the expedient of temporarily 'shelving' them, that is, of taking them for granted, so that other experiences can be taken up. In the genealogy of truth that James is developing, they are paleontological remains. But they are in principle susceptible of becoming part of the living process again, and do so whenever new data require a rearrangement or transformation of the old. The cogency of evidence does not ultimately depend on its logical form but on our predispositions as to what counts.

3. Dismantling the Building-Block Theory of Sensation

Despite James's stated intention in *The Principles of Psychology* to study cognition without any philosophical presuppositions, he apologizes in the second volume for introducing so much

Erkenntnisstheorie into his discussion of sensation (*PP*, II, 658). This puzzling procedure arises because of James's mistaken belief that presuppositionless observational findings could be strictly distinguished from metaphysically constrained explanations.[19] In hindsight, we can recognize that James is actually marshaling phenomenal evidence to demonstrate the central role of selective interest. He is feeling his way toward an analysis of the structures of our human organization of experience, rather than engaging in yet another epistemological debate. New terminology better suits this new procedure. We should talk about his concrete analysis of experience rather than about his metaphysics or epistemology. The metaphysical standpoint keeps alive the dualism of being-in-itself and phenomena-for-us that pragmatism continually—if not always consistently—denies. In Dewey's words, "All we know of any situation is what it does to and with us: *that* is *its* nature."[20]

As always, James is careful to relate his arguments about competing theories of knowledge to the available evidence of individual experience and scientific reports on psychological experiments. He defines sensation and perception, for instance, according to their usage in popular speech, that is, within naive experience, and in the psychological literature, that is, within a naive but more carefully observant experience. Both sensation and perception name processes of cognition of an experienced world and need, under normal conditions, the stimulation of nerves to occur. Moreover, perception always involves sensation as part of itself, and sensation never takes place in adult life without perception. Therefore, they can be distinguished only as different cognitive functions, and not as absolutely distinct entities (*PP*, II, 651).

The nearer an object cognized comes to being a simple quality like 'hot' or 'pain,' the nearer the state of mind approaches pure sensation, while the greater the number of relations cognized in locations, comparisons, or measurements, the nearer the state of mind approaches perception. The simpler the sensation, the more it functions as a mere 'acquaintance-with' a fact, while the more relations are included, the more it is called a perception that gives us 'knowledge-about' facts. Both are alike in their distinction from 'thought' and 'conception' in that they give us the fact as an immediately present outward reality. In physiological terms, both differ from thoughts because their production involves incoming nerve currents and differ from each other depending on the amount of associative processes aroused in the cortex: the greater the number, the more likely perception rather than sensation will be invoked. It is important to note that James is drawing on these distinctions as functional differences within the prereflective level of consciousness not yet explicitly incorporated into conceptual schemas.

There are no pure sensations according to James, but belief in their reality follows from their postulation as necessarily corresponding on the cognitive side to their referential objects, namely, to simple 'qualities' or 'attributes' like 'hard,' 'hot,' 'pain.' Somewhat surprisingly, he does not question the certainty that such individuated qualities exist in nature. What such a qualitative existence apart from the existence of a correlative sensation would be, though, is not explained. He does say that sensations are the functional equivalent of the *"bare immediate natures"* by which we distinguish objects (*PP*, II, 653). This puzzling assertion of simple objective qualities unmatched by simple sensations is apparently part of the empiricist residue not yet brought to the critical 'bar' of the incompatible theses argued in "The Stream of Thought." It could also simply be an instance of his exposure of the language fallacy of assuming that simple things in nature are exactly matched by simple ideas.

The problem is not with simple sensations, though, against which he trenchantly argues, but with the assertion of irreducible qualitative existents, given James's thesis of the chaotic flux of experience and his critique of essentialism. However, his intent in the passage on bare natures is to explain how sensation has illicitly come to be thought of as discrete, and the reference to objective qualities is given only in passing. He says in the section that a 'pure' sensation can also mean the relative lack of relations adverted to. This meaning is compatible with his earlier and later explanations and the one for which he argues more consistently.

Long after *principles*, for instance, James explains the shared world of the multi-sensorially deprived Helen Keller and those who have full use of their senses by pointing out that "the great world, *the background*, in all of us, is the world of our *beliefs*. That is the world of the permanencies and the immensities, and our relations with it are mostly verbal." Everyone's access to reality is still argued as being through the senses, but sensations supply only the merest hints, which "we extend by imagination or add to by analogy." Although James says that we verbalize sensations to symbolize "the relations existing between the things," he obviously means things-as-experienced.[21]

The appeal to experience replaces foundational metaphors by directing our attention to the feedback loop it provides: beliefs as plans of actions, implementation, reflection on adequacy of both means and ends, a reworked belief that takes into consideration such findings, enactment, in a never ending but more securely appropriated practical circle of interpretation and reconstruction. Pragmatism rejects the traditional model of reducing complex texts or theories into their component parts and then univocally grounding each isolated assertion in its sensible equivalent. It reconstructs the search for foundations into a search for a satisfactory way of life. Contrary to the fallacy of omniscience, such a way of life cannot be grasped all at once. It must be constructed piecemeal in relation to the limited means to ends of the actual situations in which we both find ourselves and which we choose and to the constitution of which we contribute.

4. Pragmatic Warrant: Making Ourselves at Home in Different Worlds

We are not completely adrift without foundations. We each have a vague sense of what would constitute 'being at home in the world.' However, long-range goals are necessarily vague in comparison to the living sense of our actual, delimited situations. Pragmatists reject the rationalist assumption that local organizations must ultimately coincide in one, most desirable, utopia. In fact, the multiplicity of visions in different communities, in literature, in social movements, in political programs, in feminist and ecological demands, and the like, contributes to a pool of ever more enriched expectations. They increase the possibilities for beneficial interactions of selves and worlds and therefore should be encouraged and valued. Furthermore, as we move from the vagueness of such comprehensive purposes to realizing them in definite situations with specific goals, the actual shape of our 'home' becomes less vague and more 'concrete' or specific.

Pluralism also leads to actual clashes of implementation, and these points of conflict are pregnant with concrete rather than abstract possibility. It is not enough to encourage proliferation. We must also work out resolutions that will be cooperative rather than authoritarian.[22] As Dewey never tires of pointing out, such cooperative problem solving is not an abstract ideal of rationality, but a regulative value that has come to be held in high esteem because of the strengths it has exhibited over time. The weaknesses of communal, experimental problem solving are tolerated by those who are not willing to pay the price the alternatives demand. Simply put, these alternatives include authoritarianism, terror, ideological hegemony, warfare and torture, paternalism, cultural stasis and revolution, or appeal to the laws and rights embedded in nature or to deontological universalism. They all differ from cooperative problem solving in being coercive and presupposing privileged insight into reality in a deluded attempt to escape from temporality and finitude.

For James the question of the many and the one is the central problem of philosophy. For all of us it is of utmost importance to determine which unifications of experience are justifiable and which are not. The great problem is to determine how best to organize multiplicity without negating the perspectives that do not cohere. Among the various ways we unify experience are the intentional unity of discourse; physical continuity; political, social and economic organizations; and the generic unity of natural kinds (PM, pp. 66ff.). In his concrete analyses James shows that the particular unifying principles taken as definitive of each subuniverse are chosen because they lead toward the fulfillment of some local purpose. Since everything that exists is related to and influenced by other existents, the choice of which regularities to follow determines the ordered world that is identified.[23] But this discovery of regularity can be undermined by choosing aspects that do not cohere. Furthermore, the recognition of and insistence on these discontinuities prevents any one imposition of order from hegemonically crushing unrelated centers of organization.

Although we make ourselves at home in different fragments of the universe, James pleads for loyalty to the world that bears us (PU, pp. 10–11). The appeal to the world as mother of us all is not a repetition of sexist discourse, but a reminder that we share a common planetary fate. We are bound together organically, both biologically and socially, try as we might to envision ourselves in purely mechanistic terms. Individual differences can be valued without falling into false isolationism, laissez-faire individualism, and the hubris of self-creation apart from any shared conditions resulting from our sociality and our common ecosystem. It is important to draw attention to the evidence of our growing social, economic, and political interdependency as a precondition for cooperative action. I develop an example from ecology, however, since it so clearly illustrates the interaction of the local and the global.

From the fact that local microclimates may be radically opposed to one another, so much so that we may cherish our own conditions as part of a temperate zone community over those of the rain forest, for instance, it does not follow that we are not bound together within a larger, interconnected ecological system. We may and do neglect our mutual dependence in a celebration of local autonomy, but we now realize that there is a price to pay, and maybe even the ultimate price of the failure of the human species to survive. We are far from consensus, but if this is not taken as a goal worth pursuing, then we are willfully ignoring those present conditions that already signal impending disaster (*PM*, p. 136). James's criticisms of totalizing systems are remarkably similar to those of contemporary poststructuralists, but he would not agree with Jean-François Lyotard, who somewhat improbably contends that all cognitively informed organizations of experience are terroristic.[24] The realization of our common planetary ecosystem is not a terroristic imposition from without. It is we ourselves who have come to discover our connectedness, despite our ethno-, andro-, species, national, and every other variety of 'centrism.' This discovery has been possible only by reflection on the new facts we ourselves have caused to emerge by our actions, such as the widespread pollution caused by the burning of fossil fuels and the continuing destruction of rain forests. Many particular economic and technological goals have been ignorant of, or indifferent or deliberately hostile to, any larger relationships. Therefore, these goals have been local to the point of recklessness.

Reflections on the present state of ecological affairs show that merely local legitimations are seldom, if ever, merely local. Such isolated localism is an illusion, and an extremely dangerous one at that. It is of paramount importance to learn how to change local concerns into global ones without destroying the richness and the value of local variation. We are implicated whether we will or no. The question we should be raising is not whether we ought to reach some consensus as to how to increase the odds both for survival and for survival of a more desirable way of life, but how such consensus is to be achieved. Do we want to be driven to consensual action by the terrorism of the imposition of force, or do we want to bring ourselves to consensual action by voluntary cooperation, both as to means and to particular ends? We can also refuse consensus as not a valuable goal in the first place, as Lyotard seems to argue, but we cannot by this understanding escape the consequences of our actions.[25] We can and do disagree what those consequences are, but they are neither limited to the choice of language games nor can they be interpreted away. "Every experience enacted and undergone modifies the one who acts and undergoes, while this modification affects, whether we wish it or not, the quality of subsequent experiences."[26]

For pragmatists, feminists, Marxists, and everyone with an agenda for social change, the question "Whose choice?" is not an idle one. Our particular plans of action, ways of life, and visions for the future are as various as the hues of a rainbow, but like the rainbow, such socially conscious choices also enhance and are more continuous with each other in their pursuit of a nonexclusionary, better society than they are with those whose privileging of some segments of the community requires oppressing others. Since the rainbow also draws its existence from the very particular conditions without which it could not exist, it does not symbolize a utopian, ethereal ideal, but one grounded in and intimately related to its surroundings.

How much alike and how different—both within the various communities of interest under one heading, like the feminist, and with other centers of organization of experience—must constantly be renegotiated. We cannot presuppose, even within one movement, a univocal community of shared interests, history, and future prospects. We can, however, deliberately elicit and seek to enact such cooperatively unified communities. That such sharing of differences and forging of common alliances will be benign and contribute to growth rather than destruction cannot be presupposed but must be actively pursued if it is ever to be accomplished.

The individuating complexities of persons and the multiplicity and fluidity of communities of which we are members makes unity more difficult to achieve, but no less necessary and desirable both for a sense of belonging and to accomplish goals effectively in the larger social, economic, and political spheres outside local communities.

Like a bridge, a rainbow also arises from and plunges back to earth after soaring aloft. But it draws its limited means of survival from atmospheric rather than geological conditions. The bridge, however, must be securely embedded in the earth if it is going to successfully support weight. To impose the conditions for the survival of either structure on the other would be an exercise in futility. But it would be just as reckless to assume that there are no conditions they share. Destroy the planet, and both the rainbow and the bridge disappear. "The great point is to notice that the oneness and the manyness are absolutely co-ordinate here. . . . In our general dealings with the world of influences, we now need conductors and now need non-conductors, and wisdom lies in knowing which is which at the appropriate moment" (*PM*, p. 68). But since James, like the poststructuralists, takes hegemonic centralizations of power as more immediately dangerous in his concrete, social situation, he repeatedly criticizes philosophy's characteristic failing as being the privileging of the rationalizing drive for simplification and unification over the complementary drive for diversity and plurality. He does not often stress their reciprocity, but rather the dangers involved in the premature imposition of "this ultra-monistic way of thinking" (*PM*, pp. 73–74). This emphasis distinguishes his style and positions from Dewey's, which are characteristically reconstructive, rather than deconstructive, since he is more concerned with investigating the conditions conducive of postmodern, liberating communities than with exposing the conditions that have generated hegemonic ones.

James, even more than Nietzsche, speaks out for those who have been left out of consideration, for those who have been excluded from dominating communities of interest. He says, for instance, that "pragmatism, pending the final empirical ascertainment of just what the balance of union and disunion among things may be, must obviously range herself upon the pluralistic side" (*PM*, p. 79). This is 'empirical,' not in the sense of what is fated to be factually, but in the sense that we cannot presume to know what a perfectly unified world would be like until we and others cooperatively bring it about.

In concrete experience we can and do appeal to moral, economic, political, and social ideals and directives developed over time out of the funded character of experience and conceptually refined. However, these should be taken as guidelines only, which ought to be continually reevaluated in light of present conditions and understanding. Our thinking is dangerously utopian if we think we already know concretely in what a perfect world consists, without having to continually revise our beliefs in light of the experiences of those participating in the construction of actual communities. Furthermore, the good intentions of utopian visionaries should not blind us to the oppressiveness of imposing such visions on those who do not share them. We do not have any privileged access to being as such that would enable us to build up an accurate model of the world, brick by brick, as the foundationalist model assumes. We weave the chaos of experience into particular patterns of living for aesthetic and practical purposes. Both ephemeral rainbows and solid bridges continue to exist in sovereign ignorance of each other, indeed, of anything. But our ignorance of the conditions of each other's survival and growth, both of what distinguishes us and what we have in common, is fraught with deadly peril.

Notes

1. C. S. Peirce, *Collected Papers of Charles Sanders Peirce*, ed. Charles Hartshorne, Paul Weiss, and Arthur Burks (Cambridge: Harvard University Press, 1960), 1:1.

2. *The Principles of Psychology*, 3 vols., in *The Works of William James*, ed. Frederick H. Burkhardt, Fredson Bowers, and Ignas K. Skrupskelis (Cambridge: Harvard University Press, 1981), 2:656–57. Hereafter abbreviated as *PP*, followed by volume number and page.

3. James is often taken as adhering to this empiricist principle. See, for instance, H. S. Thayer, *Meaning and Action* (Indianapolis: Hackett, 1981), pp. 139–40.

4. *Some Problems of Philosophy*, in *The Works of William James* (Cambridge: Harvard University Press, 1979), p. 51. Hereafter abbreviated as *SPP*.

5. In a 1944 letter, for instance, Dewey explicitly says that "the quarrel between 'idealist' and 'realist' goes on and has to go on forever—until they give up their common premise. But, as far as it goes, it rests upon a sort of recognition, neither of them can help, of the 'circularity between knowings and known.'" *John Dewey and Arthur F. Bentley: A Philosophical Correspondence, 1932–1951*, ed. Sidney Ratner and Jules Altman (New Brunswick: Rutgers University Press, 1964), p. 208.

6. "The Sentiment of Rationality" (1879), in *Essays in Philosophy*, in *The Works of William James* (Cambridge: Harvard University Press, 1978), p. 51. Hereafter abbreviated as *EPH*.

7. Even in one of his last writings James still distinguished the philosopher from the mystic by the fact that the philosopher, as philosopher, "seeks to grasp totality," even though she or he will be forever doomed to fail because "there is no complete generalization, no total point of view, no all-pervasive unity." "A Pluralistic Mystic" (1910), in *EPH*, pp. 177 and 189.

8. *The Will to Believe* (1897), in *The Works of William James* (Cambridge: Harvard University Press, 1979), pp. 68–69. Hereafter abbreviated as *WB*.

9. This paragraph summarizes the model of James's reconstruction of rationalism developed in my *William James's Radical Reconstruction of Philosophy* (Albany: State University of New York Press, 1990).

10. Lewis E. Hahn, "Dewey's Philosophy and Philosophic Method," *Guide to the Works of John Dewey*, ed. Jo Ann Boydston (Carbondale and Edwardsville: Southern Illinois University Press, 1970), p. 17.

11. Dewey quotes this passage from James as encapsulating "the epistemological problem." "Substance, Power, and Quality in Locke," *Freedom and Experience*, ed. Sidney Hook and Milton R. Konvitz (New York: Cooper Square, 1974; 1st ed.: Cornell University Press, 1947), p. 207.

12. *A Pluralistic Universe*, in *The Works of William James* (Cambridge: Harvard University Press, 1977), p. 116. Hereafter abbreviated as *PU*.

13. *The Meaning of Truth*, in *The Works of William James* (Cambridge: Harvard University Press, 1975), Appendix II, p. 291. Hereafter abbreviated as *MT*.

14. John Dewey, *Experience and Education* (New York: Macmillan, 1938), pp. 43–44.

15. For an explanation of the methodological centrality of James's appeals to "concrete experience," see my "William James's Phenomenological Methodology," *Journal of the British Society for Phenomenology* 20 (January 1989): 62–76.

16. See *Essays in Psychology*, in *The Works of William James* (Cambridge: Harvard University Press, 1983), p. 7, n. 3. Hereafter abbreviated as *EPS*.

17. *Pragmatism*, in *The Works of William James* (Cambridge: Harvard University Press, 1975), pp. 5–6; 32ff.; 162, n. 37.24. Hereafter abbreviated as *PM*.

18. See *EPH*, p. 41, and *EPS*, p. 16.

19. For James's inconsistent espousal of both pure seeing and seeing-as, see my "Poetic Invention and Scientific Observation: James's Model of 'Sympathetic Concrete Observation,'" *Transactions Charles S. Peirce Society* 26, 1 (Winter 1990): 113–30.

20. John Dewey, *Later Works, Volume 10: 1934 Art as Experience* (Carbondale: Southern Illinois University Press, 1987), p. 247.

21. Ralph Barton Perry, *The Thought and Character of William James*, vol. 2 (Boston: Little, Brown, 1935), p. 455.

22. For a reference to concrete possibility, see *PM*, p. 136.

23. Dewey develops this insight further in his "principle of continuity," which is both an aspect of experience and a means for distinguishing better and worse interpretations. It is succinctly stated in *Experience and Education*, pp. 33–50.

24. Jean-François Lyotard, "The Postmodern Condition," *After Philosophy*, ed. Kenneth Baynes, James Bohman, and Thomas McCarthy (Cambridge: MIT Press, 1987), p. 89. For an explanation of how James's postmodernism differs from both Richard Rorty's and Lyotard's, see my "Weaving Chaos into Order: A Radically Pragmatic Aesthetic," *Philosophy and Literature* 14, no. 1 (1990): 108–16.

25. Lyotard, *After Philosophy*, p. 88.

26. Dewey, *Experience and Education*, p. 35.

Eight

Pragmatism and the Reconstruction of Metaphysics: Toward a New Understanding of Foundations

SANDRA B. ROSENTHAL

Though the understanding of a particular philosophic method is perhaps the key to understanding any philosophic position, this is more than usually crucial to understanding the position of classical American pragmatism—that movement incorporating the thought of William James, John Dewey, Charles Peirce, C. I. Lewis, and G. H. Mead.[1] Various forms of inadequate appreciation for the systematic significance[2] of the pragmatic understanding of the creative dimension within scientific method and of its relation to human biologic activity had far-reaching results. Pragmatism was viewed as, on the one hand, foundationalist in its episte-mological and/or metaphysical claims, and, on the other hand, antifoundationalist, historicist, and, at the extreme, heralding the end of metaphysics. This latter view has of course been appropri-ated in the recent deconstructionist focus on pragmatic philosophy. However, a focus on the complexities of the pragmatic understand-ing of scientific experimentalism and biological activity will reveal them as the essential pragmatic tools for fashioning a new pathway toward metaphysics with a resultant new understanding of the nature of the metaphysical enterprise. Such a pathway, fashioned by the paradigmatic novelty of pragmatism, is neither foundationalist nor antifoundationalist but, rather, undercuts the frameworks within which such alternatives make sense.[3] The ensuing discussion first turns briefly to the pragmatic understanding of scientific method as the structure of inquiry as such, exemplified by any and all experimental activity. Such an understanding avoids reductionistic tendencies to confuse or conflate scientific method and scientific content; avoids formalistic attempts to confine scientific thinking within fixed rules and decision procedures, thus robbing scientific method of its speculative directions; and sets the stage for an understanding of knowledge in general that eludes the alternatives of foundationalism or antifoundationalism as well as other family related sets of traditional alternatives.

The beginning phase of scientific method, not as a formalized deductive model, not as a metaphysical enterprise illicitly reifying scientific contents as supposed ultimate truths, not as a causal analysis of humans and their environment,[4] but as lived experimental activity, exemplifies human creativity. Scientific creativity arises out of the matrix of ordinary experience and in turn refers back to this everyday experience. Though the contents of an abstract scientific theory may be far removed from the qualitative aspects of everyday experience, such contents are not the found structures of some "ultimate reality of nature." Rather, they are abstractive transformations of lived experience, and the possibility of their coming to be as objects of scientific knowledge requires and is founded upon the qualitative experience of the scientist. As Mead observes, "the ultimate touchstone of reality is a piece of experience found in an unanalyzed world. . . . We can never retreat behind immediate experience to analyzed elements that constitute the ultimate reality of all immediate experience, for whatever breath of reality these elements possess has been breathed into them by some unanalyzed experience."[5] In Dewey's terms, the refined products of scientific inquiry "inherit their full content of meaning within the context of actual experience."[6]

However, the return to the context of everyday or "lived" experience is never a brute return, for, as Dewey continues, "we cannot achieve recovery of primitive naiveté. But there is attainable a cultivated naiveté of eye, ear, and thought, one that can be acquired only through the discipline of severe thought."[7] Such a return to everyday primary experience is approached through the systematic categories of scientific thought by which the richness of experience is fused with new meaning. Thus the technical knowing of second-level reflective experience and the "having" of perceptual experience each gain in meaning through the other.

Further, such creativity implies, for the pragmatist, a rejection of the "passive-spectator" view of knowledge and an introduction of the active, creative agent, who, through meanings, helps structure the objects of knowledge, and who thus cannot be separated from the world in which such objects emerge. Thus James notes of scientific method that there is a big difference between verification as the cause of the preservation of scientific conceptions, and creativity as the cause of their production.[8] As Dewey emphasizes this noetic creativity in science, "What is known is seen to be a product in which the act of observation plays a necessary role. Knowing is seen to be a participant in what is finally known." Both perception and the meaningful backdrop within which it occurs are shot through with the interactional unity between knower and known.[9] Without such a unity there is no scientific world and there are no scientific objects.

Such a creative noetic structuring of a world brings objects into an organizational focus from an indeterminate background and, as constitutive of meanings as dispositional modes of response, yields purposive, teleological, or goal-oriented activity.[10] The system of meanings both sets the context for activity and rigorously limits the direction any activity takes, for such meaning structures are constituted by possibilities of acting toward a world.

Finally, the adequacy of meaning structures in grasping what is there, or in allowing what is there to reveal itself in a significant way, must be tested by consequences in experience. Initial feelings of assurance, initial insights, initial common assent, or any other origins of a theory do not determine its truth. Only if the experiences anticipated by the possibilities of experience contained within the meaning structures are progressively fulfilled— though of course never completely and finally fulfilled—can truth be claimed for the assertions made. Such unfolding of experience in conformity with projected anticipations represents a self-corrective rather than a building-block model of knowledge. The meanings or rules governing the organization of experiences are judged by their ability to turn a potentially indeterminate situation into a resolved or meaningfully experienced one. Thus Peirce stresses that scientific method is the only method of fixing belief, for it is the only method by which beliefs must be tested and corrected by what experience presents.[11]

The role of scientific method in understanding everyday experience within pragmatic philosophy is evinced in several brief but telling remarks. As Dewey observes, awareness, even in its most primordial state, "represents a general trend of scientific inquiry." It means things entering, via directed activity, into a condition of "differential—or additive—change."[12] Or, as he summarizes, "There is no difference in kind between the methods of science and those of the plain man."[13] Peirce emphasizes the same point in his claim that the creative interpretations of scientific endeavor shade into everyday perceptual claims without any sharp line of demarcation between them.[14] Or, in Mead's terms, scientific method is embedded in the simplest process of perception of things in the world.[15] Again, Lewis attempts to clarify the noetic creativity ingredient in scientific objects by turning to the understanding of "thinghood" within common sense.[16]

The use of the model of scientific method in understanding everyday experience is in no way an attempt to assert that perceptual experience is really a highly intellectual affair. Rather, the opposite is more the case. Scientific objects are highly sophisticated and intellectualized ways of dealing with experience at a second level, but they are not the product of any isolated intellect. Rather, the total concrete human way of being, a way rooted in praxis, is involved in the very ordering of any level of awareness, and scientific knowledge partakes of the character of even the most rudimentary aspects by which a world of things emerges within experience. The abstractly manipulative and instrumental purposes attributed to science have their roots at the foundation of the very possibility of human experience in general.[17]

Pragmatism, in focusing on scientific method, is providing a phenomenologically or experientially based description of the lived-through activity of scientists that yields the emergence of their objects. In so doing, it is focusing on the explicit enlarged version of the conditions by which anything can emerge within experience, from the most rudimentary awareness of things within everyday experience to the most sophisticated objects of scientific knowledge. In providing a description of the lived experience within which the objects of science emerge, pragmatism is uncovering the essential aspects of the emergence of any contents of awareness. The pursuit of scientific knowledge is an endeavor throughout which are writ large the essential characters of any knowing, and it partakes of the character of even the most rudimentary ways in which human activity involves anticipations of future experience.

Further, if scientific method is indicative of the dynamics of all levels of intelligent activity, then it is indicative of the dynamics of philosophic activity, including metaphysical reflections. And, like science, philosophy involves a second-level system of meanings. Thus, in grasping the systematic interconnections with the structure of pragmatism, its assertions must be understood as arising from, yet going beyond in the sense of making meaningful through philosophic interpretation, the immediacies of lived experience. And, in turn, the test for the adequacy of such philosophic assertions must be found in their continual verification in lived experience. Thus, the pragmatic focus on scientific method, far from leading to an antispeculative position limited to a theory of meaning and truth, provides the direction for understanding the nature of a speculative metaphysics. As Dewey so succinctly notes in separating scientific method from scientific content in the development of philosophic system, "The trouble then with the conclusions of philosophy is not in the least that they are the results of reflection and theorizing. It is rather that philosophers have borrowed from various sources the conclusions of special analyses, particularly of some ruling science of the day."[18] However, the ensuing discussion temporarily sets aside this philosophic direction in order to explore the implications of the above account of scientific method for clarifying both the biological activity that reflects and is foundational for it, and the resultant noetic activity that eludes the confines of the foundationalist-antifoundationalist alternatives.

A proper understanding of the lessons of scientific method reveals that the nature into which the human is placed contains the qualitative fullness revealed in lived experience. In addition, the grasp of nature is permeated with the meaning structures by which humans and their world are interactionally or intentionally bound, at the levels of both commonsense experience and scientific reflection. Thus, scientific method itself reveals that purposive biological activity, insofar as it is the foundation of meaning, cannot be understood in terms of the scientific contents or scientific categories that presuppose it. Rather, it is the "lived through" biological activity of the human organism and, as such, is capable of phenomenological description. Habits, dispositions, or tendencies are immediately experienced and pervade the very tone and structure of immediately grasped content, thus incorporating an intentional relationship that can be phenomenologically studied from within. There is a twofold sense of purposive biological activity running throughout pragmatism, one ontological, the other epistemic or phenomenological, both of which undercut the level of the biological in terms of the contents of scientific analysis. There is an inseparable relationship between the human biological organism bound to a natural environment and the human knower who through meanings constitutes a world. From the context of organism-environment interaction there emerge irreducible meanings within the structure of experience. Such meanings are irreducible to physical causal conditions or to psychological acts and processes; yet they emerge from the biological, when the biological is properly understood, for the content of human perception is inseparable from the structure of human behavior within its natural setting. Thus, Dewey and Mead each stress that meanings can be expressed both in terms of the ongoing conduct of the biological organism immersed in a natural universe and in terms of the phenomenological description of the appearance of what is meant.[19]

The significance of dispositions or habits, not as objective ontological categories but as epistemic or phenomenological categories, is that such "felt dispositions" provide a fixity and concreteness to objective meanings that outrun any indefinite number of experiences to which they give rise precisely because felt dispositions and tendencies are felt continuities that outrun any indefinite series to which they give rise. As Peirce observes concerning a certain "unboundedness" inherent in dispositional modes of response as a readiness to respond to more possibilities of experience than can ever be specified: because they are, as felt continuities, "immediately present but still embracing innumerable parts . . . a vague possibility of more than is present is directly felt."[20] Or, in

Lewis's terms, such an absence of boundedness gives rise to our "sense of the experientially possible but not experientially now actual." [21]

The minimal experience always involves a durational flow, for it is filled with the rudimentary pulsations of the temporal structure of habit as anticipatory. The sense of the future involved in anticipatory activity is not an induction from past experience but is at the heart of experience in the durational present. Such a durational flow is essential for the pragmatic understanding of experience as experimental, for it involves an anticipation of a next experience to come, something for which we are waiting, an expectation set in motion by the temporal stretch of human activity. Embodied in the actuality of our meaning structures as habits of response, then, is a sense of a reality that transcends actual occasions of experience.

The temporally rooted structure of human behavior as anticipatory both requires and makes possible the creatively regulative features of meaning as habit. Such regulative features, as Dewey notes, are "no exclusive function of thought. Every biological function, every motor attitude, every vital impulse as the carrying vehicle of experience . . . is regulative in prospective reference; what we call expectation, anticipation, choice, are pregnant with this constitutive and organizing power." [22] This regulative feature rooted in activity, he further stresses, "makes possible the subject-matter of perception not as a material cut out from an instantaneous field, but a material that designates the effects of our possible actions." [23]

Both the ontological and phenomenological dimensions of habit relate to a fundamental feature of pragmatic philosophy, the creative, interactive unity of humans with that which is independently there. Experience is this rich ongoing transactional unity, and only within the context of meanings that reflect such an interactional unity does anything emerge for conscious awareness. Experience is always experience within a world, and the things that come to awareness within the world, and the world itself, as the outermost horizon of meaningful rapport with the independently real, as the encompassing frame of reference or field of interest of organism-environment interaction, reflect as well this interactional unity. Lewis captures the import of this in his claim that "it may be that between a sufficiently critical idealism and a sufficiently critical realism there are no issues save false issues which arise from the insidious fallacies of a copy theory of knowledge."[24] The position intended can be captured neither by the traditional epistemic alternatives of realism or idealism, nor by the more recent alternatives of realism or antirealism or of foundationalism or antifoundationalism. As Peirce so well summarizes, though "everything which is present to us is a phenomenal manifestation of ourselves," this "does not prevent its being a phenomenon of something without us, just as a rainbow is at once manifestation of the sun and the rain."[25] For all the pragmatists, the flux of life as it concretely occurs contains already a phenomenological dimension of human thrown-outness onto the universe through a vital intentionality constitutive of the nature of experience as experimental. Thus, the being of humans in the natural universe and the knowing by humans of the natural universe are inseparably connected within the structure of experience.

Such a transactional unity is more than a postulate of abstract thought, for it has phenomenological dimensions. The interactive ontological unity of organism-environment transaction is reflected in the phenomenologically grasped features of experience. That which intrudes itself inexplicably into experience is not bare datum, but rather evidences itself as the over-againstness of a thick reality there for my activity. Thus, Lewis asserts that independent factuality "does not need to be assumed nor to be proved, but only to be acknowledged,"[26] while Dewey observes that experience "reaches down into nature; it has depth."[27] This description of the ontological dimension of experience is well evinced in Mead's claim that, in becoming an object, something has the character of "actually or potentially acting upon the organism from within itself." He calls this character that of having an inside.[28] Such an acting upon the organism cannot be understood in terms of passive resistance, but as active resistance, resistance to our organic activity.[29] Thus, the phenomenological description of the characteristics found at the heart of experience itself reveals the incorporation within experience of an ontological dimension or ontological presence.

Pragmatism, in attempting to unite meanings freely created with the coercive thereness from which they have emerged, has at times emphasized meanings freely brought, and at times what is there to coerce. What must be emphasized and distinguished is the epistemic and ontological unity at the heart of experience as providing the corridor from one to the other. Such an interactional unity contains a three-directional openness: the primordial openness of the character of experience itself opens in one direction toward the features of the human modes of grasping the independently real, and in the other direction toward the features of the independently real, for the character of experience emerges from an interaction of these two poles and thus reflects characteristics of each, though it mirrors neither exactly. In the interactional unity that constitutes our worldly experience, both poles are thus manifest: the independently there otherness onto which worldly experience opens, and the structure of the human way of being within whose purposive activity worldly experience emerges.

Abstract knowledge claims do not constitute our main access to the natural universe; concrete experience does. Yet the beginning infiltrations of meanings as embodied in human activity are immediately present in even the most rudimentary grasp within our natural embeddedness. Conversely, the semiotic relationships embodied in pragmatic meaning are not the products of the free play of linguistic signs, but rather are contoured within limits by the historically grounded dynamic forces operative in that within which we are embedded. It can be seen again that this position undercuts the dichotomy of foundationalism or antifoundationalism and, along with it, the closely related dichotomies of realism or antirealism and objectivism or relativism since each, in its own way, represents the alternatives of an absolute grounding of knowledge or skepticism. At the very heart of the temporal stretch of human behavior as anticipatory is a creativity, expressive of the experimental nature of experience, that is at once unified with that ontological presence but that renders its grasp in terms of any absolute grounding impossible. The unity denies the arbitrariness of antifoundationalism or antirealism or relativism. The temporally founded creativity denies the absoluteness of foundationalism or realism or objectivism. Experience, as an interactional unity of the poles of ontological presence and creative noetic activity, reflects characteristics of each but mirrors neither exactly.

The failure to recognize this interactional "reflection" at the heart of all experience, and as a result to substitute for it a mirroring either of the ontologically real alone or of our selective activity alone, leads to the contemporary dichotomies of foundationalism-antifoundationalism, realism-antirealism, objectivism-relativism. Further, the failure to recognize that this reflecting that constitutes the structure of experience not only is not a mirroring of an independent pole alone or a selective activity alone, but also is not a reflection of itself, leads to the failure to see that the categories of metaphysics must undercut this interactional unity to get at the character of the independent pole such unity in part reflects. A further discussion of this natural ontological embeddedness in its primordial dimensions as the pathway to metaphysics, however, requires a return to the significance of scientific method.

It has been claimed that the dynamics of everyday experience reflect throughout the dynamics of scientific method. Just as "the object" of science is an abstraction from a richer or more concrete transactional experience and hence cannot be hypostatized as absolute, so the perceptual object is likewise an abstraction from a richer, more concrete experience and hence cannot be hypostatized as absolute. The things of the everyday world, like the objects of science, are unified in terms of their function, not in terms of some underlying essence.[30] In opposition to the foundationalist claim, the objects that come to awareness do not exist independently of or prior to human activity, nor can we work back in experience to a direct grasp of anything that is as it is prior to its emergence within the context of experimental activity. Yet, in opposition to the antifoundationalist claim, there is incorporated in human experience a concretely rich ontological presence that constrains the interpretive nets through which it can reveal itself as a world of objects. Thus Peirce can claim, "There is no *thing* which is in itself in the sense of not being relative to the mind, though things which are relative to the mind doubtless *are*, apart from that relation."[31] Or, in a similar vein, he makes the seemingly paradoxical claim that "the object of final belief, which exists only in consequence of the belief, should itself produce the belief."[32]

The pragmatic characterization of the concrete matrix of activity that makes possible the dynamics by which the everyday perceived world emerges through the experimental activity of organism-environment interaction is a philosophic claim that helps fund with meaning the philosophical understanding of the dynamics of experience as experimental. Thus, Dewey's characterization of the concrete matrix of undifferentiated activity and James's world of pure experience, as well as his radical empiricism, are interpretive descriptions that direct the manner in which one actively gazes at everyday experience, which both emerge from and bring enriched meaningful understanding to everyday experience, and which are in turn verified by the textures of everyday experience. These features of the relation between the reflections of philosophy and its meaningful grasp of everyday experience are precisely the features previously revealed through the analysis of scientific method.

But the model of scientific method, combined with the phenomenologically grasped features of experience, indicate that a more speculative level can be reached that focuses not on the pervasive textures of experience at any of its levels, but on the pervasive features of the independently real in its character as independent of experience. This speculative endeavor, which is rooted in the previously analyzed levels of experience and which will be seen to reflect the dynamics of scientific experimentalism, goes beyond experience to that independent element which enters into all experience. The categories of such a speculative metaphysics emerge as philosophically reflective structures or tools for delineating the interwoven pervasive textures of the concrete, independent reality that provides the concrete basis for, and that intrudes within, all experience. As second-level explanatory tools, they are a step more abstract than the second-level philosophic interpretive descriptions of primary experience. But that to which they are applied and within which they delineate is one step more concrete than primary experience, in the sense that it is the concrete basis for all levels of experiencing. It is that "thereness" upon which or within which the intentionality of purposive activity operates in giving rise to the interactional unity that is experience.

The passage from temporality as the basis of meaningful experience to process metaphysics as the basis for understanding its ontological character is operative in all the pragmatists. It is found in Lewis's claim that "the absolutely given is a specious present fading into the past and growing into the future with no genuine boundaries. The breaking of this up . . . marks already the activity of an interested mind."[33] Or, as Mead states in similar fashion, "at the future edge of experience, things pass, their characters change and they go to pieces."[34] The role of human constitutive activity in transforming a processive, "independently there" matrix into structured things unified in terms of their function within a world is succinctly indicated in Dewey's claim that "structure is constancy of means, of things used for consequences, not of things taken by themselves absolutely."[35] Further, the "isolation of structure from the changes whose stable ordering it is, renders it mysterious— something that is metaphysical in the popular sense of the word, a kind of ghostly queerness."[36] For all the pragmatists, the structures of things grasped by the knowing mind do not reach a reality more ultimate than the processive interactions of temporally founded experience, but rather, the lived-through grasp of felt temporality opening onto a processive universe is the very foundation for the emergence within experience of meaningful structure. The two-directional openness of experience carries temporality from one pole to the other, from a phenomenology of worldly experience toward a process metaphysics. Thus, when James asks "how far into the rest of nature may we have to go in order to get entirely beyond" the overflow characteristic of pure experience,[37] his answer is clear. One may "go into the heart of nature," one may grasp the most pervasive textures of its most characteristic features, and one will not get beyond its overflow. Humans are natural beings in interaction with a natural universe. And at the heart of nature is process. Conversely, process metaphysics reinforces the pragmatic understanding of knowledge, for as James observes, "when the whole universe seems only . . . to be still incomplete (else why its ceaseless changing?) why, of all things, should knowing be exempt?"[38]

Like any system of meanings, the categorial system of meanings that constitutes a metaphysical interpretation must arise out of the matrix of experience, provide an organizing perspective that directs the way we approach experience, and in turn must be verified by the intelligibility it introduces into the ongoing course of experience. As Peirce indicates, metaphysical endeavor is like "that of the special sciences," except that it "rests upon a kind of phenomena with which everyman's experience is so saturated that he usually pays no particular attention to them."[39] Thus, James compares the method of science and metaphysics as ideal systems of thought yet allows for a disparity of content,[40] whereas

Dewey points out that philosophy, like science, legitimately theorizes about experience but can legitimately begin not with the contents of science, but with the "integrity of experience."[41]

Pragmatists as process metaphysicans are led, in accordance with the experimental model of gaining knowledge, to a "speculative, interpretive description," via a speculative extrapolation from experience, of what that independent reality must be like in its character as independent to give rise to the primordial level of experience and to "answer to" the meanings by which it reveals itself to us. And, it should be well noted here that there is a vast difference between the illicit reification by past philosophies of common sense or scientific meanings, and the speculative extrapolation from within experience of the pervasive tones and textures of the processive "thereness" that enters into all experience. Because of the nature of the categories as creative speculative extrapolations from experience, Peirce can claim both that his metaphysics is scientific and that it is "metaphorical."[42] Indeed, the creativity of science itself can be said to contain a metaphorical dimension. The categories of metaphysics provide the illumination by which traits of "what is there" can come into focus. Such categories represent the persistent attempt to illuminate and articulate, through a creative scheme or explanatory structure, the processes and textures present within all experience.

The vision of a "thick," "dense," processive "thereness" not of our making, and of an indefinite richness of potentialities for ordering within it, is gained by a sophisticated elaboration of or extrapolation from the reference to the primitive experience of anticipatory potentialities and unactualized possibilities as this occurs through the actual functioning of concrete living meaning in the flow of time. A disposition or habit as a regulative rule, it has been seen, is something whose possibilities of determination no multitude of actually generated instances can exhaust. The primordial sense of the unactualized creative potentialities of habit as experienced in the actual temporal continuity of the durational present gives a concrete content to the concept of a metaphysics of process, of a real lawfulness that governs unactualized possibilities, of potentialities that can never be exhausted by any number of actualities. Human potentialities or dispositional tendencies to respond are precisely lawful tendencies of behavior potentially capable of structuring emerging activities. Further, the sense of unactualized possibilities embedded in meaning as dispositional brings a sense of real alternatives—the could do or could be otherwise—into the heart of perceptual awareness, founding a sense of freedom and of what Lewis refers to as a "primordial sense of probable events,"[43] thus providing an experiential basis for the rejection of deterministic hypotheses. This move from the character of experience to the character of the independent pole is not anthropomorphically fashioning the independent pole in the likeness of human experience, but rather showing the natural conditions within which human experience emerges and functions, and with which human experience, both in its phenomenological and ontological dimensions, is inseparably intertwined.

Such a processive universe that reveals itself in the pervasive textures of experiencing is the home of the whole of the sensory, with its richness and spontaneity, the home of the brute otherness of the independently real with which I interact and to which I respond; the home of the continuities and regularities that pervade my commerce with it and allow me to anticipate the type of presence to be contained within the approaching moment. Thus all the pragmatists, through their respective terminologies, converge toward a process metaphysics of nature that can be characterized in terms of the categories of qualitative richness, diversity, spontaneity, possibility; interaction, over-againstness, shock, presentness; dispositional tendencies, potentialities, lawful modes of behavior. These categories are understood and interrelated in terms of ways in which a thick, natural, processive reality functions.

This emerging metaphysics thus envisions a universe in which humans are at home and with which their activities are continuous; a universe in which their lived qualitative experience can grasp real emergent qualitative features of reality and in which their creative meanings, embodying dispositionally generated noetic potentialities, can grasp the real dynamic tendencies of reality to produce operations of a certain type with a certain regularity. A universe, in short, that is both grasped by, and reflected within, the pervasive textures at the heart of all experience and at the foundation of all meaning.

It has been seen that the categorial contents of such a metaphysics are in no way intended as a grasp of being in some spectator vision. But they are also not merely hypothetically supposed at the beginning without our having some experiential awareness of them. Like all knowledge claims, these metaphysical claims elude the confines of the alternatives of foundationalism or antifoundationalism, of an absolute grounding of knowledge or skepticism, or, within this more specific context, of a metaphysics of presence or the demise of metaphysics. The second-level reflections of philosophy must be grounded in lived experience and be constantly fed by this experience. Such an open system is explanation rooted in and answerable to lived experience, not direct grasp of "being in itself." Though rooted in the lived level, it is never completely adequate to the lived level. It is open to change and development, just as all claims are open to change and development. Indeed, Peirce nowhere indicates that his categories are absolute or eternal and in fact states quite clearly that though his selection seems the most adequate, alternative series of categories are possible.[44] Similarly, though Lewis speaks of metaphysics as providing the presuppositions for an understanding of the knowledge situation, he notes that though a presupposition is logically prior, the ideal of necessity must be given up.[45] Nor is such a presupposition known by some "higher" type of knowledge, but rather it is an interpretive structure that gains, within lived experience, "partial and inductive verification."[46] Because of its openness, and the conditions within which it emerges, such a system must be recognized as tentative, not certain, and thus Peirce received "the pleasure of praise" from what "was meant for blame" when "a critic said of me that I did not seem to be absolutely sure of my own conclusions."[47] Pragmatism, then, gives rise to a new understanding of metaphysical system as an open system or explanatory structure, and to a view of explanation rooted in, rather than opposed to, a history of evolving change.

Here it may be objected that the view of metaphysical system as perspectivally and temporally rooted involves antifoundationalism, relativism, and historicism, both for metaphysical claims and for knowledge in general, of which it is a kind. However, such objections again sever experience from its creative, interactive unity with, and openness upon, that which is independently there. As has been previously indicated, the interactive unity denies the arbitrariness of antifoundationalism, antirealism, relativism, a historicism of present happenstance, the demise of metaphysics. The temporally founded interactive creativity denies the absolute- ness of foundationalism, realism, objectivism, the absolute grasp, a metaphysics of pure presence. Instead of the stultifying self- enclosement of an antifoundational relativism in terms of arbitrary conceptual schemes, this pragmatic view houses an open perspec- tivalism in which perspectives open onto the common concrete ground of their possibility. Instead of an historicism of present happenstance, it involves a temporalism in which historical rooted- ness is at once ontological rootedness, and in which the ontological rootedness of perspective emerges within the context of a past that presents itself in the richness of the potentialities and possibili- ties of a processive present oriented toward a novel and indefinite future. Like all knowledge claims, the metaphysical claims of prag- matic philosophy are fallibilistic, perspectival, and temporal but nonetheless ontologically situated.

Because the independently real, as ontological presence within experience, enters directly into interaction with our creative cate- gories or meanings and the possibilities they allow, coherence is not a sufficient criterion for truth. There is an ontological dimen- sion to what appears within experience that limits our meaning projections in terms of workability. But, true knowledge, even ideally true knowledge, could not be correspondence, for the nature of our creative link with the indefinite richness of the in- dependently real makes the relation of correspondence literally senseless. A true belief works in anticipating possibilities of ex- perience but works not because it adequately copies, but because it adequately "cuts into," the independently real as a function of the world or conceptual contour or paradigmatic structure that makes the belief possible. The independently real, which provides the dimension of ontological presence within experience, answers our questions and determines the workability of our meaning struc- tures, but what answers it gives are partially dependent on what questions we ask, and what meaning structures work are partially dependent upon the structures we bring. The very possibility of truth thus emerges from the backdrop of the transformation of the independent richness of the "independently there" into worldly encounter. Truth is relative to a context of interpretation, not be- cause truth is relative, but because without an interpretive context the concept of truth is meaningless. Truth as pragmatic is thus both made and found. We create the interpretive frameworks—whether in common sense, science, or philosophy—within which beliefs can emerge and be found true or false. The creative intelligence involved in radical changes and shifts of interpretive frameworks is influenced by sociocultural conditions but is ultimately founded not in a relativistic, perspectivally closed historicism, but in an ontologically grounded, perspectivally open temporalism. Indeed, though differing philosophies put forth differing positions embedded within, and reflecting the influence of, differing cultural, sociohistorical conditions, yet they can do so only because they are further and more deeply rooted in the conditions that make possible the emergence of any reflection, and because the philosopher is rooted in the concrete richness of these conditions that ground the alternative possibilities of formalized articulations.

The contemporary unease with the traditional notion of systematic speculative metaphysics is thus embedded in the very structure of pragmatism as a philosophic system. The history of metaphysical speculation, as embodied in philosophic system, is a history evincing positions that have systematically denied or rejected the sense of temporality, creativity, novelty, fallibilism, pluralism, perspectivalism, and openendedness—in short, the key dimensions of pragmatic philosophy—in favor of the eternal, the fixed, the final, the certain, the absolute grasp, the ultimate completion, the perfected whole, the indubitable foundation. The supposed philosophic foundations thus asserted were, according to this pragmatic view, reflective creations grounded in a foundational richness ignored by foundationalist and antifoundationalist thinking alike. The categories of a speculative metaphysics within pragmatism attempt to draw one toward an awareness of the interactive openness, at the heart of experience, of humans and that which is independently there, and in so doing provide the path for freeing thinking from premature ontological assertions, from illicit reifications, and from a tradition of philosophy that, in its search for supposed foundations, lost the illusive but pervasive experiential-ontological foundations of its search. These latter tendencies of metaphysical thinking, as well as contemporary attempts to throw out the metaphysical baby with the foundationalist bathwater, ignore the fundamental, creative, indefinitely rich interactive epistemic and metaphysical unity at the heart of lived experience. The language of philosophy is born of a tradition that ignores this interactive unity, and hence it reinforces problems and alternative solutions that the present position eludes.

Much of contemporary philosophy, operating within the seemingly novel paradigm of linguistic analysis, or within other seemingly novel paradigms radically restrictive of the nature and limits of philosophical pursuits, and thus denying metaphysical system, has yet not succeeded in breaking with the alternatives offered by, and hence the possible solutions allowable by, traditional paradigms stemming from substance metaphysics and spectator theory of knowledge. Though the alternatives and possible solutions may take distinctively new turns, and though seemingly new alternatives and new limitations emerge, too often they can be seen as new paradigmatic twists to old paradigmatic offerings. The alternatives, whether expressed in newer or older fashion, of foundationalism-antifoundationalism, realism-antirealism, objectivism-relativism, subjectivism-objectivism, correspondence-coherence, realism-idealism, empiricism-rationalism, are all alternatives that grow out of reflective frameworks that ignore the fundamental, creative, interactive unity at the heart of lived experience. As long as pragmatic doctrines are understood within, or developed in terms of, one of the family-related sets of the very alternatives it has rejected, then though specific aspects of its position may be further developed for specialized purposes, the significance and uniqueness of its systematic vision is lost. Pragmatism, in illuminating the creative interactive unity at the heart of experience through its focus on biologically rooted experimental activity, develops a position that eludes the false alternatives and misplaced dichotomies that still haunt philosophy today and that tend to form the backdrop for questions concerning the demise of metaphysics. It rejects key elements of the tradition it inherits, not by destroying the enterprise of creative metaphysics, but by reconstructing the pathway for its ongoing development. Though in some ways this pragmatic endeavor manifests the end, as demise, of metaphysics in the traditional sense, yet it also represents its end as newly focused aim. To take a typical Dewey statement out of context, no ending is absolute, but rather every ending is at once at a new beginning.

In conclusion, and as a sort of postscript, a few general, inadequately brief remarks are in order concerning not the justification of systems as understood within this pragmatic framework, but rather the justification of this entire pragmatic framework, though even this will of necessity draw from its own perspective. This pragmatic framework of course cannot be self-justifying; no system can justify itself. Any attempt at self-justification already presupposes features of that which it is attempting to justify. However, the philosophical tradition, as a tradition that has articulated itself through a history of incommensurable systems in conflict, seems, like the history of science, to point toward a nonformal evaluative sense of the adequacy of formal conceptions, for it has shown an ability to come to a loose, albeit contingent, consensus concerning a loss of vitality of the most soundly developed systems, of certain lines of questioning and possible types of answers, through a vague sense of lifelessness, even though there is a formal incommensurability among these systems concerning the nature of truth, evidence, justification, and the issue of foundations. Indeed, many of the possible formalizations of philosophy, though emerging with continued logical vigor, are today beginning to emerge as peculiarly devoid of vitality. Thus, Lewis holds that philosophy "can be nothing more at bottom than persuasion."[48]

The switch from proof to persuasion, however, is not the switch from foundationalism to antifoundationalism, or from rationality to psychologism or irrationality, or from absolutism to fiction or arbitrary relativism, or from rule-structured reason to capriciousness, but rather a recognition that rationality as articulated second-level reflection emerges in philosophy as an attempt to render intelligible imprecise, tentative, often initially inarticulate perceptions. The persuasiveness of a system does not lie in a strictly logical force, or in a strictly empirical force, in the sense of pointing out supposed trans-systematic facts that other philosophical positions must accept, but rather in its forcefulness in arousing basic insights that "ring true to life," infusing its paradigmatic structure with vitality even as another takes on the lifelessness of artificiality. In the language of pragmatism, a philosophy is ultimately judged not by its roots but by its fruits. Any philosophic system will hold persuasion only if others, through such a system, find that it throws into focus initial prephilosophical glimmerings that were before vaguely inexpressible or submerged through the weight of distortive structures. The ongoing philosophical tradition itself would seem to indicate that the reflections of reason are ultimately rooted in, and accountable to, a prephilosophical vitality of life within which is embedded a rich, inexhaustively creative intelligence that underlies, overflows, and ultimately deabsolutizes any attempt to impose formalized demands upon it. Thus, James characterizes the process by which one accepts a philosophical view as "life exceeding logic . . . the theoretic reason finds arguments after the conclusion is once there."[49]

Indeed, this is the only kind of evaluation that can really keep any system alive, no matter how solid its arguments or how numerous its intrasystematic "facts." If, however, as pragmatism holds, the pulse of human existence at its very core is, both ontologically and epistemically, creatively and perspectively intertwined with, and thus attuned to, that which reveals itself in various ways both within and among various levels and modes of human activity, then this free, creative, prethematic evaluative sense can be at once both a more demanding and more tolerant master than any of the diverse second-level articulations to which it gives rise. The alternatives of foundationalism or antifoundationalism have been seen to ignore, respectively, the dimensions of free creativity or of ontological presence, which are unified at the heart of human existence. The paradigmatic novelty of classical American pragmatism, by breaking out of the confines of the foundationalist-antifoundationalist debate, can give philosophical legitimacy to the prethematic evaluative sense that is embedded in concrete human existence and that allows for creative diversity while yet issuing compelling constraints.

Notes

1. By the term 'pragmatism' in this essay is always intended the position of the classical American pragmatists. That these philosophers provide a unified perspective is assumed herein, but this claim is defended at some length in my book, *Speculative Pragmatism* (Amherst: University of Massachusetts Press, 1986; paperback ed., Peru, Ill.: Open Court Publishing, 1990).

2. Some of the pragmatists, of course, make frequent denials that their respective philosophies constitute a system. The systematic character of pragmatism's shared philosophic vision is also defended at some length in *Speculative Pragmatism*.

3. The pragmatists will at times deny the validity of metaphysics in favor of ontology only to proceed with their own developments of positions that they themselves label as metaphysical. They are, in their respective ways, rejecting the traditional metaphysical enterprise and working toward a new understanding of the nature of metaphysics. The present essay can proceed in either of two ways. It can follow the trend of labeling as metaphysical the products of what it sees as the errors of past philosophies, reserving the term 'ontological' for the present position. Not only is this one strand to be found in the writings of the pragmatists, but it is also in line with the distinction as made in some other contemporary positions. However, pragmatism *is* concerned with issues of metaphysics, though with a metaphysics that reaches the richness of reality in its foundational concreteness, and in a way that renders foundationalist claims inadequate. The position intended is traditional in its endeavor; it is concerned with metaphysical speculation; it is consciously speculative, although its speculations cannot be grasped within the distinctions, dichotomies, and presuppositions of past metaphysics. Thus, the present essay follows the second strand to be found in the pragmatists—the indiscriminate use of 'metaphysics' and 'ontology'—for, the negative sense of metaphysics to be found in the pragmatic attacks on past positions notwithstanding, this alternative seems best in keeping with the spirit of pragmatic philosophy. The "process metaphysics" that results from the pragmatic focus cannot be conflated with a Whiteheadian type, which, in spite of its emphasis on process, nonetheless embodies the traditional metaphysical enterprise of translating the textures of experience into some type of explanatory ultimates.

4. Causal connections are always expressed as relations among particular types of objects or events, and the nature of the events or objects being connected enters into the very understanding of the nature of the causal relationship sustained. This focus on scientific method as the method of causal analysis is thus still not purified of content and represents a lingering influence of modern worldview thought. This brief sketch of the distinction between scientific method and scientific content within pragmatic philosophy, as well as the ensuing discussion of its understanding of scientific method, is examined and supported in some depth in *Speculative Pragmatism*.

5. G. H. Mead, *Philosophy of the Act* (Chicago: University of Chicago Press, 1938), p. 32.

6. John Dewey, *Experience and Nature*, vol. 1 (1981) of *The Philosophy of John Dewey: The Later Works*, ed. Jo Ann Boydston (Carbondale and Edwardsville: Southern Illinois University Press, 1981–), p. 37.

7. Ibid., p. 40.

8. William James, *The Principles of Psychology*, 2 vols. (1981): *The Works of William James*, ed. Frederick Burkhardt (Cambridge: Harvard University Press, 1975–), 2: 1232–34.

9. Dewey, *The Quest for Certainty*, vol. 4 (1984) of *The Later Works*, pp. 163–65.

10. For example, see James, *Principles of Psychology*, 2: 961; Peirce, *Collected Papers of Charles Sanders Pierce*, 6 vols., ed. Charles Hartshorne and Paul Weiss (Cambridge: Belknap Press of Harvard University, 1931–1935); vols. 7 and 8, ed. Arthur Burks (Cambridge: Harvard University Press, 1958), 7: 498.

11. Peirce, *Collected Papers*, 5: 384.

12. John Dewey, "Does Reality Possess Practical Character?" in vol. 4 (1977) of *The Philosophy of John Dewey: The Middle Works*, ed. Jo Ann Boydston (Carbondale and Edwardsville: Southern Illinois University Press, 1976–1983), pp. 137–38.

13. Dewey, *Studies in Logical Theory*, vol. 2 (1976) of *The Middle Works*, p. 305.

14. Peirce, *Collected Papers*, 5: 181. Peirce's technical term for such creative activity is "abduction." This shading of scientific abductions into everyday perceptual claims is not a continuity of content organized but of method of organization.

15. Mead, *Philosophy of the Act*, p. 25.

16. C. I. Lewis, *Mind and the World Order* (New York: Dover Publications, 1929), Appendix A, esp. pp. 395–97.

17. Science is detached from our world of commonsense engagement because its *objects* are detached abstractions from it. Scientists, however, are significantly and actively engaged with their world of scientific objectivities, though such engagement is more deliberately controlled and more narrowly focused.

18. Dewey, *Experience and Nature*, p. 37.

19. Dewey, *The Quest for Certainty*, p. 142; "The Experimental Theory of Knowledge," in vol. 3 (1977) of *The Middle Works*, pp. 114–15. Mead, *Philosophy of the Act*, pp. 115–16.

20. Peirce, *Collected Papers*, 6: 138.

21. Lewis, *An Analysis of Knowledge and Valuation* (La Salle, Ill.: Open Court, 1946), p. 17. Thus, even the most rudimentary conscious experience, according to Dewey, "contains within itself the element of sugges-

tion or expectation." "The Existence of the World as a Logical Problem," in vol. 8 (1977) of *The Middle Works*, 9.

22. Dewey, "Experience and Objective Idealism", in vol. 3 of *The Middle Works*, p. 136.

23. Dewey, "Perception and Organic Action," in vol. 7 of *The Middle Works*, p. 13. Thus Peirce notes that within such a temporal flow, "feeling which has not yet emerged into immediate consciousness is already affectible and already affected. In fact this is habit by virtue of which an idea is brought up into present consciousness by a bond which had already been established between it and another idea while it was still in futuro" (*Collected Papers*, 6: 141). As James states, we can hardly get hold of an impression at all in the absence of an anticipation of "what impressions there may possibly be." *Pragmatism* (1975), *The Works of William James*, p. 119.

24. Lewis, *Mind and the World Order*, p. 194.

25. Peirce, *Collected Papers*, 5: 283.

26. Lewis, *An Analysis of Knowledge and Valuation*, p. 361.

27. Dewey, *Experience and Nature*, pp. 12–13.

28. Mead, *Philosophy of the Present*, ed. Arthur E. Murphy (La Salle, Ill.: Open Court, 1959), p. 137.

29. Ibid.

30. For a good analysis of this point, see Dewey's discussion of "the table," *The Quest for Certainty*, pp. 189–90.

31. Peirce, *Collected Papers*, 5: 311 (emphasis added).

32. Ibid., 7: 340.

33. Lewis, *Mind and the World Order*, p. 58.

34. Mead, *Philosophy of the Act*, p. 345.

35. Dewey, *Experience and Nature*, pp. 64–65.

36. Ibid., p. 65.

37. James, *A Pluralistic Universe* (1977), *The Works of William James*, p. 129.

38. James, *Essays in Radical Empiricism* (1976), *The Works of William James*, p. 37.

39. Peirce, *Collected Papers*, 1: 282; 6: 2.

40. James, *Principles of Psychology*, 2: 671.

41. Dewey, *Experience and Nature*, pp. 37, 19.

42. Peirce, *Collected Papers*, 5: 119. Peirce characterizes our knowledge of "the premises of nature" as an "imaginative" comparison with fundamental features of experience.

43. Lewis, *An Analysis of Knowledge and Valuation*, p. 320.

44. Peirce, *Collected Papers*, 1: 525, 526.

45. Lewis, "The Structure of Logic and Its Relation to Other Systems,"

The Collected Papers of C. I. Lewis, ed. John Goheen and John Mothershead, Jr. (Stanford: Stanford University Press, 1970), p. 378.

   46. Ibid.

   47. Peirce, *Collected Papers*, 1: 10.

   48. Lewis, *Mind and the World Order*, pp. 207, 23.

   49. James, *A Pluralistic Universe*, p. 148.

Nine

Metaphysics without Mirrors

BETH J. SINGER

In his well-known book *Philosophy and the Mirror of Nature* Richard Rorty attacks the mentalistic and epistemological foundationalism and universalist, antihistoricist pretensions of "mainstream" Western philosophy from René Descartes to contemporary "analytic" philosophy, and proposes a new approach to philosophizing. Along with Ludwig Wittgenstein, Martin Heidegger, W. V. O. Quine, and Wilfrid Sellars, he credits John Dewey with revealing the arbitrariness and confusion of the entrenched ways of doing and conceiving philosophy and with opening the way to a new and more appropriate approach. He nevertheless finds none of these philosophers to have articulated an adequate program, and in some ways he sees Friedrich Nietzsche and Jean-Paul Sartre as more nearly approximating the model of philosophy he takes to be desirable. Dewey, like Sellars and Paul Feyerabend, "point[s] the way toward . . . a nonepistemological sort of philosophy" but only "partially exemplif[ies] it."[1]

In general I accept Rorty's diagnosis of most modern and contemporary philosophy. I also accept his call for philosophy that is not epistemology-centered, that stands outside the mind-body problematic, and that comes to terms with the inevitable historicity and cultural conditioning of knowledge without succumbing to skepticism. But the model he proposes—philosophy that is "edifying" rather than systematic, hermeneutic rather than epistemological, reactive rather than constructive, eschewing all metaphysics and refraining from commitment to any position or conceptual frame—sacrifices too much and is not the only way to escape the pitfalls of foundationalism. I intend to show that there can be and in fact is "philosophy without mirrors" that is nonetheless systematic and does not extirpate metaphysics.

I

Dewey was not the only American philosopher to reject epistemological foundationalism and the traditional conception of "the mind."[2] William James paved the way, and there were others. Challenging the notion of subjectivity associated with the "mental mirror" concept and ingredient in both classical empiricism and idealism, George Herbert Mead presented a new model of mind and self. The human mind, he says, "is essentially a social phenomenon."[3] In order to interact with others, the individual must learn to take their attitude toward himself. "When this occurs [he] becomes self-conscious and has a mind" (MSS, p. 134). Self-consciousness is not introspection but an inner conversation, in which one alternately takes the attitudes of self and other. Mind or intelligence is the ability of the individual to reflexively modify and refine this process. Knowledge is no mirroring or remembering of percepts, but the exercise of intelligence.[4] Things known, like knowers, are social objects, located in social space as well as in physical space and in time. Rejecting the "identification of the object of knowledge with the so-called percept, whether a percept by virtue of the eye or of the imagination," Mead claims that "[this] rejection sweeps out a vast amount of philosophic riffraff known as epistemology, and relieves one of the hopeless task of bridge-building from a world of one's states of consciousness to an outside world that can never be reached" (PA, p. 94).

In the United States it is not only pragmatists who have challenged the epistemological orientation of modern philosophy. Alfred North Whitehead's "philosophy of organism" obliterates the "mind" and "body" of the tradition and gives metaphysics priority over epistemology, rather than vice versa. Reacting primarily against the then prevalent versions of idealism, the "New Realists" repudiated the psychologism they saw to be also characteristic of classical empiricism. With it, they repudiated the effort to ground philosophy in epistemology.[5] These writers represent a persistent trend in American philosophy, one that is still alive. For example,

Sandra Rosenthal, in her book *Speculative Pragmatism*, develops an ontology for pragmatism.[6] Rather than an attack on foundationalism, Rosenthal's approach to metaphysics is designed to undercut the conflict between foundationalism and antifoundationalism. It does so, not by eliminating epistemology, but by showing conventional epistemology to be too narrowly conceived.[7] The dichotomy between foundationalism and nonfoundationalism "represents the alternatives of an *absolute* grounding of knowledge or skepticism" (*SP*, p. 79; emphasis added). But for the pragmatists, knowing is a function within experience, and experience is interaction with an environment. The only "ground" of knowledge is its functional status in the relation between the knower and the environment, and any analysis of this grounding must be ontological as well as epistemic. In Rosenthal's version of pragmatism, the objects of awareness, potential objects of knowledge, are an "ontological presence" within the experiential field, but they are not present to experience as things in themselves.[8] Being anticipatory and experimental, even the most rudimentary experience—and hence the experiential field or "world"—is already informed with referential meanings. Therefore, we cannot "work back in experience to a direct grasp of anything that is as it is prior to its emergence within the context of experimental activity" (*SP*, p. 79). Thus there can be no absolute grounding for knowledge. But since the meaning structures are tested in the same experiential field in which they have their source, skepticism is as arbitrary as foundationalism.

As a pragmatist, Rosenthal takes experience to be representative of its experiential/existential setting. Characterizing this setting, Rosenthal is not trying to state eternal truths about reality. Philosophy, she holds, must be understood as emerging from experience, and experience as emerging from its own history, a thesis Rorty should endorse.

> A philosophy, like any knowledge structure, does not conform to a pregiven world that is "there" and that one philosophy will "find" in spectator fashion. Rather it is a perspective on a common-sense world infused with the meanings of various derived worlds. This world is constantly in the process of remaking, and as it changes, the philosophic reflection upon it changes . . . in turn infus[ing] with new meanings the world from which it emerged.[9]

II

I have elsewhere cited the philosophy of Justus Buchler as the most consistent and thoroughgoing representative of this strong antidualist, antifoundationalist and anti-epistemological trend in American philosophy.[10] Another important representative is John Herman Randall, Jr., repeatedly cited by Rorty but only as a historian. Randall, who consciously builds on Dewey, is a metaphysician as well as a historian and philosopher of history. Like Dewey, he is reacting against the foundationalism and mentalism of the dominant philosophic schools. Again like Dewey, he rejects reductivism and the atomistic and essentialist assumptions Rorty also condemns. Unlike Dewey, however, he is deliberately systematic, although not in Rorty's sense. It is on Randall's philosophy that I wish to concentrate, but to show how it responds to Rorty's critique of the tradition, I must discuss that critique in somewhat greater detail.

Rorty's critical analysis of the history of philosophy is complex and many-sided. Very briefly, his central thesis is that "mainstream" philosophy has illegitimately set itself up as the neutral, authoritative judge of the validity of any and all knowledge-claims. It has sought to be "an all-encompassing discipline which legitimizes or grounds the others" (*PMN*, p. 6), the arbiter, for every culture and institution and for all time, of what counts as "knowledge of reality" and what does not. Rorty shows this to be an inappropriate task, both because it is impossible to establish universal criteria by which all knowledge-claims can be justified and because the very notion of the "problem of knowledge" that epistemology tries to solve rests upon untenable assumptions.

One such assumption is that philosophy addresses perennial problems. But these problems arise out of historically evolved frameworks or problematics, and the problem of knowledge is no exception. Philosophy's quest for epistemological guarantees, as well as its failure to find them, is historically rooted in a conception of knowledge derived from Descartes and John Locke, a conception resting on a visual model, with the mind taken to be a sort of mirror and knowledge to consist in mental representations. After David Hume showed the implications of a consistent, Lockeian psychology, making God, the human soul, and the "universal laws" of science all equally dubious, Immanuel Kant restored the mind to its central position, now as a transcendental faculty of uniting the diverse representations. Having found an a priori grounding for scientific knowledge of the (now phenomenal) world, he appealed to the same faculty to provide an epistemological justification, which science could not supply, for the metaphysical presuppositions of religion and morality. Epistemology, not science, had taken the place of metaphysics as the most basic discipline. To put it another way, as an attempt to find out what one can be objective about, metaphysics became epistemology and, in the hands of the post-Kantians, metaphysics-epistemology became philosophy and installed itself as cognitive dictator.

In the meantime, Rorty points out, Kant was still trying to "answer the question of how we could get from inner space to outer space" even though "his paradoxical answer was that outer space was constructed out of the *Vorstellungen* that inhabited inner space" (*PMN*, pp. 147–48). Distinguishing between the formal constituents of our representations and their sensory content left him with another problematic duality, that of the given and the "postulated theoretical entities in inner space" by means of which we unify the sensory manifold and synthesize our intuitions. Not only have we "no introspective ground" for these "psychological goings-on"; Quine was later to show the impossibility of defining the boundary between the a priori and the empirical. Moreover, in trying to solve the problem of knowing whether our inner representations are accurate, both Locke and Kant confuse causal explanation with justification.[11] This confusion resulted from their thinking of knowledge as "knowledge of," rather than "knowledge that"; as a confrontation with an object rather than as justified true belief that something is the case (that is, belief that a sentence is true). The ambiguity in Locke between the content of an idea and the judgment that it is the idea of an object is symptomatic of this confusion. The Kantian theory "confuses predication (saying something about an object) and synthesis (putting representations together in inner space)" (*PMN*, p. 148). That is, Locke never made, and Kant started to make but failed to complete, the move from "knowledge of" to "knowledge that," that is, from viewing knowledge as consisting in mental representations to viewing it as consisting in stated beliefs, sentences.

What happens if this move is made? Some philosophers merely substituted words for ideas, treating language as a representational scheme, a public "mirror of Nature," just as the mind is a private one. This generated an analogous problem of justification. But Ludwig Wittgenstein and Martin Heidegger taught us not to take belief-statements to be representations or externalizations thereof. If they are not, their truth is not a function of correspondence at all but of the reasons for them, that is, of their relation to other statements in some context of discourse. Truth, then, and meaning as well, can be understood only holistically, that is, contextually. But this means that we must give up the quest for certainty and objectivity. Generalizing Thomas S. Kuhn's analysis of "normal" and "abnormal" science, Rorty holds that, in every sphere, the evaluation of truth-claims and of what count as good reasons rests upon social agreement rather than upon universal or transcendental criteria. Canons of inquiry and criteria of truth and reality, such as the concept of objectivity, are only historically evolved ways of reaching agreement that are definitive of "normal discourse." There is no ultimate justification. As Sellars contends, we are given the right to make certain assertions but not others by the epistemic rules of a community. The logical space of reasons is the space occupied by these rules, which are products of discourse, conversation, social practice.

Every cultural community establishes its own rules of normal discourse. In Rorty's words,

> We can get epistemological commensuration only where we already have agreed-upon practices of inquiry (or, more generally, of discourse) —as easily in 'academic' art, 'scholastic' philosophy, or 'parliamentary' politics as in 'normal' science. We can get it not because we have discovered something about 'the nature of human knowledge' but simply because when a practice has continued long enough the conventions which make it possible—and which permit a consensus on how to divide it into parts—are relatively easy to isolate. (*PMN*, p. 321)

There can be no "permanent, neutral framework" for assessing truth-claims, but only a multiplicity of "disciplinary matrices" and vocabularies. Monitoring the search for justified true beliefs is not an appropriate task for philosophy. What it ought to do, according to Rorty, is to adopt a "bifocal" view: It should pragmatically take normal discourse on its own terms, in the light of its own motives. But then it should take the broader view and admit that what counts as justified true belief may be no more than conformity to the norms of the day. Adopting the first stance, Rorty himself accepts the physicalism he takes to be dictated by natural science.[12] But rather than trying to show how it is that science is closer to reality than religion or art or moral judgment, he tells us to recognize the impossibility and the needlessness of establishing this, accept their incommensurability and historicity, and abandon the epistemological project of universal commensuration.

This means that systematic philosophy must be given up, because it "centers in epistemology." (For philosophy to be systematic, in Rorty's sense, is for it to be inherently epistemological and to establish itself as canonical.) Furthermore, if discourse is not representational, we should cease to view any discourse as being about the way things are. We will then cease to do metaphysics, which, as a search for the most general traits of reality, is a search for accurate representations, and a mistaken enterprise. "When experiment and 'meaning analysis' fail," Rorty says, "philosophers have traditionally turned to system-building—inventing a new context on the spot, so to speak" (*PMN*, p. 89). Metaphysical alternatives to dualism simply posit a new kind of unprovable underlying reality. To take metaphysics as trying to go beyond science, to find out what science cannot, is to try to combine within it both normal and abnormal discourse. But to take it as an attempt to find out what one can be objective about is to identify it with the epistemological enterprise. In either case it is to be repudiated.

More generally, philosophers should cease to think of themselves as engaged in inquiry. Instead of constructing and defending positions, we should devote ourselves to revealing the ahistorical error of the epistemologists, the error of elevating one vocabulary or one brand of normalcy to universal, prescriptive status. Recognizing the legitimacy of alternative and incommensurable vocabularies and attitudes, we should stand outside the normal and react against it. Rather than trying to solve the traditional philosophic problems of "normal philosophy," we should devote ourselves, in Dewey's words, to "breaking the crust of convention." That is, we should try "to find new, better, more useful ways of speaking" but not in the attempt to establish a new normal philosophy. Philosophic discourse should be only "edifying" conversation: edifying because it invokes "the fact or possibility of abnormal discourses, undermining our reliance upon the knowledge we have gained through normal discourses" (*PMN*, p. 386). To be edifying, philosophy must be hermeneutical, not epistemological. Rather than an attempt at commensuration, it is "discourse about as-yet-incommensurable discourses" (*PMN*, p. 343). Therefore, it must be frankly and self-consciously abnormal, setting aside the conventions of any form of normal discourse and avoiding any pretense of universality. It must be "existential," refraining from the attempt to gain objective knowledge of the world or the self. From time to time in the course of the conversation new forms of normal discourse may happen to emerge, but these are no longer part of the abnormal conversation, and the achievement of normality is not an appropriate aim for philosophy.

"Edifying philosophy," Rorty tells us, "aims at continuing a conversation rather than at discovering truth." To take a position is to make a claim to truth, which can be meaningful and justifiable only within a normal framework. Edifying philosophy will take no positions but only "attempt to prevent conversation from degenerating into inquiry, into an exchange of views" (*PMN*, pp. 373, 372).

III

Randall is a systematic philosopher, not in the sense that his philosophy is justified by an epistemology, but because the dimensions of his thought are interdependent and informed by the same historicist and instrumentalist outlook. His fundamental, Deweyan, hypothesis is that existence is at least what we find it to be in experience, at least what we can successfully understand it to be. Since history, culture, and communication are found in experience, he approaches the analysis of existence by generalizing the fundamental concepts he has found to apply to the analysis of history, communication, and language, testing them further in the analysis of other subject matters. All are shown to be intelligible when construed in terms of the continuous adjustment of means and ends, an analysis that is elaborated in a theory of the functional structure of all existential processes. Randall's metaphysical categories are considered by him to be analogous to the institutions of culture as he understands them. That is, they are instruments for dealing with existence as it is encountered in experience. They are formulated in process terms because this encounter is a process, an interaction with factors that are disclosed as "acting and interacting with us and with other[s] . . . as doing things to us, as something to which we do things in return."[13]

Randall's general metaphysics or ontology is systematic also in the narrower sense of being a categorial system, a framework of interrelated concepts. These categories are not descriptions of a single, underlying reality. Instead, they formulate in language distinctions or "discriminations" found in all forms of experience. Derived from the comparative analysis of particular subject matters, the categories are put forth as applicable to all existence, that is, existents taken distributively. Despite its intended universality, Randall's categorial scheme is not conceived as an expression of necessary conditions of experience but as a hypothetical generalization from experience. Not from "brute" or "raw experience": that is only an abstraction; and not "subjective" experience, for Randall shows experience to be a process in nature and in interaction with other natural processes. The categories arise in the critical analysis of the conceptualizations of reflective experience: traditional discriminations, historically conditioned understandings embodied in cultural institutions and disciplines, critically analyzed in the light of other experiences of diverse kinds in an effort to identify discriminations common to all.

Randall is not searching for eternal truths, but is consciously playing a part in cultural history and the history of philosophy. Viewing that history as the ongoing interplay between established understandings and practices and new experience, he draws upon both the classic tradition of Western philosophy and the Deweyan critique of that tradition for metaphysical insights.[14] Reflecting the same view, he portrays metaphysics itself as at one and the same time a critical endeavor and as subject to criticism in the light of further experience.

The history of ideas, Randall says, teaches us "to look upon history as the continual readaptation of materials in the light of changing needs and problems" (*NHE*, p. 5). As Dewey contends, philosophy has a special, critical role to play in this process.

It is . . . conflicts between traditional beliefs and novel experience which drive men to construct philosophies, to fit opposing or irrelevant ideas together into some not too chaotic scheme, to adjust warring values so as to give some direction to life without excluding too much. . . . The problems which give rise to philosophies emerge when the strife of ideas and experiences forces men back to basic assumptions in any field. They have varied from age to age, and are to be understood only as expressions of fundamental conflicts within a culture, leading men on to thoroughgoing criticisms. (*NHE*, p. 6)

That philosophy is a form of criticism does not mean that it is not at the same time a form of inquiry; it only illustrates the fact that inquiry itself is intrinsically critical. We see this in the history of natural science, which "is the history of the continual criticism and modification of the basic assumptions in terms of which the structure of nature has been pieced together and expressed" (*NHE*, p. 16). Science is knowledge only in this functional and instrumental sense of a critical reconstruction of previous understandings calling for further testing. "Knowledge . . . is not an immediate seeing, is neither the intellectual apprehension or vision of rationalism, nor the sensible vision and perception of empiricism, but is mediate and functional, an active process of criticism directed toward a selected end" (*NHE*, p. 16). Whatever its form in particular situations, the general end of all knowing is the redirection of continuing experience. In this ongoing process ideas are to be understood and evaluated, not as "images" of "reality," but as conceptual tools whose function is to give us greater control over the world we encounter in experience by making it intelligible.

Randall describes metaphysics as a science, "the science of existence as existence." It is science in the sense of intelligently directed, critical inquiry; the "scientific method" broadly construed. Science, so understood, is "the technique of cultural change." Its "method is a continued criticism of experience by reason and reason by experience," illustrated by the natural sciences. Metaphysics employs the same method, but at another level.

Operating at a deeper level of this same interaction than our natural science is the philosophical tradition out of which it grew and in terms of which it is itself understood and criticized. . . . When scientific tests have left too much unexplained, when they have failed to make intelligible too large an area of experience, it has recalled them to a confrontation of experience again. (*NHE*, p. 9)

The consequence of this confrontation with experience is to "remind . . . them of that universal pattern of what is, those fundamental concepts and distinctions, which whatever the language of a particular thinker or a particular tradition, seem forced on the mind by a common world and somehow expressed" (*NHE*, p. 9). Randall finds in Aristotle's analysis of process a cogent formulation of those fundamental concepts and distinctions forced upon us by the world. But "although without what Plato and Aristotle first said, all words would be meaningless, they did not say the final word. . . . [N]either the limitations nor the power of the classic tradition they created can be fully appreciated until it is seen from the perspective of all that we have since experienced and learned" (*NHE*, p. 11). Metaphysics is the continuing search for more adequate formulations of the fundamental distinctions.

We must not conclude that this is a new version of foundationalism. Even though it is in part a critique of the sciences, Randall insists that metaphysics is not a "super-science" dictating to the others. Metaphysics does not try to tell scientists or anyone else what they can and cannot know. Rather than ranking disciplines and modes of discourse as more or less accurate approximations of reality, metaphysical inquiry endeavors to find a language more adequate than any yet provided by the culture in which to express pervasive experiential discriminations. In a passage that invites comparison with Rorty, Randall states that in

metaphysical inquiry . . . language [can] free us from the tyranny of having to construe the world crystallized in the forms so essential to practice and so bound down to it. It can free us from bondage to the metaphysics enshrined in ordinary language, developed to serve well the immediate needs of daily living, the metaphysics of "common sense." Through a suitable manipulation of language, we can talk . . . in new ways . . . that will permit and encourage us to explore new ideas, to push them, to generalize them and apply them in novel situations, in new fields and new subject-matters, that will make us see those fields and subject-matters in a new light, and discern relations and structures we had not before been aware of. (*NHE*, p. 141)

Nevertheless, metaphysics is not conversation about conversation. It is an empirical discipline whose starting point and touchstone of validity are in the world experientially encountered. And it is a theoretical discipline in the sense that it endeavors to make that world more intelligible.

Metaphysics is not an alternative to natural science, a competing description of nature. But its subject matter includes that of science, together with those of all the other disciplines, and it must start with critical analysis of the terms in which those subject matters have already been conceived. "The metaphysical analysis of any specific subject-matter . . . is to be defined as a critical analysis of the distinctive traits of that subject-matter, of the intellectual instruments, the concepts and distinctions, for dealing with it, and of its implications for the nature of existence" (*NHE*, p. 137). This criticism is not aimed at those concepts as employed in their own universes of discourse. "What constitutes 'understanding' or 'intelligibility' in any particular case is defined by the end or use for which it is sought. . . . the test of whether it is adequately understood—of whether the understanding is adequate for its determinate function—is whether it can serve as an effective means to that determinate end" (*NHE*, p. 137). The end of metaphysics is not the same as that of the sciences. Metaphysical categories are more general than those of any other discipline, including physical science, and are designed to apply to existence insofar as it is disclosed in all forms of experience. "Knowledge [is] only one among many human activities" and the world is not limited to the subject matter of cognition (*NHE*, p. 11). "To be adequate, metaphysics would have to include also an analysis of other types of human experience besides those primarily cognitive . . ." (*NHE*, p. 135). Art is but one of these. It is imperative, therefore, to avoid "the traditional errors of metaphysics, identifying nature with the latest [scientific] formulations of its structural aspects," for to do so leaves us "facing the insoluble problem of explaining all the rest of the experienced world that is left over" (*NHE*, p. 4).

All the "basic types of human activity" are alike ways of dealing with existence. All have been generated and sustained by existence, and metaphysics seeks to embody in its conceptualizations the implications of the fact that existence can be so dealt with. "Philosophies of experience have taught most when they have tried to place the world stated and known in the context of the world experienced in other ways, in order to learn and state more" (*NHE*, p. 145). "The test of a metaphysical distinction or concept," Randall says, "consists in the illumination and clarification it can bring to a wide variety of subject-matters—ideally, if we are seeking complete generality, to any subject-matter" (*NHE*, p. 138). To recognize complete generality as only an ideal is not to invalidate the pursuit of generality as such. "Metaphysical discovery—or progress in metaphysical inquiry—depends on the finding of new ideas that can be so generalized with fruitful results" (*NHE*, p. 138).

Metaphysics seeks the traits of existence as such, of "what must be accepted, worked with, inquired into, manipulated, transformed, and reconstructed in practice and in art, controlled and enjoyed" (*NHE*, p. 147). These traits can be discriminated only in experience. Although inquiry (which is linguistic) can start only by examining discriminations already formulated in some way, metaphysical reflection, Randall maintains, "leads beyond that linguistic formulation to [the] subject-matter [of experience], to the world as 'directly' or 'immediately' experienced, to the context in which reflective experience takes place" (*NHE*, p. 145). If by 'immediate' experience be meant "brute," unconditioned awareness, this would be opaque and meaningless. In no sense does Randall take metaphysics, or any kind of knowledge, to be "grounded in immediacy" or justified in immediate experience. But the traits formulated in reflective experience are those discriminated in action and manipulation and guiding further action and manipulation. These discriminations and formulations can be tested in new experience to reveal more clearly the traits of that which is actively encountered. It is this encounter, now reconstructed and reconceptualized, that constitutes "direct" or "immediate" experience. (Randall always uses these names with quotation marks around them.)

That which is encountered and whose traits are discriminated, the subject matter of experience, is its context or situation, which Randall identifies with Substance, *ousía*. Though it may be more than this, Substance must be at least what it is encountered *as*. Experience is an interaction of factors in an ongoing situation, a process or, more precisely, processes in interaction. Substance, the Situation, is thus encountered as a "complex" or "cooperation of processes." Metaphysics attempts to discriminate the structure of that cooperation. But Substance is never encountered in general or as a whole: what we encounter is Substances, Situations. Substance is a multiplicity; its *formal* structure, its constitution, is that of a complex. And, discriminated in terms of our aims and interests, particular situations overlap. "Every complex process can be *analyzed* into cooperating processes" (*NHE*, pp. 174–75). To distinguish a particular process is to discriminate a complex of processes in interaction with others.

Every process or substance thus has a constitution, a formal structure. But the structure of a process qua process is a temporal, *functional* structure, in which one phase leads to another. It is a structure of means and ends. Experience and histories, including the history of culture, while at a higher level of formal organization, are no more illustrative of this than physicochemical processes. The formal structure of anything is the way it is put together, invariant from one situation to another. Its functional structure is its "nature," in the sense of the ways its formal structure permits it to behave. But the way it does behave in any context is a function of the structure of the environing situation as well. The formal structure is a means to its behaving or operating in the ways it does, a set of enabling conditions that interact with selected situational conditions. (This conception allows Randall to analyze values as traits of existence. Values are functional structures, discriminated in existence as the ways in which means lead to particular ends.)[15] But the distinction between means and ends, as Aristotle showed, is itself always relative to a specific context. What is means to an end in one situation is itself an end in another; the enabling conditions are themselves products of prior conditions, and vice versa.

This relativity, together with the complexity of all processes, all substances, means that "There is . . . no 'ultimate substance'; or 'ultimate context'; there is no 'absolute' or 'unconditioned' *überhaupt*." "Isolability," whether of contexts and their constitutents, or of the dependency relations of means and ends, "is always a relative and functional distinction in a determinate context or process" (*NHE*, p. 164). Therefore, contrary to the foundationalist principle, "metaphysical inquiry has no particular starting-point" (*NHE*, p. 194). As inquiry into the categories applicable in the analysis of substances, none of which is ultimate, metaphysics cannot be a search for any underlying or transcendent "Being" or fundamental "Reality." To contrast 'reality' with 'appearance' is to make "a distinction of value and importance, not one of existence." It is to distinguish "between the real as initially encountered and the real as analysed and understood" (*NHE*, p. 131). However encountered, no part of Substance—nothing that exists—is more or less real than any other.

Speaking of processes and components of processes, Randall uses the name 'factor' as a technical term of identification ('thing' is an informal substitute). Construing Substance in terms of process, his categories are five ways in which a factor may be functioning in the situations in which it is encountered. "There is nothing that can function in only one of these ways and no other, nothing that is only a single type" (*NHE*, p. 177). Moreover, the categorizations, each of which also expresses a grammatical function—a function in discourse—are linguistic alternatives, mutually translatable or convertible. A metaphysical analysis that identifies particular *Operations* (verbs) can also be formulated in terms of the *Powers* (nouns) those operations exemplify. What we can analyze as a *Way of Operating* (adverb) we can also analyze as a *Kind of Power* (adjective). Powers can be analyzed as ways of operating and vice versa. The category of *Connectives* includes signs, symbols, concepts, interpretations of all kinds. That they are produced and used by humans does not mean that they are "outside" nature, and, moreover, Randall finds Connectives to be species of more pervasive existential relations. They must be analyzed and appraised as ways of operating. "All Connectives are used to *do* certain definite things, to perform certain definite functions." Their "validity [is] to be judged and appraised by *how well* they perform their respective functions" (*NHE*, p. 269). A comparative value such as this, expressible grammatically as the comparative of an adverb, is a kind of power—a comparative power, a way of functioning in Substance, in an existential situation.

Randall analyzes *mind* in terms of all of these categories. In the course of this analysis, the "mental mirror" vanishes. Even the name 'mind' is rejected as a technical metaphysical term, because "it has become inextricably bound up with the ontological dualism and supernaturalism—what Dewey calls the 'extra-naturalism'— of modern philosophy." The idea of "a mind" as an immaterial substance or thing, Randall says, "seems to convert the operation of a 'power' into its own mechanism and conditions" (*NHE*, p. 219). All we can examine of such an entity, or of so-called mental processes, is specific, public modes of behavior: ways of operating. We have no privileged access even to our own "inner workings." "The appeal to 'immediate experience' is never the starting-point or the first step in metaphysical inquiry. It is always an intermediate stage in the process of criticising reflective experience—of criticising the experienced world already formulated in some scheme of interpretation" (*NHE*, p. 146). The immediate, as we have seen, is never given; it is only discoverable in analysis.

The metaphysical question concerning mind is, what are the ways of operating we call 'mental'? What are the factors that condition these operations?

> To construe 'Mind' as a unique kind of substance . . . is to make these conditioning factors wholly private and inaccessible, and to remove them from the possibility of any scientific investigation and analysis. It obscures all the cultural and environmental factors which are in reality necessary conditions of any 'functioning mentally'. (*NHE*, pp. 219–20)

'Mind' is most intelligible, Randall holds, construed as a power to act in certain ways (the power of 'operating mentally').[16] But what are those ways? Is it awareness or consciousness that distinguishes the mental? Randall finds this inadequate. Conceived as a quality, awareness is private and inaccessible. It is not impossible that oysters have some level of awareness, but we cannot tell. Nor do we find them behaving in ways we associate with mental functioning. Awareness can be conceived as itself a way of behaving or responding, but this gives us no sure basis of discrimination. If we arrange processes in a scale of increasing selectivity and specificity of response, for example, the attribution of "awareness" at a certain point along this scale must be arbitrary.

'Mind' is sometimes taken to be unique in having the power to function universally. Randall rejects this on the grounds that we encounter a rudimental universality, in the broadest sense of this term, in natural interactions. Every characteristic way of reacting, from chemical reactions to responding to signs and symbols, is an instance of universality. Operations, powers, are particular; *ways of* operating, *kinds of* power, are universal and are pervasive traits of our experienced world, not only of thought.

'Mind' has been identified historically with the power to know. But in what does this power consist? Perception is not knowledge but only "a stimulus to inquiry, or to the enjoyment and use of knowledge already gained." Knowing "is an active process, involving the use of many Connectives—hypotheses, ideas, and procedures." It is functioning intelligently, thinking, not vision, whether sensory or intellectual. If Mind is the "power to know," it "can be said to be the power to find 'intelligibility' or 'rationality'—the way things act, what a thing with a specific constitution or formal structure *can* do [its powers]." But then we know the "nature" of that thing, "the way it can act as a means to an operation or end" (*NHE*, p. 231). This we discover through experimentation, not through passive observation. The other side of intelligibility is control. To have made anything (any process) intelligible, to have control over it as a means to an end or ends, is to understand it. This power of understanding, Randall says, "is Mind in the fullest sense" (*NHE*, p. 232).

But, we may ask, what is it that *has* this power? *What* thinks, inquires, understands? The question conceals a trap. "To concentrate solely on the 'agent' or active mechanism involved in thinking, on the human thinker, leads to the neglect of the other necessary conditions present in the thinking situation and obscures the continuity between the process of thinking and other natural processes."[17] The question "What thinks?" is translated by Randall into the question "What are the different powers that cooperate in the process of thinking?" And the answer to that question must take into account all the factors in the thinking situation, not only the brain and nervous system, but "all those cultural and environmental factors which are equally necessary conditions of any 'mental situation', of any case of 'functioning mentally'" (*NHE*, p. 222). And not only these, not only language and other culture patterns, but also the intelligible structure of the subject matters encountered. The thinker, the "I" or "Self" or "person," is better understood as "individuality and personality," as "Substance individualized," "Substance personalized," a way of functioning continuous with its environmental context.

Intelligent activity is an interaction within that context. Mental functioning is a cooperation of powers in nature. Thus it is not an epiphenomenon. Understanding is a power, an instrument of control—control of experienced subject matters together with our ways of dealing with them. Inquiry, inherently critical, is the means of rational cultural change. Philosophical and metaphysical inquiry are phases in this process of change, instruments whereby our fundamental understandings and interpretations can be revised.

Randall's "metaphysics of cultural change" does not dictate how the institutions of culture are to be changed. It

> supplies an attitude, a perspective, and an intellectual method, for determining what must be done in each of the many complexly interrelated institutions of our changing culture, from metaphysics to the family, from epistemology to religion. What must be done will be clarified when that attitude and method are brought to bear upon the materials, traditional and revolutionary, of that changing culture itself. (*NHE*, p. 19)

Randall's own systematic philosophy must be understood as an intermediate step in this process of clarification, his contribution to an ongoing philosophic conversation designed to have consequences in the real world.

Notes

Presidential Address, The Society for the Advancement of American Philosophy, Pennsylvania State University, March 4, 1988. I am grateful to the late Emmanuel G. Mesthene for his suggestions concerning this paper.

1. Richard Rorty, *Philosophy and the Mirror of Nature* (Princeton: Princeton University Press, 1979), p. 381. Hereafter cited as *PMN*.

2. See, e.g., Arthur O. Lovejoy, *The Revolt against Dualism* (La Salle, Ill.: Open Court, 1930), chap. 5, "Mr. Whitehead and the Denial of Simple Location," and discussions of E. A. Burtt, G. H. Mead, A. E. Murphy, and the New Realists (passim).

3. George Herbert Mead, *Mind, Self and Society: From the Standpoint of a Social Behaviorist*, ed. C. W. Morris (Chicago: University of Chicago Press, 1934), p. 133. Hereafter cited as *MSS*.

4. See George Herbert Mead, *The Philosophy of the Act*, ed. C. W. Morris, et al., (Chicago: University of Chicago Press, 1938), pp. 94–95. Hereafter cited as *PA*.

5. In his contribution to a group effort to establish the principles of

this school, Walter P. Marvin bluntly asserts: "1. Epistemology is not logically fundamental. 2. There are many existential, as well as non-existential, propositions which are logically prior to epistemology." And in a footnote: "The terms 'knowledge,' 'consciousness', and 'experience' found in common sense and in psychology are not logically fundamental, but are logically subsequent to parts at least of a theory of reality that asserts the existence of terms and relations which are not consciousness or experience. E.g., the psychical is distinguished from the physical and the physiological. . . . [E]pistemology has not thus far made itself logically independent of psychology nor has it freed itself logically from the common-sense dualism of psychology. On the contrary, epistemology from Locke until today has been and has remained, in part at least, a branch of psychology." Edwin B. Holt, Walter T. Marvin, W. P. Montague, Ralph Barton Perry, Walter B. Pitkin, E. G. Spaulding, "The Program and First Platform of Six Realists," in Herbert W. Schneider, ed., *Sources of Contemporary Philosophical Realism in America* (Indianapolis and New York: Bobbs-Merrill, 1984), p. 37. First published in *Journal of Philosophy* 7, no. 15 (July 1910).

6. Sandra B. Rosenthal, *Speculative Pragmatism* (Amherst: University of Massachusetts Press, 1986). Hereafter cited as *SP*.

7. "The following epistemological discussions are not setting the framework for proving an external world or for showing how a subject can bridge the gap to know an object. Rather, such problems emerge as epistemological problems because epistemology has tended to ignore our primordial sense of ontological presence by splitting subject and object asunder" (*SP*, p. 21).

8. For want of space I omit discussion of Rosenthal's concept of "anteception" (experience in what she takes to be the broadest sense) and the "anteceptive field."

9. *SP*, p. 198. "To understand speculative pragmatism as philosophic system from within its own perspective is to view it not just as one more system in a tradition of systems in conflict, but rather as a system that recognizes that to understand itself, it must view itself as an emergent perspective that is an outgrowth of that tradition, and which in turn accounts for, or makes meaningful, that tradition through a reinterpretation of it as a past that yields, and is explained by, this novel emergent perspective" (*SP*, p. 197).

10. See my *Ordinal Naturalism: An Introduction to the Philosophy of Justus Buchler* (Lewisburg, Pa.: Bucknell University Press, 1983).

11. *PMN*, pp. 155, 140. Rorty takes "Sellars's criticism of the Myth of the Given" and Quine's criticism of the notion of truth by virtue of meaning as two detailed developments of this more general criticism [that the

epistemological tradition confused the causal process of acquiring knowledge with questions concerning its justification]" (*PMN*, p. 209).

12. "I shall be saying that the wholehearted behaviorism, naturalism, and physicalism I have been commending in earlier chapters help us avoid the self-deception of thinking that we possess a deep, hidden, metaphysically significant nature which makes us 'irreducibly' different from inkwells or atoms" (*PMN*, p. 373).

13. John Herman Randall, Jr., *Nature and Historical Experience: Essays in Naturalism and the Theory of History* (New York: Columbia University Press, 1958), pp. 150–51. Hereafter cited as *NHE*.

14. "I am attempting to restate Aristotle, with those modifications and additions suggested by the present state of metaphysical inquiry and its recent rapid progress. I am trying to extend the Aristotelian analysis of 'process' or *kinesis* by applying Dewey's analysis of 'the situation' and other similar analyses found in our recent philosophies of experience" (*NHE*, p. 149).

15. See *NHE*, p. 180.

16. Randall's view here bears comparison with that of Gilbert Ryle in *The Concept of Mind* (London: Hutchinson, 1949; paperback, New York: Barnes and Noble, 1949): " 'My mind' does not stand for another organ. It signifies my ability and proneness to do certain sorts of things, and not some piece of apparatus without which I could not or would not do them" (p. 168).

17. *NHE*, p. 221. "Strictly speaking, and in the full sense, Mind as a power belongs to the *process* of encountering, the process which includes the cooperation of all the various factors involved as necessary conditions in the mental situation. We can indeed *encounter* Mind as a power exhibited by the agent, the 'animal body' or human organism, taken as the locus of the 'active powers' involved. But we cannot hope to *understand* mind if we take it in isolation from all the other manifold powers and conditions involved in the thinking situation" (*NHE*, p. 221).

Ten

Metaphysics and Validation

KATHLEEN WALLACE

Metaphysics, it has been reputed, is dead, or has at least run out of things to say. Presumably at least some of us do not ascribe to such a view, even if we sometimes feel at a loss to articulate what it is that we do when we do metaphysics. I do not think that there are any easy answers to this, in part because I do not think we can overcome our perplexity on purely methodological grounds. In other words, in the spirit of Martin Heidegger, *what* metaphysics is, is itself a metaphysical question. In what follows, I first review a few key points in several contemporary approaches to metaphysics, namely, those of Richard Rorty, Nicholas Rescher, and Donald Davidson (section I). I then suggest an alternative nonfoundationalist way of looking at the matter (section II) and, by raising some of the questions involved in the issue of validation, indicate how this nonfoundationalist approach might be more fruitful (section III).

My approach is nonfoundationalist in two respects. It is based on a rejection of a Cartesian view for which the legitimacy of any inquiry, and therefore also metaphysics, depends on securely grounded self-evident starting points, which themselves cannot be doubted, revised, or affected by subsequent inquiry. On my view, the legitimacy of categories and arguments in metaphysics does not require epistemological certainty. On the contrary, validation in metaphysics is determined through the ongoing work of the categories, not their alleged irrefutability. Second, I reject the view that a metaphysical system of categories itself provides *the* foundation for all further query, or that its goal is to identify *the* foundation of Being.

Rather, I suggest in section II that metaphysics be looked at as a categorial perspective or framework, the goal of which is conceptual [re]-orientation.[1] In section III, I examine which *metaphysical* assumptions about the world and our knowledge of it we would have to revise or give up in order to account for the possibility of validation of any perspective, including that of metaphysics itself.[2] Specifically, if there is no foundational starting point, then validation has to be reconceptualized.

I

One recent approach argues that metaphysics is dead because its epistemological foundations are bankrupt. If it cannot be the case that all the competing universal claims of different metaphysical systems are true and if we have no way of deciding which are—because there is no perspicuous vantage point or secure foundation on the basis of which we could make a definitive assessment—then we may as well act as if none are or could be true. In other words, we should give up the enterprise altogether and reconceive philosophy in general as edifying discourse. This is the view, here only sketchily presented, of Rorty.[3]

Another approach is that of Rescher, who argues, not that no metaphysical claims or views are true, but that all are.[4] Each theory or conceptual system is true relative to itself. We can assess the superiority of one framework over another on "technical" or purely internal, but not on substantive, grounds. Each theory is basically self-contained, but what lends philosophy importance is that each theory is grappling in its own way with the "Big (pre-systematic) Issues" that are important to human beings.

Finally, there is a third approach that views metaphysics as the abstractive process of identifying the beliefs we all cannot help but hold as true about reality. These beliefs can be abstracted from language, since in order for successful communication to take place in speech, the speakers must share beliefs about the way the world is, and those beliefs are embedded in their linguistic utterances. This is the view of Davidson, who then further argues, against conceptual relativism or the incommensurability of theories, that the translatability of language implies that beliefs are shared by speakers of different languages (and, therefore, by analogy, that

there are shared beliefs between translatable conceptual frameworks).[5] Hence, Davidson would reject Rescher's self-referential
relativism of truth. However, what we should note as important to
my purposes is that metaphysics consists in abstracting and identifying the shared beliefs common to translatable languages. Metaphysics, then, is simply that which is collectively and distributively
believed (albeit compulsively) about the world.

Now, these are admittedly nutshell representations of views that
in all fairness are more complicated and subtle than I have just
characterized them. That notwithstanding, these views share three
common assumptions:

First, that validation in metaphysics is a function of method or
epistemology, and when those fail, so too does metaphysics.

Second, that philosophy in general and metaphysics in particular is not a discipline with distinctive aims and subject matter.

Third, that the only or primary cognitive value is truth.

Let us briefly examine why that is the case for each of the three
approaches just described.

Rorty's argument is that if there is no epistemological foundation
for certainty and truth, then there is no validity to the metaphysical
aim of trying to find *the* foundational, necessary, and universally
true theory about the world. But, notice that he accepts the criteria
for metaphysics of the very tradition against which he launches his
critique. He accepts the requirement that metaphysics be universal
and that it be validatable from a perspectiveless (necessary and universal) standpoint. Since that perspectivelessness does not seem
to be attainable, the metaphysical enterprise is devoid of meaning
and validity. But this does not follow at all. That *this conception*
of metaphysics as requiring epistemologically secure foundations
proves to be barren or wrong does not necessarily mean that metaphysics cannot be otherwise defined and practiced, even if you do
accept the impossibility of the perspectiveless, validating standpoint. Rorty's conclusion would be like saying cubism is barren,
therefore, painting is over, an exercise in futility. Metaphysics may
need to redefine what it means by universality and generality, and
hence, what count as validating conditions, but that one tradition
has not worked, or has run its course, does not entail that there
are no others and that we are reduced to edifying conversation.
To accept this conclusion is to give up the idea of philosophy or

metaphysics as a discipline. For on this view, philosophy, including metaphysics, makes no substantive intellectual contributions, but is purely commentative ("the edifying discourse") on other intellectual activity. Hence, there is really not much, if any, difference between philosophy and literary criticism or cultural commentary in general.

Part of the problem here, I might add, is that Rorty assumes that there is a model of metaphysics that is or ought to be prescriptive for metaphysics. He simply appropriates the model as he sees it of a dominant tradition in modern philosophy and argues that if the model fails, then so too does metaphysics. It is fair to ask on what grounds we should accept some model as legislative for all possible metaphysics (Immanuel Kant notwithstanding). This is not established by Rorty. That one approach has been historically dominant does not establish its right to function prescriptively, and certain contemporary tendencies to regard it as signaling the collapse of metaphysics may rather attest to a failure of conceptual imagination.

Rescher's approach reduces the disciplinary character of philosophy and metaphysics to a merely technical matter. As far as positive and distinctive intellectual contributions go, philosophy looks to be pretty gratuitous. There is no distinctive subject matter to metaphysics because ultimately all the philosophical conceptual frameworks are about *extra*-systematic, that is, pre- and therefore *non*philosophical "Big Issues." By the way, why this should be characteristic of *philosophical* but not scientific frameworks is not defended by Rescher. Anyway, Rescher concludes "that the boundaries between philosophy and non-philosophy (between philosophy and geography, say) are so murky that we would have to accept as a philosopher anyone who claims to be doing philosophy and whose discourse has some connection with the traditional issues of this field."[6]

But to say that any distinctively philosophical concept or concern, such as substance or the nature of possibility, is only a form of some "big issue," but that it is the Big Issue that is important, is again to abandon philosophy. The nonphilosopher and more specifically the nonmetaphysician does not worry about or attempt to understand the nature of possibility *as such*, even though, of course, everyone makes use of or sometimes even refers to some idea or other of possibility. This continuity between abstract and general metaphysical concepts and their everyday use or presence in familiar contexts is deceptive. It does not entail that metaphysics is merely an abstraction from what goes on and is otherwise of concern to everyone. Rather, it accounts for both the difficulty in defining the subject matter of metaphysics and the potentially wide accessibility of metaphysical ideas to the nonphilosopher.

Rescher's view would also entail that the subject matter of philosophy never changes because the "Big Issues" do not. But that cannot be right. Whatever else Aristotle did, he also changed the subject matter and basic issues of philosophy by criticizing and transcending pre-Socratic presuppositions. René Descartes and Thomas Hobbes did the same to Aristotelianism and in doing so changed philosophy. Justus Buchler's ordinal metaphysics effects a similar kind of transcendence of the metaphysics of modern philosophy.[7] In each case the metaphysical system produced renders intelligible the world in some, indeed, many respects. The subsequent critical or commentative question is how well rendered is the world by the terms or categories. Both the categories and their systematic interrelation *and* the world as articulated by the categories are Aristotle's, Descartes's, Hobbes's or Buchler's, and other philosophers' subject matter, not the world "in itself" nor the morally gripping Big Issues of human life in general.

Finally, Davidson assumes that we can identify shared beliefs about reality through the right analysis of language and the truth conditions of sentences. If the beliefs are sufficiently widespread and function as the basis of the possibility of communication that can be successful only on the assumption that we do share true beliefs, then that is grounds for regarding them as being true about the world. Whether this is true or not I do not know, but I am content to let the matter remain unresolved here. What his argument entails is that the identification of what everyone believes in common as true satisfies the metaphysical requirement of generality.

Now, Davidson is right that generality is a legitimate, indeed characteristic, aim of metaphysics, but he has mislocated it. It is not, as he suggests, a matter of how widespread even true beliefs are, but of formulating categories that articulate the world or features of it at a high level of generality or encompassment. Generality, then, has to do with the kind of concepts and distinctions made, and I warrant that recognition of these, let alone belief, is rather thinly spread.

There are three points from the preceding discussion of some contemporary views of metaphysics that are worth extracting and preserving:

1. The possibility of metaphysics does not require a perspective-less epistemological foundation, as if one could guarantee the conditions of validation before even starting the enterprise.
2. If validation in metaphysics allows for the possibility that more than one metaphysical view has legitimacy, then validation in metaphysics may have to involve more than simply an appeal to the criterion of truth.
3. Generality, in at least some sense, is characteristic of metaphysics.

II

What I would like to now do is shift our ground and offer a positive alternative to these views of metaphysics. I suggest that we consider metaphysics as the constructing of a categorial framework. What would this commit us to?

First, it would commit us to the view that metaphysics is not merely investigating or discovering "the" metaphysical facts or beliefs, but is itself an active contributor of subject matter, namely, the categories themselves and indirectly, that dimension of the world which those categories make intelligible. Second, this would entail that metaphysics is a function as well as a subject matter—in other words, metaphysics is not equivalent to general ontology, but is the function of constructing categories at a given level of generality. So, it would be intelligible to say that one could do a metaphysics of general ontology, a metaphysics of human nature, of consciousness, of God and of society, to name a few. Generality would have to mean both the generality of the subject matter as well as adequate encompassment by the categories. So, on the one hand, it makes sense to do a metaphysics of human nature, but not of fingernails, and on the other, the categories should always admit of exemplification at their level. So, while human beings qua human should exemplify categories of a metaphysics of human nature, qua being they should also exemplify the categories of ontology, since the categories of general ontology should never fail of exemplification whatever the being. In other words, categories of general ontology should be exemplified by any being; categories of human nature should be pervasively exemplified by human beings.[8]

But perhaps we are getting ahead of the game here. What is a categorial framework? What does it aim for—besides generality of a certain kind? Are we committing the sin we accused Rorty of, namely, attempting to prescribe what any metaphysics ought to be? Well, perhaps, but the only way to tell whether a distinction is legislative or generic, that is, identifying a kind of philosophic function, is by following out what it would commit us to. If we admit that metaphysics is the constructing of a categorial framework, would we be committed to a sort of hopeless relativism and have rendered moot the question of validation?

I think it would be very difficult to say what a category is without running into the prescriptive question. So, for the moment, I would like to approach the question of what a categorial framework is—not by listing traits, as Stephan Korner, for example, does in his *Categorial Frameworks* (New York, 1984)—but obliquely, by asking what is its purpose?

If it is a framework, it must be a way of mapping the world in a given respect, rather than an explanation of the world. In other words, metaphysics might frame the conceptual terms of an explanatory theory without itself being such a theory. For example, Aristotle notwithstanding, the goal of metaphysics is not to explain the origin of life as such, or how quarks behave; rather, its aim would be to articulate what life is in its most general terms, or to figure out what causality is. Aristotle, the biologist and scientist, may have been interested in biological explanations, but as a metaphysician he moves to the abstractive and generalizing mode of formulating concepts and categories to frame the analysis and to transpose it to a broader conceptual level. The practice and discoveries of science may supply evidence showing that the concept of causality that had been presupposed is defective or perhaps not sufficiently general, but the question then posed, what is causality, is a metaphysical one.

But what is categorial framing? What does it do? I am going to borrow Buchler's notion of "conceptual orientation" to help advance the discussion at this point.[9] When we frame with concepts we are orienting—or reorienting—ourselves. A framework defines a standpoint from which we get our bearings conceptually and gives direction to further inquiry. To construct a framework, or a conceptual orientation, is not necessarily to make a truth claim. Rather, it can be better understood if we think of Plato for a moment and consider the function of myth and allegory.

In the following I am going to refer to Plato to help advance my points about the idea of conceptual orientation. I am not asserting here an interpretation of Plato for consideration by Plato scholars. In general the use of other philosophers in this essay is primarily as illustrative of a theoretical point and not with the systematic integrity of their works as such.

The function of myth and allegory is to effect a conceptual reorientation within a dialogue and to show how a subject can be introduced or approached obliquely rather than by attempting to define it directly.

In the *Republic* the idea of the Good cannot be plausibly established on the basis of the dialectic as it had thus far—up to book VI —been argued. Rather, Plato introduces it as a new and distinct concept through the image of the divided line and the allegory of the cave. He is constructing a new way of conceptualizing the issues by placing them in another context that transforms the issues, raises the discussion to a new level, and hence redirects and reanimates the inquiry. Neither the simile nor the allegory is true; nor are they false. But neither are they merely self-referential nor self-justifying. Their validity depends on how well they reconceptualize or reorient things, on what [new] possibilities of understanding they create and which ones they foreclose. The only way to tell how well they do any of that is through their actualization, namely, by following out the movement of thought they generate and make possible. Having initiated it, the concepts introduced also enter into a new or transformed inferential process that is pursued in the sections following.

The idea of the Good reorients the inquiry into whether the just person is the happy person. First, it reveals the reality of ideals, not as the conclusion of argument, but rather as "foundational" to further query. That is, they are not necessary for natural life—for life in the first state constructed in books III and IV—for survival, or for life in the cave, but they are indispensable for genuine improvement, for getting out of the cave. Second, through the idea of the Good as the vitalizing principle of justice, Plato can now argue that justice is not merely a matter of order or the equilibrium of the parts of the city on purely natural or eugenic grounds, but that it depends on what the animating ideal of order is. Hence, Plato is able to show that the more remote from the ideal—the genuinely just—order, the more unhappy the society and the soul, as in the case of the tyrant.

Plato effects another such conceptual transformation in the *Phaedrus*. Recall that the third speech on love is introduced first through a redefinition of madness as divine and hence, beneficial, rather than merely uncontrollable desire. This is followed immediately by the myth of the charioteer and his horses. The myth reconceptualizes the nature of the soul, allowing Plato to transform the understanding of love from desire of possession to desire for the good through and for another. Hence, from the preceding discussion of love as something to be positively avoided because it produces only misery, obsession, and lack of control, love becomes the soul's own good, enabling it to strive for the good.

The myth serves at least two functions.[10] One is to reorient and transform the terms of our understanding. The second is to *exhibit*, not offer a truth claim about, features of the soul and of love.

In the *Republic* it is precisely because Plato's point, that the just man is also the happy man, contravenes the assumptions and opinions of Socrates's interlocutors that Plato would not be likely to effect a conceptual reorientation by simply refuting or ridiculing their assumptions (much as Socrates fails to effect a transformation, for example, in Euthyphro, with whom the purpose of the dialogue was, of course, rather different). This is not merely a matter of rhetoric or persuasion. Rather, it is a methodological and substantive point about philosophy in general and here about metaphysics in particular. Philosophy's intellectual contribution is substantive and constructive as well as critical. It introduces a subject matter— concepts, ideas, and categories. They map or frame the world or some portion or dimension of it, in order to orient or reorient the way we think about it, to create new possibilities for interrogation while cutting off others.

I have used Plato to help articulate what conceptual construction and orientation could mean for two reasons:

First, one of the roles Plato assigns to myth, metaphor, allegory exemplifies how a conceptual construction can effect a conceptual orientation;

Second, the explicit use by Plato of literary devices and constructions helps to focus our attention on the idea that in shaping concepts and categories, philosophy, and more specifically, metaphysics, *exhibits* some feature, relation, dimension, or possibility in or of the world, rather than asserts a truth claim.

But, of course, a myth, an allegory, or a metaphor is not a category, although Plato is not the only philosopher who attempts to introduce concepts and shape categorial insights through explicit literary devices. George Santayana is at least one other philosopher who immediately comes to my mind. Philosophers are, however, more accustomed to thinking of categories in terms of universal principles and concepts. This brings us to a second aim of metaphysics—namely, the goal of achieving generality. We are not abandoning our first point, that metaphysics aims for conceptual orientation, but are adding that it seeks to do so at a general level. Aristotle and Kant were each introducing a categorial system in order to effect a reorientation in our understanding. Aristotle is thought of as having done so comprehensively. If nothing else, Aristotle established the legitimacy and desirability of categorial generality as a metaphysical goal. Aristotle's categories are not, however, merely "empirical generalizations," along the order of "all crows are black." The categories are substantively new concepts, the result of both abstractive and constructive processes. Aristotle's own investigative proclivities exemplify a method and goal of validation somewhat different from Plato's. Aristotle is interested in establishing the generality of his categorial distinctions by showing their distributive pervasiveness. (Note, however, that he is never able to demonstrate their collective completeness.) Thus, Aristotle's method is "empirical" and is evidentially directed to establishing the comprehensiveness of the conceptual orientation he is effecting. Plato, I think, was more interested in effecting the conceptual orientation and exhibiting how an inferential or theoretical process could be redirected, enriched, and made more fruitful and satisfying.

But let us pursue the notion of generality for a moment. What is it? This is, of course, very complicated. Minimally, generality implies comprehensiveness or inclusiveness. At the level of general ontology, presumably generality would mean universality of some kind. The "of some kind" is important because if metaphysics, even at the level of general ontology, is the shaping of a categorial framework, then it is still *a* framework or perspective and therefore, cannot be literally all-inclusive. But let me hold this point until section III and here make two other points about generality. First, generality cannot be so vague as to admit of no distinctions. "Everything is" would be very general, but very useless philosophically. Generality, at least as far as categories go, must involve the making of distinctions. Therefore, generality must mean *relevant* or apt generality. If this is the case, then obviously not every true belief—no matter how widely shared—will constitute a metaphysical insight. We all believe "there are events" or accept as true that "human beings are featherless bipeds." But, the first is too isolated to function as a category or a basis for further distinctions. The second may be true, but it fails metaphysically because it does not distinguish the metaphysically relevant traits. What justifies my saying that it is not metaphysically apt? Certainly not some empirical observation that finds human beings who are feathered bipeds, but the theoretical point that it fails to orient the analysis or understanding of what is distinctive of human beings, or that it fails to stimulate further discourse.

Partially as an aside, but also to forestall the criticism that I fail to provide criteria of relevance: I cannot really offer *the* criteria for what count as apt or relevant general traits. Whether a categorial distinction is made compelling will depend on how it is articulated and what kind of inquiry it fosters and enhances. I think that in metaphysics, as in art, we may not know in advance what count as *the* legitimate or relevant criteria of inclusion. Aristotle's categories may "respond" to those of his predecessors, but they also required inventive insight on Aristotle's part, just as the myth or the allegory had to be invented by Plato.[11] I do not think that prior to Plato's or Aristotle's query we could have prescribed or legislated what they ought to have done or achieved. Metaphysics in the contemporary world has more predecessors than either Plato or Aristotle did.[12] But even so, I am very hesitant to announce what *the* task of a specific metaphysics is or ought to be, because it depends on how a philosopher can define it. But I am suggesting that however that task is conceived and articulated by a thinker, its aim will be conceptual orientation or reorientation at a high level of generality.

Second, if by generality we mean relevant generality, and if we accept the idea that metaphysics is supposed to make and promote the further making of distinctions, whatever the level of generality, then metaphysics requires interrelated concepts or categories. Aristotle could not have gotten very far with just the concept of *ousía;* he had to shape a whole system of categories that together articulate each other and what *ousía* means. Just as one true belief does not a categorial distinction make, so too does a catalogue of true beliefs no metaphysical framework make. There is a good reason why metaphysics tends to be *systematic* in character. It is not a matter of circularity or mere consistency, but of how well the categories and concepts shape a framework. How well the framework hangs together, whether its underlying principles or systematic commitments are commensurate with one another, whether a distinction is arbitrary or violates another distinction or principle within the system, these are questions concerning the dimension of what I would call *systematic resonance*. Validation of this dimension may be largely nonevidential and non-"empirical." But the point I am making here is that the kind of generality involved in metaphysics seems to require that it be systematic in at least some sense or degree.

So far I have advanced the following suggestions about metaphysics:

1. Metaphysics is the constructing of a categorial framework.
2. It has the aim of achieving conceptual orientation or reorientation and generality or comprehensiveness.
3. A category or framework is neither true nor false.
4. Metaphysical categories function as a basis for making distinctions (classification itself being a kind of distinction). Therefore, metaphysics involves the dimension of systematic resonance or the hanging together of the categories and principles.

Let me point out the implications of what I have thus far been advancing. If metaphysics is the shaping of a categorial framework, then it is a perspective, albeit one at a high level of generality. If the goal is conceptual [re-]orientation, then when I say that categories function as the basis for making distinctions, that means they open up and introduce possibilities of explanation and articulation, not that they necessarily "ground" every subsequent distinction. On the other hand, the generality of metaphysical categories is such that although they do not "ground" every less general concept or inquiry, they should be exemplified by categories and concepts of lesser generality.[13] There is a great deal more that can be said about metaphysics. We will have to bracket those other possibilities for now if we are going to move to the question of validation.

III

Validation is not a dimension of experience or of metaphysics that we can evade. It is a human compulsion to seek it. It matters to us whether we get it right or not, whether our choices are right or wrong, whether our professed goals and allegiances are good or not. If these goals are legitimate, then how do we conceptualize the terms in which we frame the issues? Is there a way to account for legitimate diversity *and* for the compulsive effects of the world, without which validation would reduce to mere psychological need or cultural agreement and understanding?

I am not equating validation with truth, logical validity, or empirical verification. These are species of validation, but the concept is broader than these options would suggest. Validation is not equivalent to verification. The latter would be a species of the former, but by no means the only or even the most important form validation can take. I think metaphysically or ontologically we would have to say that validation is a species of actualization; what kind will depend on what is being validated and in what contexts. If this is right, then validation does not necessarily gain us finality. With respect to metaphysics—as with any other human endeavor—this would also entail that validation may be incomplete.[14] We may be able to exhaust evidence in a given respect, where evidence is the relevant consideration, but we could never claim to have completely realized all its possibilities, since these are not defined by a system or author alone, but are a function of the ideas entering into relation with other ideas and in new perspectives of inquiry. An idea or a system of ideas may die a timely or an untimely death, but if this is so, whether it be the result of accidents of fate or of more deliberate events, it would have to be due as much to the fact that possibilities expire or cease to arise for it as that all its possibilities had been actualized—as if they had all been defined in advance in the first place—and the product "completed."

Second, validation in metaphysics is not a matter of identifying *the* correct method, for gathering evidence or anything else, because first, unlike science, metaphysics not only tolerates but encourages methodic diversity,[15] and second, not all validation in metaphysics is evidential, as for example, with respect to the dimension of what I called systematic resonance. I have, of course, not provided justification of the first. Although I think that the history of metaphysics would bear me out on this, it is also the case that methodic diversity follows from the twofold aim of conceptual construction and [re-]orientation. Metaphysical systems and ideas stimulate, initiate, interpret, and respond to one another, but they do not aim for the ideal of cumulative accretion into unified and encompassing explanatory theory.[16]

If we cannot prescribe *the* steps or *the* evidence that would validate a metaphysical view, what can we say about validation? In the remainder of this essay I will suggest some of the conditions that make validation possible and the implications for metaphysical validation. I focus on the following:

1. What saves the aim of achieving conceptual orientation from mere relativism where any one system would be as good as any other?
2. How is generality validated?
3. Whether it is evidential or not, is validation suspect if it is not "empirical"?

If we think back to my initial discussions of Rorty and Rescher, my suggestion that metaphysics is the construction of a categorial framework that defines or effects a conceptual orientation would seem to play right into their hands and implicate me in either a sort of intellectual nihilism (as with Rorty) or relativism (as with

Rescher). But their conclusions rest on several metaphysical dogmas:

1. That mind—and its ideas, concepts, and so forth—is radically different from the [rest of the] world and is hidden or cut off from the [rest of the] world. Another way of putting this would be to say that perspectives are constituted independently of the world. As a corollary to this,
2. That there is a way the world is that is wholly independent of mind's perspective, and therefore we have no way of ascertaining if our perspective has anything to do with the way the world is since we cannot get out of mind and its perspectives. And
3. Knowledge is a function of mind and consists in achieving truth.

Whatever mind is—and I am not offering any definitions, although I am doubtful that it is a thing or an entity of some kind— there is no evidence that "it" is so distinct from other beings in the world as to be unrelated to or uninfluenced by them. There is no evidence that supports the view that the world as we know it is so radically different from the world as it is in at least some respect. A belief that the world is flat is wrong, but for those who once held it, the belief was not not based on facts. Once the sphere of relevant facts was widened, the belief was abandoned because the world turned out to be different than the more limited range of facts about the world suggested. The original belief was wrong, even when it was consistent with the available perceptual evidence, because the sphere of relevant facts had not been appropriately identified. More accurately, the world in one respect, namely, as it appears in perceptual experience, *is* flat. The perceptual experience is not wrong. Rather, the mistaken belief consists in the inappropriate generalization of traits of the world in one respect to the world in other respects. Beliefs or theories that are eventually abandoned are not merely products of mind. They are about the world even if only in limited contexts or pragmatic respects. Or consider David Hume's argument that we never observe causation or necessary connection. That does not entail that what we believe is merely or only a product of our minds. The idea of causation, even if we do not observe it, may give us knowledge insofar as it enables us to understand and manipulate the world in ways that we would not otherwise be able to do. That is a form of validation, albeit not one based on a notion of empirical verification of a belief as true.

However bizarre, biased, or arbitrary some ideas or beliefs may seem to be, they are not evidence that mind is not part of the world or is cut off from the way the world is, but rather are evidence that the world is plurally determinate, and in different contexts and relations, features of it may produce different results. The bag lady living on the hot-air vent and carrying on arguments with nonexistent people is not cut off from the world but has assimilated parts of it and is responding to other parts of it in a unique way. However demented she may, sadly, be, her mind is in and of the world as much as yours or mine is. So, of course, are the contents of her ravings. Her perspective may be highly restricted, disconnected from other perspectives and resistant to evidence, but I do not think that it entails that mind is cut off from the world. My grandmother who watches on television a golf match that took place in Arizona and then reports to my cousin when he subsequently visits that she is exhausted, "weak in the pins," from having just returned from Arizona where she went to see this golf match—true story, by the way—is not cut off from the world but is assimilating and manipulating it in a unique way. Does her belief have nothing to do with the way the world is? No, of course not—there was a golf match in Arizona, and there even was a sense in which she was there, even if she got it wrong in exactly which sense.

I am not here defending the bag lady's or my grandmother's sanity, but only pointing out that even highly unusual views of the world and of one's participation in it are not a product of mind alone, but of a relation between the self and the world. In fact, the necessary condition for ascertaining that both the bag lady and my grandmother are wrong, is that the world is not inaccessible to us. My cousin and I both know with certainty that my grandmother did not go to Arizona in the spatiotemporal sense. How do we know that we are right and she is wrong? Because we have unrestricted access to the space-time world in the relevant respects and she, because of the deteriorating effects of old age, does not; second, because we have the power of critical self-reflexiveness and she, like the bag lady, does not; and finally, her belief is impotent. She would be unable to manipulate the world in some way that would support her belief and persuade others of its correctness, whereas my cousin and I can do just that with respect to ours. Therefore, we can claim knowledge and she cannot. Validation of belief does not require perspectivelessness, but access to the relevant ones. Nor does the fact that validation is perspectival entail that everything is equally valid.

The possibility of validation depends on

1. the fact that a perspective itself is already a relation between the self and the world, not a box that the self alone constitutes and in which it is contained, and
2. the extent to which we can occupy and move between multiple perspectives and discriminate the right or relevant ones.

Therefore, the possibility of validation does not require the securing of an absolute foundation or perspective, but rather the ability and willingness to identify and "move into" the relevant perspectives. In other words, I am suggesting that no single perspective may be sufficient to validate the truth of a claim, the aptness of a concept, or the correctness of an insight. At this point, we would also be in a position to formulate why Davidson may be on to something about true beliefs, even if not about metaphysics. Namely, the translatability criterion for shared beliefs can be rendered, in ontological terms, as recurrent validation through multiple perspectives. In other words, the recurrence of a given belief in a variety of *relevant* perspectives constitutes cumulative evidence of its correctness, even though recurrent presence alone may not be sufficient to establish truth. It might still require further testing in the relevant perspectives or respects. The criterion here is not mere invariance, but recurrence in the relevant respects. Validation, then, does not consist in conformity of a belief to invariant, mind-independent, or nonperspectival traits. We would be unable to recognize such conformity. Rather, the only rational assumption is that the world does not cease to be itself in relation to us as knowers or inquirers. The flatness of the world in a perceptual experience is a trait of the world; the world is in relation to visual perception and has traits in virtue of that relation. Other human perspectives may not have such direct or literal relation to the spatiotemporal, public world we normally think of as "the world," to wit, my grandmother's and the bag lady's. But, however we interpret their perspectives, they are not wholly mind determined. And whatever else validation consists in, it is not nonrelative, but "relative to" or "related in the relevant respects."

Rather than its being the case that our mental constructs or our conceptual frameworks erect a barrier between us and the world, it seems to me that they are just as, if not more than, likely to reveal dimensions of the world that had hitherto or otherwise not been available to us. Hypotheses in science function in this way. A metaphysician who shapes a categorial framework, as well as the scientist who searches for the right explanation, is compelled by the world or by dimensions of it. The one looks for conceptual understanding; the other, an explanation. But, unlike the experimenting scientist, who aims to have her or his conclusions further compelled by specific facts to produce the right answer, the metaphysician's compulsion produces a beginning, not an end.[17] The metaphysician is aiming to push the terms of conceptualization in one direction rather than another. Whether the product, the categorial scheme, is compelling in pushing its conceptual orientation has to be tested, like Plato's allegory, by seeing how it functions in a variety of perspectives.

Validation of the allegory of the cave consists in how it advances understanding of education, knowledge of the good, the possibility, or rather, impossibility, of the philosopher-king, the discussion of ideal and degenerate states. These are issues germane not only to Plato's dialogue but to a more general understanding of education, the tension between the intellectual and the political life, and the tension between the moral and the political life. Nor were Plato's allegories and myths shaped in a vacuum. Yes, they are Plato's constructions, but they were also compelled by social, political, and human realities that Plato presumably felt he could not ignore and that cried out to be made intelligible.

The point of this somewhat digressive discussion is that there is no reason to assume that we have given away the game to the relativists or the nihilists by suggesting that metaphysics is a conceptual framework. Rather, the possibility of validation depends on giving up the dogmas, one, that mind is cut off from reality, and two, that there is "the" way the world is that our admittedly perspectival knowledge cannot know.[18] Not only can our perspectives reveal something about the ways the world is in a variety of respects, but the world, as Charles S. Peirce said, compels us. I would go so far as to say that even that poor bag lady is being compelled by dimensions of the world, in her case, let us say, by poverty, disease, deprivation of privacy, harassment, and the like. Her garbled harangues may be better understood as exhibiting her distress and isolation rather than as assertions to or about her imaginary interlocutors. And my grandmother is exhibiting her dislike for the immobility that old age has forced upon her by traveling imaginatively.

We produce our ideas and frameworks. But neither do we do so in a vacuum, nor does the fact that we produce them entail that in so doing we also produce the world, much less the only version of it that we can know. Metaphysics is not mere speculative fabrication. Sometimes speculation is unfocused, sometimes it is propelled by awareness of ignorance or a gnawing dissatisfaction with prevailing ways of categorizing or a restless craving to transform the scope of analysis and understanding. So, in metaphysics, the question may well be whether the proposed transformation or orientation is intellectually compelling, rather than whether it is *the* right explanation. Are the distinctions made soundly formulated? Can they be made compelling to anyone else? Are they qualified in the right respects, or are they overgeneralized? Are they sufficiently general? Are they apt distinctions when generalized? All this and more can and ought to be asked. But, to assume, as both Rorty and Rescher do, that validation is impossible because we cannot get out of mind's perspective, that we have no access to evidence or other perspectives and that communication is impossible, rests on a failure to recognize the compulsive element in belief, knowledge, and experience. To repeat, it seems to me that Peirce is right. There is a limit to how far and how long we can go purely on the basis of preference before the world—whether in the form of other people, events, facts, failures to get desired results, or whatever—forces itself upon us.

The third dogma that needs to be exposed is the assumption that the only cognitively and therefore philosophically relevant value is truth and that the only knowledge that counts as knowledge is the having of true beliefs.[19]

It seems to me that I know something when I understand what

Plato's allegory of the cave *exhibits*. Henry Moore's knowledge of women's bodies is not at all a matter of true belief but is revealed and grasped exhibitively in his sculptures. Mozart's knowledge of human feeling, emotion, and motivation is exhibited musically.[20] The swimmer's knowledge of the distance at which to begin the underwater flip; lovers' knowledge of one another's characters. The swimmer enacts it; the lover anticipates a reaction or a mood or has a tactile knowledge of what arouses or calms.[21] Most of these are not a matter of truth, although there is a difference between getting it right and getting it wrong. Does it count as knowledge only if it can be translated into true assertion? I think not, and in fact in the translation into another form much of the cognitive value may be lost.

It is important to recognize that knowledge and cognitive value are broader than truth, because otherwise there is a great deal in human experience and in philosophy as well that would be misunderstood or underrated. What then is knowledge? It must be a power of manipulation of some kind—of concepts and ideas, of stone, musical notes, one's own actions. Sometimes the manipulation may be primarily [self-]reflexive, as perhaps in cases of self-examination.[22]

So, what does all this have to do with validation in metaphysics and specifically of conceptual orientation? Well, if we are willing to give up the three dogmas, then a metaphysical system is not *merely* a mental construction but is potentially a means to enable us to understand and manipulate dimensions of the world, and it may give us knowledge, even if the system as such is not true. In other words, we have not necessarily cheapened cognitive value of metaphysics by allowing this. A categorial system can render intelligible in a variety of ways, both by exhibiting dimensions of the world through its concepts and principles, as Plato exhibits a set of ideas in the allegory, as well as by the assertions it supports or would commit us to.

If there are "competing" metaphysical views—say, materialism and idealism—that do not seem to be able to outright refute one another, it may be because each is exhibiting the world in a different way and like Plato's allegories are just different, but not in competition for our allegiance. But, of course, that cannot be the whole story, that cannot be all right, because even if we were to accept the idea that as conceptual orientations they are neither true nor false, still we want to be able to determine if one is better than another. And, even if we accept the idea that metaphysics itself is multidimensional, still there are superior and inferior metaphysical systems. I say superior and inferior, because a system may be surpassed without necessarily being refuted. How can we evaluate it?

Well, if categories make distinctions and together in a system function as a basis for making further distinctions, then we can assess whether the distinctions the system supports or requires are apt. So, for example, on Hobbes's materialistic metaphysics, a painting would be nothing but bodies in motion. Now, this is either false or not apt as an ontological classification, or, as I think, both. But is this a limitation in my thinking? Not quite. Even if neither of these is just revealed by the painting as a fact, we can show what such a classificatory scheme presupposes and what it would commit us to saying about paintings. And, even if a Hobbes were to say, "but that's all it *really* is, everything else about a painting being secondary," you could still show that the materialist's metaphysical commitment or compulsion (which I would call a kind of reductionist foundationalism) comes with a high price, for example, because its assumptions generate paradoxes. Even if you do not persuade the materialist (who may persist in the metaphysical allegiance on nonevidential grounds—for example, because of a commitment to a methodological standard of testability by "the facts") or *refute* materialism as such, you could show that if the aim is intelligibility and *apt* generality, then it ought to be surpassed, that is, abandoned for a view that would provide a more just basis for classifying and distinguishing beings. You can do so, of course, only from another perspective, but that is the point. For the metaphysical perspective, such a classification may be too restricted or may generate paradoxes, even if *when restricted* to the perspective of the physicist, the classification identifies traits relevant to that perspective of inquiry.

Or, on another tack altogether, one can show that categorial distinctions themselves are not compelling, as might be said of some of Alfred North Whitehead's many categories. Sometimes categories are conceptual cul-de-sacs, as is Santayana's concept of substance. Sometimes the principles of a system generate and support paradoxes. These could be "internal"—as with Whitehead's concept of God—or "external"—as when a metaphysical scheme would support or require claims that contradict established scientific theory. Thus, even if the system is neither true nor false, it supports and is either reinforced by the true claims or undermined by the false ones that it supports. Whether it is a matter of proof or disproof, in any case, we can show why a metaphysical system does not get it right, and the respects in which it does not. That a metaphysical system is "coordinated" with established scientific theory contributes to the validation of and cognitive value of the metaphysical system, although it does not guarantee its validation or value with respect to a new context of scientific inquiry, or when there is what Kuhn calls a paradigm shift. But one of the strengths of a metaphysical system will consist in its persisting or recurrent power to interpret, to move with paradigm shifts or possibly even to facilitate them. If, on the other hand, a metaphysical system stands or falls on the basis of a given scientific outlook, it may be too restricted in its categories and commitments and hence will be simply abandoned.

Another dimension to validation in metaphysics consists in a process similar to what Plato does with myth. Myth—like a categorial system—introduces a conceptual orientation, but whether it is any good or not is determined by following out the ideas and distinctions it makes and seeing where you end up. Sometimes you find out that it is right, in at least some respects, by what it allows you to analyze conceptually, as in the *Republic* and the *Phaedrus*, and sometimes you discover that it is wrong, or deficient, or needs to be transcended, as with the first "noble lie" in the *Republic*. Whether Plato's conclusions made on the basis of the orientation are right or not is determinable by reenacting the process for ourselves, which we do when we study the dialogue, examining what, if any, paradoxes are generated, whether further distinctions and analyses are apt, compelling, and the like.

Much of what I have just cited—aptness of generalization, generation of paradoxes, noncontradiction of established scientific theory, dialectical consequences, other distinctions the categories allow one to make—does not sound much like validation. But that is because we are accustomed to thinking of it in "empirical" terms, as evidential verification, bringing ideas to the table of the "facts."

This brings me to another of the three issues involved in validation that I said I wanted to address: Whether it is evidential or not, is validation suspect if it is not also "empirical"? This issue is not wholly separable from that of generality, which we had suspended discussion of in section II and which we can now bring back into the discussion.

Because of the level of generality typically involved in metaphysics, whether a particular metaphysical scheme renders the world intelligible or not can be answered at least in part by appeal to conceptual and dialectical evidence—what does it allow us to analyze, to understand at perhaps very abstract and theoretical levels? This is not a defect of metaphysics, but one of its functions. I referred earlier to the metaphysician's concern with the nature of possibility. A sufficiently general and apt conception of possibility should be exemplified by any possibility. But possibility as such is a rather abstract concept, and its connection with and exemplification by "facts" or particular possibilities may be somewhat remote, and in any case not something we can simply point to as if the aptness of the general concept were immediately obvious as, say, under standard optical conditions is the color of a dress. Rather, it may take a great deal of analysis and theoretical work to get to the point where the categorial distinction is recognized as relevant, as making something about the world in more concrete terms or respects intelligible. At the level of general ontology anything can count as evidence, but that it does depends on whether it is aptly analyzed. There are no raw "facts" that will just step forward and apprise us of their suitability, like eligible bachelors announcing themselves to the right girl, or, in this case, category.

Moroever, what if you are trying to render intelligible or establish the reality and influence of ideals or of love—as Plato was in the *Republic* and the *Phaedrus*? What "facts" would qualify as validating or disconfirming the allegory—or the orientation—in these cases? There are many issues in metaphysics that are not empirical at all, or at least not on the more common appellation of the term: whether there are ontological simples, the nature of possibility, as I said, or of necessity, whether there are eternal possibilities, the nature of God (insofar as that is a categorial rather than a dogmatic question). You cannot just point to some factual example to confirm or validate the categorial analysis. Spinoza tried to show how the consequential nature of God could render intelligible human emotional and moral life and ultimately religious experience by being its necessary and animating condition.[23] If you want to show that Spinoza's conception of God is deficient, you would try to show that and how God is not a necessary condition for these experiences at all; or that the analysis of human life is wanting—yes, perhaps by pointing to instances of experience that fail to exemplify Spinoza's points, but also by demonstrating what its implications are and that these are ultimately unacceptable or generate paradoxes or come with a high price.

Yet even if you show that Spinoza got some things wrong, there is an intellectual value to his work that persists. I think we would have to be prepared to admit that when this is the case with a philosopher's work—and of course, it is not always the case, since much of philosophy does die a timely death and fortunately so—but if this is so, it must be the case that through recurrent actualization of the categorial framework, it does render the world in some respect(s) intelligible, or challenges us intellectually to render it better, or rotates around the world or a set of concepts in such a way as to provoke thought and *advance* understanding. It may do so, as I suggested earlier, as much by exhibiting the relevant features of the world as by making truth-claims. Plato does this by the explicit use of literary devices, but there are other ways of exhibiting. Among other things, Spinoza's use of the geometric method *exhibits* the consequential nature of God and the relation of human experience to God as its necessary condition. Spinoza's intellectual contribution to our understanding of the human being's relation to God and the universe is perhaps to have shown our smallness as well as our opportunity for greatness in the intellectual love of God. This in itself is a great intellectual achievement, and as for us philosophers, even if not scientists, it must give us pause and command our respect, even if not our belief.

If there is a respect in which metaphysical systems do not invalidate one another—and I say only a respect, because there is another respect in which they cannot all be equally good or equally valid—one reason is because the goal of conceptual orientation admits of great latitude. And, if this is so, it must be that the world itself, when more broadly conceived, is plurally determinate and indeterminate, and accessible. Moreover, the aptness of one metaphysical system relative to some range of available evidence may not be expandable or transferable to another perspective. So, although another metaphysical system may be wider in the scope of its aptness—more pervasively validated—it might not strictly invalidate the first one. Part of its superiority, though, would be its greater pervasiveness or generality.

Finally, a word about generality. At the level of general ontology, where presumably one is talking about everything insofar as it is, is a being, generality cannot mean literally all-inclusiveness in the sense (*a*) that one is talking about everything distributively; or (*b*) that one is talking about everything collectively. So, when Aristotle says that to be a being is to be an *ousía*, it is not that *ousía* includes or subsumes all particular differences of any being, or that we can sort of look around the world and observe "*ousías*"—or monads, actual entities, or natural complexes, for that matter. Rather, I think the generality of such categories is better understood (*a*) as identifying *an aspect* of beings—forgive the barbaric language, their being-ness, if you will, and (*b*) as entailing that they are always presupposed (even if only implicitly) or exemplified by distinctions of lesser generality, but not vice versa. That is, generality would mean, on the one hand, comprehensiveness in the formulation of the relevant or apt characteristics of being in general and, on the other, pervasiveness of exemplification. On this view, instead of metaphysics, meaning here general ontology, being a perspective that *includes* all perspectives—an impossible claim to validate since we would have to be able to transcend all perspectives in order to determine this—it would rather be a or the perspective that is presupposed and exemplified by other perspectives. Determination of whether the relation obtains or not does not require the perspectiveless standpoint. We would also be able to compare the scope and categorial aptness of different metaphysical systems: we could compare whether one metaphysical system is more general than another; whether the concepts of special disciplines exemplify the categories and principles of a metaphysical system; whether the categorial interpretations of the presuppositions of a special discipline by one system are better (for example, richer, less forced, more accessible) than those by another system. Although on my analysis one could never claim certainty or proof of the truth or correctness of a metaphysical system, validation as a recurrent and reliable process of probing, testing, and interpreting is at least possible. Thus, we would not have to give up metaphysics altogether, as Rorty would have it. Nor do we have to renounce the possibility of assessing and adjudicating between metaphysical systems, as Rescher, applying Kuhnian ideas to philosophy, concludes.

I have suggested that we redefine metaphysics as being concerned with apt generality and conceptual [re-]orientation, not foundationalism, universality, and perspectivelessness. If there is diversity in metaphysics, it is, at least in part, because the world, as well as our own experience, demands that we keep starting over again. If more than one metaphysical theory has validity, and if we can know the world in a variety of ways, it is both because the world *is* in a variety of ways and because we can construct concepts and categories that create new possibilities for knowing the ways of the world.

If the purpose of metaphysics is conceptual [re-]orientation, then there is a sense in which metaphysics is, in one respect, like art. The goal of metaphysics is to *transform* the way or the terms in which we think about the world, not to identify what we do believe, as Davidson would have it. Like the myth—and like art—a metaphysical scheme may be neither true nor false, but *exhibits* something about the world. Mozart's music gives a compelling characterization of Donna Elvira and Don Giovanni (which can be grasped ultimately only by listening to the music) and in doing so, it exhibits aspects of human emotional and psychological life. The broad range of human experience that resonates with Mozart's musical articulation validates and extends the meaning of the musical characterization. In metaphysics, it is not enough to just construct the myth or the framework. You also have to explain what it means, follow where it takes thought, what it implies, and actualize the categories by seeing what intellectual work they can do. The philosopher constructs and analyzes, suggests further areas to probe, problems to solve, and some of the implications of her or his own product. So, unlike art, in metaphysics, one may not experience that sense of completeness in the product itself. I think philosophy in general and metaphysics in particular is characterized by this tension between the craving to get it just right, to be able to rest satisfied with a categorial structure, much as one would with a felicitous and exquisite rendition of Donna Elvira's enraged but loving loyalty, on the one hand, and the restless urge to push the ideas, to interrogate further, on the other. Unlike art, metaphysics also demands evidential validation, even though the scope of what could count as evidence is indefinitely great. But even that is not exhaustive of metaphysical validation. If the kind of knowledge we achieve in metaphysics is breadth and commensurateness of understanding, then maybe it is not so terrible that we have to keep starting over again.

Notes

Acknowledgments: I would like to thank David Weissman, Eric Steinhart, and the editors of this volume for their very helpful suggestions and criticisms of this essay.

1. I use brackets to identify phrases or material that should be read as part of the subsequent word or phrase and that, although technically optional, renders the meaning more precise.

2. I also pursue this issue in "Making Categories or Making Worlds, II," *Texas A & M Studies in Philosophy*, ed. Robert Burch (College Station: Texas A & M University Press, 1991).

3. Rorty develops his views in several places, the most notable of which are *Philosophy and the Mirror of Nature* (Princeton: Princeton University Press, 1979) and *Consequences of Pragmatism* (Minneapolis: University of Minnesota Press, 1982).

4. Nicholas Rescher, *The Strife of Systems: An Essay on the Grounds and Implications of Philosophical Diversity* (Pittsburgh, Pa.: University of Pittsburgh Press, 1985). All references are to this work, but see also Rescher's article, "Aporetic Method in Philosophy," *Review of Metaphysics* 41, no. 2 (December 1987): 283–97. I discuss Rescher's view in more detail in my review of *The Strife of Systems: An Essay on the Grounds and Implications of Philosophical Diversity* in *Journal of Speculative Philosophy* 1, no. 4 (1987): 318–24.

5. See, for example, Donald Davidson, *Inquiries into Truth and Interpretation* (Oxford: Clarendon Press, 1984), especially "The Method of Truth in Metaphysics," pp. 199–214. (This article was first published in *Midwest Studies in Philosophy, 2: Studies in the Philosophy of Language*, ed. P. A. French, T. E. Uehling, Jr., H. K. Wettstein [Minneapolis: University of Minnesota Press, 1977].)

6. Rescher, *Strife of Systems*, p. 213.

7. See Justus Buchler, *Metaphysics of Natural Complexes* (1966), 2nd, expanded ed., edited by Kathleen Wallace and Armen Marsoobian, with Robert S. Corrington (Albany: State University of New York Press, 1989).

8. Elsewhere, I address the issue of greater and lesser pervasiveness: " 'Fundamental' or 'foundational' marks a functional and relative distinction. Some distinctions or categories are more fundamental than or are foundational to others. So, for example, Aristotle's category of *ousía* is more fundamental than that of soul or psyche because it is more widely applicable and because it is presupposed by the latter, but not *vice versa*." Wallace, "Making Categories or Making Worlds, II."

9. Justus Buchler, "Reply to Anton: Against 'Proper Ontology'," *Southern Journal of Philosophy* 14, no. 1 (1976): 85–90. Reprinted in part in Justus Buchler, *Metaphysics of Natural Complexes*, 2nd ed., pp. 200–206. Some of Kuhn's insights regarding the function of conceptual frameworks in science may resemble aspects of my view of metaphysics, although I have not drawn my points from Kuhn. But see Thomas S. Kuhn, *The Structure of Scientific Revolutions* (1962), 2nd ed., enlarged (Chicago: University of Chicago Press, 1970). My views are drawn more from Buchler's work in general, from the implications of his ordinal metaphysics as well as from his tripartite theory of human judgment: assertive, active, and exhibitive. The former is developed in *Metaphysics of Natural Complexes*, the latter in *Toward a General Theory of Human Judgment* (1951), 2nd, rev. ed. (New York: Dover Publications, 1979), and *Nature and Judgment* (1955; rpt. Lanham, Md.: University Press of America, 1985). The notion of compulsion in section III has its origins in Buchler's theory of experience, or *proception*, where one of the basic categories is that of compulsion. See *Toward a General Theory of Human Judgment*.

10. Myth, of course, has many functions for Plato, not all of them positive. I am here being quite selective in the discussion of myth. My concern is not with the complexity of myth in Plato's work, but with one aspect of myth in order to develop what I mean by conceptual [re-]orientation.

11. Aristotle thought that to be a master of metaphor is a sign of genius: "But the greatest thing by far is to be a master of metaphor. It is the one thing that cannot be learnt from others; and it is also a sign of genius, since a good metaphor implies an intuitive perception of the similarity in dissimilars." *Poetics*, 1459a 5–7, trans. I. Bywater. If constructing categories is like making metaphor, then it, too, would be a sign of genius, and criteria for good categories would be hard to specify in advance of their invention.

12. Learning the history of philosophy is minimally an apprenticeship, orienting oneself to the conceptual arena as thus far defined. This is another reason why it is not the case that anyone who claims to be

doing philosophy and whose ideas have some connection with the traditional issues of philosophy is therefore doing philosophy, as Rescher would have it. And the knowledge of the history of philosophy is important to metaphysics because it defines the backdrop of any reorientation and, in a sense, whether it even is a reorientation.

13. This would be one consequence of what I have called "systematic resonance."

14. This is one of the senses in which my view of metaphysics is non-foundationalist. Epistemologically, neither can it be grounded with certainty at its starting point, nor can its subsequent validation definitively secure it as *the* irrefutably correct conceptual foundation for every other mode of inquiry.

15. Methodological foundationalism—that all we have to do is hit on the right method of construction or validation or both—is a species of epistemological foundationalism, a requirement that my approach denies. Not only Descartes, but I think even John Dewey falls into the trap of methodological foundationalism. Although he is not fully consistent, Dewey's optimism about scientific method and its ability to sort out problems in metaphysics as well as ethics borders on a kind of methodological foundationalism. Moreover, though science, too, has many methods, they must be duplicable. The same cannot be said of the methods of any metaphysical system.

16. And if Thomas Kuhn is right, neither do the results of science.

17. The experimenting scientist practices what Kuhn calls "normal science." "Extraordinary science" may, like metaphysics, lead to a new beginning, ultimately a new paradigm. However, not only are its methods different from those of metaphysics, but its beginning will be directed to achieving explanatory and research goals different from those of metaphysics.

18. Goodman's view seems to make these assumptions. For Goodman, since we construct perspectives and facts, we in effect make the world or worlds that we know and encounter. But the "fit" between our constructions and "*the* world" is a matter of practice or convention. In my view, and in spite of his asseverations to the contrary, Goodman's nominalistic ontology stands in the way of his developing an adequate account of the "fit" or "rightness" of theories, categories and art. If only individuals are "real," then it would be difficult to define what the "fit" of constructions, which necessarily are constituted by relational traits, is to the "real" world of individuals. See Nelson Goodman, *Fact, Fiction and Forecast*, 4th ed. (Cambridge: Harvard University Press, 1983; earlier eds. 1955, 1965, 1973), and Nelson Goodman, *Ways of Worldmaking* (Indianapolis: Hackett, 1978).

19. If there is no single right way of knowing, it would seem that

neither an epistemological nor a metaphysical foundationalism could be successfully defended.

20. These would be instances of "exhibitive judgment." (See note 9.)

21. These would be instances of "active judgment." My point is that any mode of judgment has cognitive value, not just true beliefs or assertions. (See note 9.)

22. See Buchler, *Nature and Judgment*, p. 33.

23. By "consequential" I mean that God's nature is logically necessary and sequential. The existence of any thing is entailed by the very nature of God, and the ultimate explanation for any thing is its relation to Substance, that is, God. The rational necessity of these relations, and in the last analysis of our dependence on God, is *exhibited* by the geometric method of exposition. (My use of the term "consequential" has no connection to Whitehead's phrase "the consequent nature of God.")

About the Contributors

Gary Calore is Assistant Professor of Philosophy at the Ogontz campus of the Pennsylvania State University. He has written on the concept of time in classical and contemporary philosophy and on such figures in philosophy as John Dewey and Alfred North Whitehead.

Joseph Margolis is Professor of Philosophy at Temple University. His most recent major work is a trilogy, *The Persistence of Reality*, with volumes entitled, respectively, *Pragmatism without Foundations: Reconciling Realism and Relativism*; *Science without Unity: Reconciling the Human and Natural Sciences*; and *Texts without Referents: Reconciling Science and Narrative*.

Emily Michael is Professor and Chairperson in the Department of Philosophy at Brooklyn College of the City University of New York. She has published papers in areas such as aesthetics, ethics and animals, the history of logic, American philosophy, renaissance philosophy, and modern philosophy.

Fred S. Michael has taught at the University of Tennessee and Long Island University and is currently teaching at Brooklyn College of the City University of New York. He has published papers on logic, on ethics, and in the history of philosophy on figures such as Pierre Gassendi, John Locke, Thomas Reid, and Charles Sanders Peirce. With Emily Michael, he has published joint papers in journals such as *Journal of the History of Ideas*, *Journal of the History of Philosophy*, *History of European Ideas*, *The Monist*, *Notes and Queries*, and the *Irish Philosophical Journal*.

Ronald Polansky edits the journal *Ancient Philosophy*. He has published articles on Greek and early modern philosophy. His book on

Plato's *Theatetus* is to appear shortly, and he is currently working on a study of hypocrisy.

Tom Rockmore is Professor in the Department of Philosophy at Duquesne University. In addition to numerous papers, he is author of *Fichte, Marx and German Philosophy*; *Hegel's Circular Epistemology*; *Habermas on Historical Materialism*; and the forthcoming *Irrationalism: Lukács and the Marxist View of Reason*; *On Heidegger's Nazism and Philosophy*; and *Hegel: Avant et Après*. He has edited *Lukács Today: Essays in Marxist Philosophy* and, with Joseph Margolis, *Heidegger and Nazism* by Victor Farías and *Heidegger and Politics*.

Sandra B. Rosenthal is Professor of Philosophy at Loyola University in New Orleans. She has published numerous articles on pragmatism and on the relation between pragmatism and phenomenology, as well as several books. Her most recent books are *Speculative Pragmatism* and *Mead and Merleau-Ponty: Toward a Common Vision*, the latter co-authored with Patrick Bourgeois.

Charlene Haddock Seigfried is Professor of Philosophy at Purdue University. She is the author of *William James's Radical Reconstruction of Philosophy* and *Chaos and Context*. Two of her articles have recently been reprinted: "Vagueness and the Adequacy of Concepts" in *Twentieth-Century Literary Criticism* (1989) and "Second Sex: Second Thoughts" in *Hypàtia Reborn: Essays in Feminist Philosophy*. Professor Seigfried was awarded a Center for Humanistic Studies grant to work on her current project of developing a specifically pragmatist feminist theory.

Beth J. Singer is Professor of Philosophy at Brooklyn College of the City University of New York and past president of the Society for the Advancement of American Philosophy. She is the editor of *Philosophy after Darwin*, a collection of essays by John Herman Randall, Jr. Her publications also include *Ordinal Naturalism: An Introduction to the Philosophy of Justus Buchler*; *The Rational Society: A Study of Santayana's Social Thought*, articles on various figures in American philosophy, and papers on concepts such as experience, meaning and interpretation, communication and community, selfhood, normativity, and human rights.

Kathleen Wallace is Associate Professor of Philosophy at Hofstra University. She has written on metaphysics, Justus Buchler, and George Santayana. She is the editor of the second edition of Buchler's *Metaphysics of Natural Complexes* and *Nature's Perspectives: Prospects for Ordinal Metaphysics*. She is currently working on a book on self and morality.

Wilhelm S. Wurzer is Associate Professor of Philosophy at Duquesne University. He studied under Eugen Fink, Werner Marx, and Wolfgang Struve and received his Ph.D. from the University of Freiburg, Germany. He is author of *Nietzsche und Spinoza* and *Filming and Judgment: Between Heidegger and Adorno*.

Index of Names

Index of Titles